Networks

By the same author

Non-fiction

It's a Dog's Life
The Making of Space 1999
H.R.H. The Man Who Will Be King (with Mayo Mohs)

Fiction

Unbecoming Habits
Blue Blood Will Out
Deadline
Let Sleeping Dogs Die
Just Desserts
John Steed, "an authorised biography" (Volume One)
Murder at Moose Jaw
Caroline R (as David Lancaster)
Masterstroke

Networks

Who We Know and How
We Use Them

Tim Heald

Guy heard of mysterious departments known only by their initials or as "So and So's cloak and dagger boys". Bankers, gamblers, men with jobs in oil companies seemed to find a way there; not Guy. He met an acquaintance, a journalist, who had once come to Kenya. This man, Lord Kilbannock, had lately written a racing column; now he was in air force uniform.

"How did you manage it?" Guy asked.

"Well it's rather shaming really. There's an air marshal whose wife plays bridge with my wife. He's always been mad keen to get in here. I've just put him up. He's the most awful shit."

"Will he get in?"

"No, no, I've seen to that. Three blackballs guaranteed already. But he can't get me out of the Air Force."

Evelyn Waugh, *Men at Arms*, 1952

HODDER AND STOUGHTON
London   Sydney   Auckland   Toronto

The typeface, Times New Roman monotype 327, was designed by Stanley Morison specifically for *The Times* newspaper. It first appeared in print in 1932 and was issued for general use in 1933.

British Library Cataloguing in Publication Data

Heald, Tim
  Networks.
  1. Elite (Social sciences)   2. Social classes –
  Great Britain
  I. Title
  305.5'54   HN400.E4

  ISBN 0-340-26487-X

For my parents
who gave me
a place in the
OBN

Contents

Contents

A vocabulary of network terms and
expressions can be found on p. 243

Prologue

The seeds for this book were sown at the end of the seventies.

In 1979 Sir Anthony Blunt was revealed as the "fourth man" in that seemingly endless spy scandal which began at Cambridge University in the thirties when he, Guy Burgess, Donald Maclean and Kim Philby were undergraduates together.

After a long siege by the Press, Blunt consented to be interviewed by *The Times*, though, following protests, the *Guardian* was present too and television was allowed a ten minute postscript. At the *Times* building in Gray's Inn Road the unmasked traitor was given smoked trout, white wine and, considering the circumstances, a surprisingly easy time.

The question of how Blunt had been recruited by British intelligence was naturally one which exercised his interrogators.

"You went to France, came back, then you joined MI5?" he was asked. "How did you join? Did you apply, or was it arranged for you, or how?"

"Well," said Blunt, playing the half volley gently back to the bowler, "like all those . . . that kind of recruitment, it was done simply. Someone who was in MI5 recommended me. I was recommended."

Evidently this was something that those present, and by extension the readers of *The Times* and the *Guardian*, understood implicitly.

"The old boy network?"

"Yes," said Blunt.

And there the matter was allowed to drop. Everyone – Blunt, the interviewers, the world at large, would, it was assumed, know exactly what was being discussed.

The old boy network.

"Oh that! Of course. Enough said, old boy. Next question."

The more I looked at those three simple words "old boy network" and visualised the meaningful smile of complicity that went with

11

them the less happy I was. I recognised the phrase and I recognised the concept. It was one of those curiously English expressions like "fair play", "conduct unbecoming" and "stiff upper lip". Everyone, me included, used it all the time. But what did it really mean? Blunt was clearly a member of the old boy network (OBN for short), but how and why? Was it because his father had been Vicar of St. John's Paddington? Was that how he had been recruited? Did someone in a leather armchair at a St. James' club murmur that young Anthony was the Reverend Blunt's boy? Did that get him in? Or was it Marlborough? Respected Wiltshire public school? Did being an Old Marlburian guarantee your passage into the security services? Or was it Trinity, Cambridge, where Blunt spent his university days? Or a combination of all three? And then the cover-up. Blunt was never prosecuted. He had bargained his immunity years earlier in a secret interview with some shadowy powers-that-be. Was this a gentleman's agreement between fellow members of the OBN? Did it have something to do with his being Surveyor of the Queen's Pictures? Blunt's friends and colleagues wrote to *The Times* in his defence; an attempt to have him expelled from the British Academy was defeated; and there seemed to be a widespread feeling that he was not a traitor at all but a rather unwell old gentleman who was being unfairly treated. Was this too something to do with his network?

The more I thought about it the more irritated I was by the way the Blunt interview had glossed over the truth behind Britain's old boy network. I wanted to know more about the idea. Which was the more important – Blunt's apparent membership of some monolithic club called the old boy network or his own highly individual and personal network of friends and colleagues? Who belonged to the OBN? Did we all have our own idiosyncratic networks or only those who had been to public school and Oxbridge? *Or* Oxbridge? Or served in the Guards?

The implication was – wasn't it? – that the OBN was only for the "haves", but what about the "have-nots"? Were there networks for them too? No particular reason why the principles of networking shouldn't apply universally, was there? Favouritism, a preference for dealing with friends, by-passing the rules and the regulations – weren't these all part of the British Way of Life?

The more I thought about it the more complex, the more all embracing and the more intriguing the whole idea of "networks" became. I wanted to know more.

1

Dr. Burchfield and a Lack of Written Evidence

A network is a club without premises, constitution, or life membership. Not simply a clique. Not quite an élite. Not exactly a trade union. But with some of the qualities of all these alliances.

Nicholas Tomalin, The *Sunday Times*, 1964

The "old boy network" is a peculiarly British invention. According to one American lexicographer, seeking to explain British idiom to his fellow countrymen: "*Old boy contacts* often referred to as the *old boy network*, which are so terribly important in England, would come out in America as *old school connections*, but compared with the English variety they are so tenuous as to be almost academic, figuratively as well as literally."

Dictionaries recognise that old boy network is part of the language, but even British lexicographers appear muddled in their definitions. Collins' New English Dictionary describes it, rather narrowly, as, "The appointment to power of former pupils of the same small group of public schools or universities". The latest Supplement to the Oxford English Dictionary maintains that an "old boy" is a "former pupil of a (particular) boys' school, esp. an English public school", though old boys of such famous Scottish public schools as Gordonstoun or Fettes would rightly take issue with this caveat. When it comes to the idea of the old boy network the OED broadens the Collins definition by saying that the old boy network is not simply concerned with "appointment to power" but is used to "designate comradeship or favouritism shown among old boys". Brewer's Dictionary of Phrase and Fable goes even further by suggesting that if you do something through the OBN you "arrange something through a friend (originally someone known at school) instead of through usual channels".

Already we have come a long way from the Collins definition. By the time we reach Brewer the OBN involves any sort of transaction at all whether it is the appointment of a new archbishop or fixing yourself up with a black market ticket to the England–Wales rugger international at Twickenham. And it is no longer restricted to old school friends. The implication is that though school is where the idea originated it has broadened out so that you can practise old boy networking with anyone you know whether it is someone you once shared a study with at Rugby or Wellington or a chap you play golf with, the next door neighbour or the boss's secretary. The only essential, according to Brewer, is that the OBN transcends "usual channels". It is a bureaucracy-buster, a queue-jumper and a red-tape cutter. Depending on your point of view and whether you are on the inside or not it is either a grossly unfair form of cheating the system or a sensible and legitimate way of getting ahead. The crucial point to the Brewer definition, unlike the Collins, is that it is open to everyone, not just old boys.

If you now look under "network" in several dictionaries you will find confirmation for this notion. The OED Supplement, for instance, admits that one meaning of network is "an interconnected group of people" while Chambers' Dictionary suggests that networks are, "Groups of persons constituting a widely spread organisation and having a common purpose." In both cases the ideas behind the OBN have been broadened and democratised. What was originally a self-improvement tool for the privileged and privately educated has become, if we are to believe the lexicographers, a weapon for life enhancement and advancement which is available to anyone with the capacity for making – and using – a friend or contact.

Old boys are, like the schools that produce them, an essentially Victorian invention. Many of the schools were in existence hundreds of years earlier but it was the nineteenth century which produced the public school revolution, public school boom and, most importantly from our point of view, the idea that going to a public school not only gave you an education but also admitted you to life membership of an exclusive and potentially useful club. The first recorded use of the phrase old boy occurs in 1868 when the *Haileyburian*, Haileybury's typically named school magazine, recorded that, "On November 30th was played our first old boys' football match." By the end of the century it was generally accepted that after you left public school you became an old boy of the school. You continued to owe some kind of allegiance and loyalty, not only to your alma mater, but also, more significantly, to your fellow old boy. There was even a sort of uniform to prove it

14

and to signal your membership to your fellow networkers: the old school tie.

Many years later Professor Max Beloff wrote in *Encounter* that, "It is obvious that personal contacts will, on the whole, be easier between those who have shared the formative experiences of early life. It is then that people make friends, rarely later." The public schools institutionalised that theory – some more consciously than others – until it seemed to many people, including by implication Professor Blunt's interrogators, that the whole of British society was dominated by one vast and all embracing OBN. The Labour party calls the public school system "an educational plutocracy based on social and economic élitism". The party's education spokesman, Neil Kinnock, complained that the public schools offer no real educational advantages over the state but that they do confer "the tribal security of an old boy network". To them it is all a hideously successful plot to run the country on the basis of friendship and connection instead of ability in the abstract.

Although born more than a hundred years ago, it was a surprisingly long time before the OBN was recognised and defined; as early as 1919, John Buchan had used the metaphor of the "net" to describe a human organisation. (He used it to explain how a disparate and disconnected collection of enemy spies – "loose ends" – were combined into an interconnected mesh. Ever since then, the spy network concept has continued in that sort of fiction, up to and including le Carré.)

No one, however, seems to have combined "old boy" and "net" or "network" until the fifties. But quite how and when remains a mystery. According to the OED, the *Guardian* and the *Spectator* started it in 1959: the *Guardian* wrote in December that year that, "Appointments boards have always . . . a certain resemblance to the 'old boy net' which they replaced," and a month before the paper wrote about, "The old boy network of the left." The *Spectator*'s contribution, in February, was to talk about Krupp's place in the *old-boy network*, of the Ruhr. The OED's line is unconvincing for all kinds of reasons. For a start, the dictionary mentions the old girl network as existing five years earlier, in 1954. Given the relative strengths of the two kinds of network (women are only now beginning to realise the full potential of networks) and the relative age and importance of the boys' and girls' public schools, it simply does not make sense to suggest that the OBN evolved later than the OGN. It must be the other way round. Even more significant, the 1952 edition of Brewer said that "old boy net"

15

was "a British military expression in World War II". In 1981 they dropped the suggestion for lack of written evidence. It also seems extraordinary that the 1959 examples concern "the left" and the Germans, rather than the original limited Collins Dictionary type of OBN: "The appointment to power of former pupils of the same small group of public schools or universities."

The only reasonable explanation for this uncertainty is that although the old boy network (or possibly net) existed in both fact and conversation, long before the fifties, it was too colloquial an expression to find its way into print. Dr. Robert Burchfield, the Oxford University Press's chief dictionary editor, confirmed this by sending me a copy of his correspondence with a colleague, Nicholas Allen, manager of the OUP showroom in Oxford.

Allen had protested that the OED was wrong and the old boy network dated from ages before the fifties. He recalled that when he was commissioned into the Gunners in 1951, the regiment was being inundated with ex-Indian Army officers and that, "The phrase 'old boy network' was very much a part of their vocabulary then."

"Doubtless you are right," replied Burchfield, "in remembering the use of the phrase at an earlier date than our entry indicates. The difficulty is to find printed evidence to support one's recollections."

So, although Dr. Burchfield and the OUP are unable to produce written evidence of the OBN in the early part of the century, that is not at all the same as saying that it didn't exist.

In an attempt to flush out a more convincing piece of early written usage I managed to persuade Godfrey Smith to run an appeal in his weekly *Sunday Times* column. Smith himself said that it was one of the few phrases he could clearly remember learning. "A fellow undergraduate used it on a walk to Iffley one day in 1950 and was shocked to hear that I'd never heard of it."

The most convincing responses came from those who subscribed to the Brewer theory that it had originated in the second world war and was not specifically related to old boys of schools. It simply meant that you knew someone well enough to call him "old boy" and to use the acquaintance to cadge a favour. Thus, as one retired wing commander put it: "Look Joe, *old boy*, can you get me a flight to Delhi on Tuesday?" Or, "That bloody fool of a brigade major of yours has made a cock of it again, can you get that last order cancelled, *old boy*?"

Smith's correspondents also seemed certain that the phrase was originally "old boy net", not "network" and derived from "the army wireless communications link – squadron net, regimental net, brigade net and so forth".

Tom Baistow, the press pundit who served in an armoured brigade in the second world war, subscribed to this theory and gave a vivid example of its working.

In the Normandy bridgehead we pulled back for refit and rest after a very rough battle but found ourselves unable to do either because of constant heavy shelling from German batteries. The brigade commander, Brigadier Erroll Prior-Palmer, a superb soldier (and father of Lucinda, his living image), sent me to ask General Barker, of 49 Division, if we could move into his more sheltered rear area.

"No!" Barker bellowed. "In the last war we were shelled all the time – it makes soldiers of you!"

"But we've been stonked non-stop since D-Day," I protested.

"Get out of my tent, you impudent young pup," roared Barker, rising. I fled.

"P-P" just grinned at my distress. "We'll just have to use the old boy net – I'll try Boofy – he was in the 9th [Lancers] with me." He called up on the corps net: "Hello, Boofy . . . that bugger Barker . . ."

Within hours we were moving in, literally, behind General Barker's back.

That was the old boy network, at its best, in operation. I doubt if we could have won the war without it."

Today, as many of the dictionaries suggest, the use of "network" to describe social organisations of many kinds is widespread. "Old boy network" (the OBN) may suggest a network whose members come only from the English (or British) public schools; but it may also, as the *Guardian* and *Spectator* of the fifties showed, refer to Herr Krupp or the cabals and mafias of the Labour party. But as long ago as the forties, anthropologists began to use the word network in academic studies and since then many other academic disciplines have jumped on the network bandwagon, notably the sociologists who even attempt to define social networks with algebraic formulae and such jargon ridden sentences as, "A Network is a social configuration in which some, but not all, of the component units maintain relationships with one another."

The one consensus which emerges is that the network is a sort of black economy of British society. On the surface, there is a well ordered system in which jobs are awarded according to your qualifications, preferment is by way of proven talent and ability, and in which you are served when it comes to your turn in the queue. The reverse side of the coin is the network, a system whereby rewards of every kind are apportioned according to who you know and how you use your contacts and friendships. At its most extreme, this network principle could completely overturn considerations of merit, so that, for instance, a totally unsuitable candidate could succeed to a managing directorship *simply* because he is the chairman's nephew or because his wife plays bridge with the proprietor's wife. On a more plausible level it means that where there are two candidates of apparently equal ability – as proved by paper qualification – the one with the contacts, the shared interests, the same network membership, is the one who will succeed.

If this is so and networking is a vital ingredient of success or "getting on" at every level from the highest level of politics, of industry, or the bureaucracy, to the most mundane areas of social or economic survival, then it seems likely that the public school dominated OBN is the most important. But just because it is the most important it hardly follows that the OBN is the *only* network which counts. I find it hard to believe that the fact that Blunt was a boy at Marlborough is the only, or even the crucial, network determinant. His contacts and friendships, formed over a lifetime of service to the Crown, the Kremlin and the Arts, constituted a Personal Private Network – or PPN – which is powerful and highly individual in character. Only Blunt himself had precisely that combination of friends in high and low places; and when you stop to think about it, each of us, no matter how solitary, has a PPN of friends and contacts which is as unique as character itself.

If, for example, a man has been educated at Eton he will be a member of the OBN – assuming for the moment that the OBN is a club comprised of all those who ever attended a public school. He will also have a more closely knit association with Eton as an institution and with other old Etonians who have a similar association. He may have a few close personal friends acquired while actually at the school. But in addition to that he will have family; friends from university; perhaps from military service; from the community in which he lives; the place at which he works; people with whom he has shared interests or tastes, be they fellow stamp collectors or balletomanes or golfers; and other friends or contacts of all kinds, no matter how they are acquired. All of us have our unique PPN, composed of any number of other network memberships. One man in his time may be Old Etonian, Grenadier Guards officer, tennis player and merchant banker. Each category may confer a network membership. He will draw friends from all of them but the friends are peculiar to him and the final composition is his own personal network. It may be similar to others but it can never be quite the same. And while some of these PPNs may be more exalted or influential than others, the principle remains the same.

We all belong to networks and we all have networks.

2

Rhubarb, Custard and Clerical Grey

SCHOOL, CLUB AND COMPANY TIES (Special Design). In addition to our stock service we are able to produce designs to customers' own specification, either stripes or motifs woven in ALL SILK or POLYESTER/ CRIMPLENE. Alternatively we can offer printed motifs. We are specialists in this type of work and all details are carefully recorded with a number given to each design to eliminate delay on repeat orders.

> Stock list of Regimental, School and Club Colours from P. L. Sells and Co. Ltd., Clifton Street, London, EC2.

Networks – particularly the OBN – have an elaborate system of codes, sartorial as well as oral. These not only have the effect of binding together network members, but also of excluding those who do not belong. Outsiders who tamper with the codes can become badly unstuck.

That immaculate Speaker of the House of Commons, George Thomas, always seemed to the breeches born but he was, when he first came to the House in the 1950s, a young inexperienced Labour member from South Wales unversed in the ways of the world and especially those of the OBN. If he had a sense of network it was in no way a network of privilege but the cohesion bred of oppression and adversity; a common background of choirs, coal and rugby football. However, as the newly elected MP for Cardiff Central he naturally wanted to cut an appropriately distinguished figure at Westminster and he therefore acquired a suit.

"It was a very nice suit," he says. "It was a dark colour we call 'clerical grey' in the valleys. And one day I saw a tie that went with it very nicely, so I went into the shop and I bought it."

In those days Mr. Thomas used to sit next to the Liberal member for Orkney and Shetland, Jo Grimond (Eton, Balliol, OBN) and it was to Mr. Grimond that he turned when he first entered the

House in his smart new tie with his smart grey suit to be greeted with uproar from the Tory benches.

"They were going frantic," he says, "so I said to Jo, 'What's wrong with them?'"

"I think it's you," said Mr. Grimond, laconically.

"Me?" said Mr. Thomas. "What do you mean, me?"

"I think it's the way you're dressed," said Mr. Grimond.

So Mr. Thomas glanced down at his flies to check, as he puts it, that "everything was in order", saw that he was not unbuttoned and looked back up to see that the Conservative chief whip, Captain Chichester-Clark, was motioning him to join him for a word. Chichester-Clark walked to neutral ground in the centre of the chamber. The member for Cardiff followed him, cheered to the echo by the Tory benches baying for their broken glass. "What's the trouble?" he asked, when he got to within earshot of the whip.

"Are you aware?" asked Chichester-Clark, trembling, "that you are wearing an Old Etonian tie?"

"No," said Mr. Thomas, "I got it at the Co-op in Tonypandy."

Mr. Speaker laughed a lot when he told me the story though it can't have seemed quite so funny at the time. He heard, subsequently, that the headmaster of Eton "wrote to the manager of the establishment to take the matter up. The manager told him he'd bought it in a job lot".

Mr. Thomas never wore the tie again. "I gave it to an Old Age Pensioner in Cardiff West. He didn't know it was an Old Etonian tie either . . . well I wasn't going to throw it away."

More recently, the erstwhile Labour backbencher, now transformed into a respected national figure, was asked down to Eton to talk to the boys. He told them the story of the Old Etonian tie from the Co-op in Tonypandy but they didn't seem to find it funny.

As that tale suggests, the Old Etonian tie, black with a thin diagonal stripe of Cambridge blue, is a vastly potent OBN symbol, only seriously rivalled by the Brigade of Guards neckpiece of dark blue and magenta stripes.

It and other old school club and regimental ties are the crucial sartorial links in the OBN. The tie is the outward and visible sign of membership. The mere act of wearing a diagonally striped tie or a tie with some form of heraldic device, or even one covered in sailing club pennants or pink elephants, is a statement. The wearer is making a public claim to membership of the greater OBN. He is also claiming membership of a much smaller network within the OBN. If he is wearing blue and black he is telling you he is an Old

Etonian; red, chocolate and blue – like Charles Ryder in the televised *Brideshead Revisited* – that he is a Wykehamist (a rare liberty with Waugh's text); black or midnight blue with a double white stripe that he is a Harrovian; green, blue and white that he was at Rugby; pink and red on a dark ground indicates Charterhouse. And so on. It is a peculiarly British convention. Other countries have a complex of network codes by which they announce their network membership to each other or the world at large, but no one except Britain has turned the necktie into such a precise form of communication.

The significance of neckwear in the OBN is regarded by outsiders as unfathomably obscure. Even perceptive social observers such as the American commentator and novelist Alison Lurie simply can't face up to it. In her otherwise fascinating study, *The Language of Clothes*, she contrives a section on "the costume of the upper-class British male" in which she doesn't mention ties once, though she does say (quite wrongly) that, "Old Etonians always carry an unrolled umbrella." Elsewhere she suggests that stripes stand for "organised effort" and conformity and that in sport the wider the stripe the more arduous the activity. She is obviously unaware of the broadly hooped caps beloved of largely lost generations of amateur cricketers – possibly the most sedentary breed of sportsmen ever to break sweat.

In fairness to Professor Lurie, however, it should be conceded that her tongue is often firmly in cheek, as when she suggests, splendidly, that, "The unusually wide spaces between the stripes of the traditional baseball uniform may represent the large portion of time during each game when the average player is inactive."

It seems to be generally agreed that the modern striped tie originated in sporting gear. James Laver, who knew more than anybody about clothing, wrote that this was, "The process by which all men's clothes develop. They start by being sports costume; they are then adopted, and adapted, for ordinary day wear; they then become evening dress and if they run through the whole gamut they end as servant's costume." In the case of network stripes, alias the old school tie, we seem still to be firmly in the ordinary day wear era.

Chaps who wear old school ties generally do so between dawn and dusk and preferably with tweed (in the country) but possibly with Mr. Speaker's clerical grey (in town).

The sporting costumes from which modern school, club and regimental ties largely derive, came into their own at the time that

22

sport and games moved from the sort of largely chaotic contest still practised from time to time as an "old English custom" to the more formal organised games we enjoy today and which are, by and large, a nineteenth-century invention. (Colours were adopted to enable players to pick out their own side from the opposition.) In some areas this began a little earlier. There is some evidence for thinking that Eton's colour has been azure blue since the seventeenth century and in 1787 the Marylebone Cricket Club were reportedly playing in the same blue, although MCC's curator, Stephen Green, says red and yellow have been the club colours "for ages" and that all the early members' lists are bound in red with gilt lettering.

Sporting colours, however, really came of age in the next century, spurred on, significantly, by the public school revolution in which organised games were a natural, manly element. This necessitated an astonishing array of colours and favours, both uniform, to distinguish individual houses and schools, and hierarchical, to distinguish the heroes of the First XV from the also-rans of the Third. The Leander Rowing Club was formed in 1820; Blackheath Rugby Club (from old boys of Rugby and Blackheath schools) in 1858; and the Football Association in 1863. Two years earlier the Cambridge cricket eleven appeared at Lord's in light blue to be followed a year later by Oxford in dark. In 1864 the Royal Engineers' footballers performed in red and blue striped stockings and by 1887 the mania for colours had reached such proportions that Professor Hoffman's "Tips for tricyclists" advised riders to purchase white straw hats complete with the club ribbon of the Cyclists' Touring Club for four shillings and sixpence. The 1878 Australian cricketers even wore red, white and blue stripes, says Stephen Green, and by the eighties and nineties jockeys who had previously worn coloured cravats under their collars were wearing neckties under stiff wing collars. (Alison Lurie suggests that, "The striped costumes of jockeys may be explained by the fact that horse racing is a competition between two-unit teams of horse and rider in which co-operation is essential.") Unlikely. By 1896 even the ladies of the Bedford College hockey team were wearing striped ties on the field of play. The striped tie had arrived.

Tricycling is no longer a voguish OBN sport, but otherwise the links between the public schools and such manly pursuits as rowing, cricket, rugby and soccer have remained strong. When I was at public school, conservative masters all wore striped ties. In practice this meant all but a handful of aesthetes who tended towards the plain knitted tie, a symbol itself of membership in an artistic, non-hearty network of bolshies. They alternated invariably between their old school ties and those of the university sporting clubs (silver crown on navy blue for Vincent's of Oxford, gold stripe on maroon for the Hawks of Cambridge) or rugger clubs such as the Harlequins (a garish multi-coloured harlequin stripe) and cricket clubs such as the I Zingari (red, gold, black).

Neckties are the most obvious of these sartorial symbols but there are others. Eighteenth-century MCC members apparently had blue coats to distinguish themselves from other teams even though they were discarded on the field of play. Blazers – derived from the heraldic "blaze" and "blazen" became popular in the sixties and seventies. They were still garish, striped, multi-coloured and obviously sporting in those days and it was not until the early twentieth century that the dark blue blazer arrived to be worn with white or grey flannel bags. Like striped neckties the dark blue blazer has become bowdlerised, for the North American market, stripped of its network symbolism of monogrammed or engraved buttons and breast pocket badge, and converted into an item of clothing much favoured by television network newscasters who wish it to be thought they were educated at Yale or Harvard. In Britain the noisy striped blazer may still be seen at the Henley Royal Regatta and the odd social cricket match. The dark blue with badge has decidedly unsmart connotations – the RAF seem to like it! In Britain the well cut plain blue job is worn by successful advertising men who would like it to be thought that they are television network newscasters.

The striped tie, however, has remained easily the most important network signal of the last hundred years. If there *is* a language of clothes then it is one of the few phrases whose meaning is unequivocal. The old school tie is the outward and visible sign of an inner emotional bond – a sartorial double entendre, a semantic double Windsor.

It might be possible for an innocent politician to buy so discreet a tie as the Old Etonian by mistake, but surely nobody could purchase the garish "rhubarb and custard" stripes of the MCC, let alone wear it, without knowing exactly what it meant. And most such ties, because of their sporting origins, tend to be vivid.

Effective communicating in this, as other languages, depends not only on the fluency of the speaker but also of the listener. At the time that George Thomas committed his outrageous faux pas in the House of Commons the sartorial language of the old school tie was as foreign to him as Swahili. Although he could tell you if it was Sunday in Swansea by looking at a man's clothes and which rugby XV was Pontypool and which Pontypridd by a glance at their shirts, he couldn't tell an Etonian from a Harrovian by his tie, let alone a former officer of the Assam Valley Light Horse from an old boy of St. Bees (a St. Beghian).

To an outsider the striped tie is a totally alien tongue and may mean absolutely nothing. If, however, he or she has a smattering of the language, the wearing of the tie – whatever the stripes – suggests that the wearer belongs to some organisation or network of which he is both proud and fond. This in itself makes one think that the wearer is a person of substance and sociability. It is, on this level, a fairly vague statement, not much more suggestive than wearing a suit or having polished shoes. But it does put across a message. As Erving Goffman, the Canadian sociologist, put it, "The social information conveyed by a symbol can establish a special claim to prestige, honour or desirable class position – a claim that might not otherwise be presented or, if otherwise presented, then not automatically granted."

Even if the recipient of the message has only the most garbled idea of what the tie is talking about the effect can be startling. The former Labour MP, Sir Geoffrey de Freitas, a keen student of the networks and a wearer of a variety of meaningful striped ties, told me of an occasion on which he was standing on the platform at the Gare du Nord wearing the maroon tie with thinnish gold stripes of the Hawks Club, Cambridge. Also at the station was a group of somewhat dishevelled Cypriots on their way to England, where, it transpired, they were to take up jobs in the catering industry.

As they were standing, waiting for the train, the leader of the Cypriots approached de Freitas and asked for assistance. Was this the right platform for the train to England? At what time did it leave? Where should he and his friends get out? And so on. De Freitas gave him the necessary information and the man went back to his friends duly grateful. When the train arrived in Dieppe the same thing happened. De Freitas directed the Cypriots on to the ferry. On docking at Newhaven he pointed the way to the Victoria-bound train. On the platform there the Cypriot leader came to make his farewells and goodbyes. De Freitas accepted these and then asked the question that had been nagging at him since the first approach was made in Paris. "Tell me," he said, "there were a lot of other people at the Gare du Nord and along the route who could have helped you. Why did you choose me?"

"It is the tie sir," said the Cypriot as if that explained everything.

"The tie?"

"I knew," said the Cypriot, "that we could trust a man who wore the tie."

The reason was that back home the district commissioner inspired absolute devotion and trust. And he always wore his Hawks tie. The lost Cypriots, recognising it around Sir Geoffrey's neck at the Gare du Nord, had homed in on it immediately. It was these particular stripes which reassured them but *any* striped tie tends to suggest authority. Perhaps that is why so many American executives have taken to stripes – notably an ersatz magenta and blue.

You can tell an American striped tie because American tié manufacturers cut their cloth face down, unlike the British, so their stripes run from the right down to the wearer's left. Ours go from left to right. Another favourite in the States is the multi-striped Argyll and Sutherland Highlanders. Paul Stuart, the New York outfitters, sell more Argyll and Sutherland ties than any other. The affectation infuriates OBN Englishmen abroad almost as much as George Thomas' breach of etiquette in the House of Commons. Englishmen will, on occasion, cross the street and accost perfect strangers who they assume are wearing ties to which they are not entitled or whose meaning they don't understand. It happened to me once when I was sitting at a pavement café in Yorkville in Toronto wearing the MCC rhubarb and custard stripes. A bristling Englishman walked across and asked icily if I realised what I had round my neck. Had I not been able to prove my membership I felt he might have confiscated it. Not that all Americans are completely resistant to the symbolism of ties. The *New York Times* magazine recently advertised, "Your Heritage Necktie – wear it with pride!" The ties, available in navy, burgundy or brown cost 9.95 dollars each from a firm in California, and have a device of crossed flags on them. All ties have a stars and stripes and you can then choose "the flag of your forefathers" from Ireland, Italy, UK, Poland, France, Canada, Israel, Japan or Mexico.

For those who do understand the language there are varying degrees of fluency. Alison Lurie and Geoffrey de Freitas' Cypriot could get the rough gist of what was being said and maybe pick up a key phrase or two. Most English people probably wouldn't do a great deal better although they might have a peculiar knowledge of local dialect. This can sometimes yield tangible results. The Bear, just behind Christ Church, Oxford, and the Trafalgar Tavern in St. Martin's Lane, London, both have collections of ties mounted behind glass, but, apart from the landlords of those two pubs, it is doubtful whether many publicans would have an even remotely comprehensive knowledge of the language of neckwear. Nevertheless, when Brigadier John Randle went into a pub in South Devon a few years ago and ordered a ham sandwich he got a "magnificent one", the best at that price that he had ever eaten, with about two inches of prime ham in the middle. Vastly impressed, he asked the landlord how they were able to provide such excellent food at such low prices.

"Everyone doesn't get it, sir," replied his host. "You just happen to be wearing the right tie."

The brigadier was wearing the regimental tie of the Devons.

Such local knowledge is probably not unusual – it is just an OBN form of dialect – but even if one were a neck fetishist it would be difficult to recognise all the different symbolic ties available. Sells of London are one of the country's leading tie manufacturers and stockists and they list – at my count – 427 different ties ranging from the common or garden Rotary International (five different specimens) or Pony Club to the rare and exotic Punjab Frontier Force and the 8th King's Royal Irish Hussars. And that list is scarcely a beginning. It only lists two ties for my own school, Sherborne, and yet Sherborne also had, among others, a school prefects' tie, a tie for those who won colours for major sports, ties for prefects from each of the half dozen or so separate boarding houses, and a "Pilgrims" tie for the old boys' sporting association. Balliol, my old college, is down for its rather nasty striped tie but not its marginally preferable crested one, let alone the Annandale, the Arnold, the Brakenbury, the Dervoguilla, the Beaufort or any of the other more or less select eating, drinking, talking or sporting clubs which flourish there from time to time and have ties to prove it.

Some of these are stocked by Castell's of Broad Street, Oxford, though Castell's say there has been a slump in demand for the more esoteric college society ties. In Sherborne the school ties can be found at Freeman's of Cheap Street (where you used to get boaters too – as readers of John Cowper Powys' *Wolf Solent* will know).

All over Britain similar old-fashioned outfitters sell similar OBN symbols, so that the total number is enormous and no single person could have a sartorial vocabulary large enough to understand them all. This is further complicated by the fact that there are only a limited number of variations on the diagonal coloured stripe theme and there is therefore some duplication. Even the Old Etonian is

27

virtually indistinguishable from the rather more socially mundane athletics club, the Thames Valley Harriers. Sherborne School's "country" tie, a highly unusual combination of light and dark green stripes, is said to have been invented specifically to avoid the confusion aroused by its "town" tie of dark blue and thin gold and slightly wider red stripes. This is very much the same as Trinity College, Cambridge, and Clayesmore School, a geographical neighbour of Sherborne's, but thought by Sherborne people to be a division or two below it. The possibility of such confusion and the concomitant social downgrading it can cause means that some people never wear the ties to which they are entitled. The writer Hugh Montgomery-Massingberd says he never wears his Old Harrovian tie since, watching cricket at Lord's one day, his neighbour turned to him and asked, "What years were you at Monkton Combe?" Massingberd was appalled.

Perhaps that clubbable Harrovian Prime Minister, Baldwin, had had a similar experience to Massingberd? His biographer, Montgomery Hyde, tells us:

> Of [his] contemporaries at Harrow, four became viceroys, ten became bishops, twelve became colonial governors, another dozen became privy councillors and sixty-four became generals. Baldwin himself was to become Prime Minister, the first Old Harrovian to do so since Palmerston . . . he was always to retain a warm affection for his old school and he could never hear the famous school song "Forty Years On", with which every Harrow function traditionally ends, without a lump in his throat. Yet he seldom wore the Old Harrovian tie, preferring the colours of the I Zingari cricketers.

Meaningful ties speak to a number of audiences. They speak to illiterate or semi-literate outsiders who will form a vague impression from the tie's wearing, inferring, probably, that the wearer is a member of the OBN though not necessarily a senior one. They speak to relative insiders who may not belong to precisely the same individual school network as the wearer but are sufficiently fluent in the language to understand what is being said. They communicate most effectively with others who are entitled to wear the same tie, guaranteeing, except in the most extraordinary cases, a response, probably favourable. And they speak, too, to the wearer.

For the wearer, the tie confers the sort of self-confidence born of belonging to an organisation or sharing an experience from which others are excluded. No matter that others may not get the message (though it can help if they do). Randolph Churchill used to say that if one's spirits were low one should buy a large Havana and walk up and down Piccadilly wearing a dark overcoat with a velvet or Astrakhan collar. It doesn't matter that these accoutrements of wealth and prosperity are false, any more than that the man wearing the Guards or Etonian tie has fallen on hard times. He is still bolstering his morale. James Laver made a similar point about the old-fashioned suits sported by Guards officers after the war. They were indulging in a self-deluding nostalgia by wearing them, he argued. They were saying to themselves, "I wish I could go back to an epoch when men of my class had all the advantages: chambers in Jermyn Street, a manservant like Jeeves and an income from investments which, if small, was assured." Actually they were doing more than wishing; they were playing make believe.

Among those who understand the language, communication is at its most sophisticated. At its simplest the information is straightforward. Wearing the MCC tie tells anyone who has reached the equivalent of an 'O' level in sartorial linguistics that the person wearing it is interested in cricket. Nevertheless its wearing establishes some sort of rapport not only with fellow MCC members but also with those others – and there are still some – who follow the game. I have found it a useful ice-breaker at drinks parties; it stood me in good stead at lunch in the officers' mess at Chelsea barracks when the GOC London District recognised it from afar (it does have an almost luminous glow); and it has led to some entertaining conversations with strangers on trains. Marginal benefits perhaps, but benefits all the same. And who knows what benefits may flow from the first response?

Under other circumstances the signal given by the tie may be more complex but the intention more blatant. Among Mrs. Thatcher's original cabinet the most regular wearers of the Guards tie, from among those several entitled to wear it, were Mr. Whitelaw and Lord Carrington. Mr. Heseltine, then Secretary of State for the Environment, served with the Welsh Guards but almost always seemed to wear a wide, kipperish blue silk number which sat well with his image as self-made millionaire, property developer and sometime magazine publisher. Late in 1981 Mr. Heseltine was due to address the annual general meeting of the

Historic House Owners' Association, better known perhaps as the stately home owners. Mr. Heseltine owns a pretty stately home himself, though it is not open to the public. Partly because he seems a bit of a "smart alec", partly because he is rich and flashy looking, partly because his time as MP for rural Tavistock was not an unequivocal success, he is not as highly regarded by the land-owning aristocracy and squirearchy as a Tory minister should be. It was not therefore surprising that he should be scrupulously careful to ingratiate himself with stately home owners. And so, apart from being affably conciliatory in the manner and content of his speech, he turned up wearing the Brigade tie. "Look," it reminded the assembled company, "I'm one of you."

It was an appropriate reminder. It was a good bet that even those stately home owners who had not themselves served in the Guards would like to have done so or would at least have some esteem for those that did. Sure enough, there, chanting an incantatory "hear hear" throughout Heseltine's speech while sitting in the middle of the very front row, was the rubicund, pin-stripe suited figure of Sir Walter Bromley-Davenport, owner of Capesthorne Hall, former stalwart of the Tory back benches in the House of Commons and once of the Grenadiers. Sir Walter, it need hardly be said, was wearing a Brigade tie. Later I asked Heseltine if the wearing of the tie was a conscious playing of the network game. By that time he had re-assumed his usual navy blue kipper. I'm sorry to say that the minister's only response was to glance down at it and grin. Sheepishly. Not surprisingly, since his time with the Guards was less than a year's national service in 1959.

Sir Geoffrey de Freitas' Hawks Club tie transmitted an even more clearly understood message one night in the House of Commons than it did with the Cypriots at the Gare du Nord. Sir Geoffrey, sitting on the Labour benches, was approached by the Sergeant-at-Arms who pointed out that a particularly noisy and difficult Tory MP, obviously much the worse for drink, was wearing an identical necktie. It was clearly in everyone's interests that the man should be removed but the Sergeant-at-Arms wanted a minimum of fuss. Since Sir Geoffrey and the offending Tory evidently had some sort of bond, could he invoke it? Sir Geoffrey knew that the Tory Hawk was particularly fond of the club and that it was probably the one bait he would swallow. He therefore crossed over to the Tory benches and whispered loudly, "Please could you come outside and discuss some important matters relating to the Hawks Club?" The trick worked and the old boy tottered out of the chamber to the smoking room where he fell asleep over his second Scotch.

Back in the chamber the Sergeant-at-Arms asked de Freitas exactly what he had said. "Oh," he said, on being told, "*Hawks* . . . I understood you to tell him there were some *whores* outside."

The semiotics become really difficult at the core of such networks because the very act of wearing the tie is subject to arcane regulations reminiscent of privileges granted to prefects and other seniors at public schools. At Eton members of "Pop" wear fancy silk waistcoats, at Sherborne only school prefects are – or were – allowed to walk through rather than round the ancient monastic conduit in the middle of town. All schools have – or had – an unbelievably obscure system regulating the buttoning of jackets, the putting of hands in pockets and the carrying of umbrellas, furled or unfurled. Some of these are carried on into adult life, though as informal affectations rather than quasi-legal requirements.

Some people consider it "not done" to wear one club tie in another club's premises. My editor, Ion Trewin, was once taken sharply to task for wearing his rhubarb and custard MCC tie in the Garrick Club. If he *had* to wear a club tie, he should have been wearing the Garrick's own pink and green. The Garrick, incidentally, is one of the very few London clubs which does have its own tie. When the idea of a tie "like other clubs" was mooted in the suggestions book at the Travellers' (traditionally a Foreign Office home from home), the secretary simply scrawled, "What other clubs?"

In much the same way some members of tie-wearing networks within the OBN regard the wearing of the thing at all as decidedly off. Proof, possibly, that the wearer is an imposter and certainly that he is claiming the superiority conferred by membership because he simply has no other superiority to claim. One Old Etonian Guards colonel told me that he had a friend who often wore the Eton tie but who, he was convinced, had never been near the place. The mere fact that he wore it at all made the colonel suspicious. Proper chaps didn't. I asked him if he had ever raised the matter and he seemed quite surprised. As far as he was concerned, if the man wished to pass himself off as an Etonian that was his affair. He was fairly sure that his friend knew that he knew he wasn't really an Etonian but it was one of those times when it was best not to say anything.

A classic case on similar lines was that of the *Daily Mirror* columnist Paul Callan who was "exposed" in *Private Eye* as a counterfeit Etonian. It was alleged that Callan was actually an alumnus of a secondary modern school in South London despite the fact that for as long as anyone could remember he had wandered about Fleet Street wearing not just an Old Etonian tie but an Old Etonian *bow tie* which, to a pukka Old Etonian, is about on a par with wearing Old Etonian braces. ("Never be caught fornicating in school braces" is said to have been one recent Eton tutor's standard advice to leavers.) State educated Fleet Street hacks fell about at what they presumed was Callan's discomfiture but Etonian journalists seemed not to care one way or the other – an interesting contrast with George Thomas' experiences. This may indicate the change that has taken place over the last thirty years among Old Etonians but seems to me more likely to indicate the differences in social sensitivity between journalists and MPs.*

Yet to the Old Etonian colonel Callan's non-Etonianism would have been evident the moment he appeared in that Fleet Street watering hole, El Vino, wearing a black tie with azure stripes. Even if he was an Old Etonian he was not the colonel's sort of Etonian; not in his particular network. The same colonel took a rather similar line on the Guards tie itself.

"You only wear a Brigade tie at the annual wreath laying in the Guards Chapel and the garden party," he explained patiently. "And in any case *never* after six p.m." The original reason for this usage is obscure but it seems to me to be largely a matter of self-confidence. Wearing the tie is, as we have seen, an effective form of communication but as such it is a touch obvious. It is a form of proclamation, a way, almost, of forcing yourself on an audience. Not wearing it suggests a greater self-confidence, an ability to rely on more individual sartorial messages and not take refuge in tribal ones.

In essence the rule seems to be that you should wear your meaningful ties on home turf and on duty: the MCC tie at Lord's, the Garrick at the Garrick, the Guards (perhaps) in the mess; but

---

* The fictional consequences of wearing a tie to which you are not entitled are often more dire than in real life. In *The Final Throw*, by Michael Gilbert, for instance, "There was a chap called Phil Edmunds in one of his other third-line companies. He pulled Blackett's leg in public about wearing a Guards tie, which he certainly wasn't entitled to, because as far as I know he was in the ack-ack. He blasted Phil out of his job and took a lot of trouble to see he didn't get another one." Gilbert, incidentally, was in the Royal Horse Artillery.

there is a dilemma here, summed up by Erving Goffman when he says, "The uniform of an officer may be a matter of pride to some, to be worn on every possible occasion; for other officers, weekends may represent a time when they can exercise their choice and wear mufti, passing as civilians."

Bamber Gascoigne, who was educated at Eton and did his national service with the Coldstream Guards, remembers an incident which vividly illustrates this division of life into week and weekend, town and country, duty and off-duty. A friend of his, also an Etonian doing his national service in the Coldstream Guards, had invited him to spend the weekend at his family's country house. Gascoigne's friend had on a civilian suit and an Old Etonian tie. As the two of them walked across the officers' mess at Chelsea barracks a figure sunk deep in his armchair suddenly lowered his newspaper and said in peppery tones,

"I understood that one never wore one's Old Etonian tie in town."

"Well, as a matter of fact, sir," said Gascoigne's friend, with what he thought was great presence of mind, "I'm just going to the country."

"Well, I understood," replied their senior, "that if one was going to the country, one changed into one's Old Etonian tie at the Chiswick roundabout."

Such "rules" are, unlike the ties themselves, open to disagreement and misinterpretation. They also change with time. On the basis only of personal observation I would guess that meaningful ties are worn less today than fifteen or twenty years ago. Others share this view. "Today," wrote Max Hastings in *Punch*, "my only stabs of awareness of the old school strike when I see the pink and red stripes of an Old Carthusian tie. Is it my imagination, or is the wearing of old school neckwear in decline, even among those who like to appeal to its spirit?" This is borne out by the experience of one or two outfitters like Castell's who no longer stock as many ties as they did because they are no longer, in the case of the more esoteric clubs, an economic proposition.

The MCC, on the other hand, reports that sales of its ties are increasing. This is partly due to a fairly recent increase in the overall number of members and also to the growing popularity of the more discreet crested tie against the vivid rhubarb and custard. If there is a shift in the wearing of old school and other related ties then it is partly a move away from vivid stripes redolent of the sports field to muted crests more appropriate to the boardroom.

33

These, however, like stripes, can also be ambiguous. The Roman Catholic public school, Ampleforth, had a silver gridiron on a dark blue background which is just like the Oxford University social club, the Grid.

The primary significance of the old school tie is a network one, but there are aesthetic considerations too. The Eton and Harrow ties are sufficiently sober to be worn comfortably with a dark city suit or clerical grey. The best known Winchester tie is a garish wide-striped number only really suitable for wearing with white fiannels and a straw hat. Likewise the MCC's rhubarb and custard. This is partly why you do not notice as many Wykehamist ties around the city as Eton and Harrow ones. And it also explains why the MCC and most schools have invented city ties either with narrower more circumspect stripes or with small monograms or heraldic devices on a discreet dark background. These are for networkers who lack the panache, the effrontery or the sartorial bad taste to carry off lurid stripes with a stiff collar and dark grey three-piece.

Other network symbols are at least as specific as the tie but their use is not as widespread. Apart from their various neckties, the Rotarians have a lapel badge in the shape of a wheel, but lapel badges have never really caught on in Britain (unlike France where the tiny glow of red in a collar indicates that the wearer holds the Légion d'honneur). Floral buttonholes occasionally have network meaning, as at the Eton and Harrow match. At this much diminished tribal ritual at Lord's, Harrovians wear cornflowers and Etonians carnations dyed pale, or Cambridge, blue. It would actually be more correct to call it Eton blue since it was Eton who gave it to Cambridge rather than vice versa. At the first Oxford and Cambridge boat race it was pointed out that Cambridge (unlike their rivals) had no ribbon on their bow. So at the last minute, the crew consisting entirely of Etonians, somebody produced an Eton blue ribbon.

The Eton and Harrow match used to be a great occasion when it was held during Long Leave (the summer half-term) and you could get an extra half day off by attending. For the rest of the year only members of "Pop" (Eton's self-electing body of prefects and the school's key network) could wear boutonnières, but at the Eton and Harrow match everyone could. And they did.

Nowadays few Etonians can be bothered to attend. One who did recently, described it sadly as not a network occasion at all, but, "If anything, the fossil of a small dead network."

Most floral boutonnières have no such significance, but merely indicate that the wearer is a snappy dresser. CND badges, so popular in the sixties, are making a comeback; Solidarity badges have enjoyed a certain vogue. Some people wear badges on blazers and sweaters and 'T' shirts, but unless the wearer is an active member of a playing team, they are unlikely to have any significant meaning.

Some of the clubs and societies which have ties also produce striped or crested cufflinks and car badges. Neither makes a lot of sense in terms of network communication. You do not know a man by his cufflinks because you simply don't notice them, and even if you do see a man driving a car with a badge which suggests that he shares some bond with you it is difficult to see what you are supposed to do about it. No car badge has had any significance since the AA patrolmen stopped saluting AA members, a practice which, if nothing else, was a great source of solace to retired army officers.

Uniforms, of course, carry very specific messages but they are only really worn within the context of their own network, whether it is regiment or ship, and not in the world at large. They have no real network effects. Clerical dress is a better example of a sort of uniform which emphasises the wearers' membership of a form of network. But it is a sign of the times that more and more clergy do not wear it, do not wear it all the time, or wear such a laicised form of it that it is scarcely distinguishable from an ordinary suit and – perhaps – white tie. The dog collar and cassock have a negative network effect. Rather than emphasising the together-ness of the clergy, they point up the separateness of the clergy from the rest of us.

Generally speaking, laws of dress are now so relaxed that only a really shrewd student of clothing can make accurate observations about network membership except by using such unambiguous sartorial statements as striped ties or Rotarian buttonholes. Some-times, however, a situation demands a particular style of clothing within which a whole range of quite specific network statements can be made. One of these is fox hunting, quintessential OBN territory. There are more than 400 hunts in Britain today and on a single day there may be as many as 50,000 riders out, dressed to the nines in honour of the fox.

Hunts do not have club neckties and there is no way of recognising a hunting man or woman *off* the field, except by employing highly fallible deductive methods involving ruddiness of complexion, cut of jacket or, perhaps, colour of shoes. Brown shoes, in conservative hunting circles, are not on. "But all right in the country?" protested the progressive niece of a reactionary hunting aunt. "Well," came the doubtful reply. "Perhaps. But only on weekdays."

On the hunting field, however, the rules are as absolute and as intricate as those governing old school ties. Everybody, of course, wears some sort of riding kit but only serious and accomplished hunting people wear "pink" coats. A pink coat is actually scarlet and its name has nothing to do with its colour but derives from a tailor named Pink who became famous for the cut and cloth (only the best Melton) of his hunting coats, so that one well dressed squire would say to another, "Damned fine coat, that. Who's your tailor?" To which the answer, invariably, was "Pink. Actually."

So the real hunting fraternity is in "pink", but the inner network of that fraternity, the privileged few, have distinctive hunt buttons and distinctive coloured hunt collars on their coats. These prized symbols are in the gift of the master and are rewards for long and distinguished service to the hunt. Its wearers constitute a small élite – though not necessarily a social élite. A relatively inexperienced follower would wear a black coat, and a top hat if he were a gentleman, whereas an experienced follower who was not a gentleman but merely a yeoman farmer, would wear a pink coat and a peaked jockey's cap, like the master and the hunt servants. Two sorts of élite, social and hunting, existing alongside each other in distinctive quasi-uniform dress. Women and children wear the same sorts of hat as master and servants unless, in the case of women, they are sitting side saddle, in which case they wear top hats or bowlers.

Apart from gentlemen, farmers, women and children there are at any meet one or two men wearing bowler hats, tweed or cord jackets and all black "butcher" boots. They are perfectly correctly dressed but their clothes tell us that they are not, within the meaning of the act, either gentlemen or farmers. When a survey of the subscribers to three more or less typical hunts was conducted recently it was revealed that there were – apart from landowners, farmers and their wives, who make up a majority – an interesting assortment of unlikelies. These included a gravel merchant, a film producer, an umbrella manufacturer, a self-employed plumber, a lorry driver, a retired policeman, an ex lady stripper, an ice cream manufacturer, a ship's chandler and a scrap merchant. It is odds on that, on the hunting field, men in bowlers and cord jackets are ice cream manufacturers and gravel merchants. Certainly they have the uneasy, though correctly dressed, air of people who feel just marginally out of place and not quite "on net".

These constituent networks of the greater OBN do employ an unusually complex sartorial language. There are others. The tartans of the Scottish clans, as prevalent in the Old Commonwealth as in Scotland itself, are a complex tongue though not one that has a huge network significance; though the tartan may help to create a band and an entity, the crucial determinant is in the surname (the clans may function as networks because they are essentially extended families). Hassidic Jews can be distinguished by their locks and their hats and their black, black suits. Mods, rockers, greasers, punks, teddy boys and others have all employed styles of dress, haircut, make-up and general appearance to differentiate themselves from the opposition in much the same way as the eighteenth-century MCC in their azure precursors of the blazer.

Apart from clothing, some networks use a variety of verbal codes to exclude non network members and to identify themselves to other members of the same network. Any Englishman who has ever travelled in North America knows that he has only to open his mouth to be identified. The response to such identification is obviously variable but should you happen to talk in an English way in an American bar with hardline Anglophiles or with English expatriates you invariably find that there is a network of sorts to be joined quite easily should you so wish – even if it only extends to the opportunity of discussing the First Division football results every week. In Britain itself the regional and class differences of accent and idiom remain so distinctive that the same rule applies. Life has not changed a great deal since *Pygmalion* because it is still quite easy to venture an intelligent guess about where a Briton comes from, socially if not always geographically, from the way he speaks.

It is still, as it was seventy years ago when Shaw wrote the words, "impossible for an Englishman to open his mouth without making some other Englishman despise him". By the same token it is impossible for an Englishman to open his mouth without making some other Englishman accept him. Idiom, inflexion, accent, dialect and argot help to put English people in their place. In most of the world that place is primarily geographical, but in England it is primarily social. And since the OBN and the hierarchies within it are primarily social, speech is a potent passport.

It is not, however, constant. A manner of speaking which would have identified one as a member of the OBN fifty years ago would render one a ludicrous outsider today. For instance, the present generation of Etonians tend towards a sort of cockney drawl, a disc jockey dialect which their predecessors of a few years back would have sneered at. When Granada TV was filming Evelyn Waugh's *Brideshead Revisited*, Sir John Gielgud, who had been around Oxford in the twenties gave the producer and director a first hand lesson in how the Sebastian Flytes and Charles Ryders of the day really did talk. To the 1980s' ear this obviously authentic mode of speech was not only unconvincing but incomprehensible. What passes for upper class, OBN speech in one generation does not in another.

Accent can still stifle a career at birth even though a recent succession of public figures with un-traditional OBN accents have dulled our sense of what is smart and what is not. In some areas such as state education "talking posh" can be as much of a disadvantage as dropping your aitches would once have been for an aspiring BBC announcer. Yet when even such an echt-OBN job as the Master of the Rolls can be held for twenty years by a man, Lord Denning, who seemed quite deliberately to accentuate his rural Hampshire accent, we know that accent is not the easy, certain network indicator that it used to be. I was told by one army officer who had recently moved on from a spell as an instructor at the Royal Military Academy, Sandhurst, that an extremely able cadet under his command had been turned down by the posh talking Black Watch because he spoke with a lower class Glaswegian accent, but my informant, an OBN member, thought that the Black Watch had since become less stuffy in its selection procedures. The Army, however, remains one of the few institutions where silly stories about vowel sounds still carry a ring of truth.

One such involves a dismally stupid but impeccably connected young man who was up for interview by the colonel of a particularly stuffy family regiment. The colonel was also notably dim and had been advised by all concerned to ask only the simplest questions.

"Good morning," said the colonel. "Please think carefully before answering my questions. Number one: How would you pronounce the word A-I-R?"

The young man hesitated. "Air," he said at last.

"Very good," said the colonel. "And how would you pronounce the word H-A-I-R?"

"Hair," said the candidate.

"Oh, first class," said the colonel. "And now L-A-I-R."

"Lair," said the candidate brightly. He felt he was beginning to get the hang of it.

"And now," said the colonel, evidently coming to the climax of the confrontation, "I want you to pronounce all three words together, one after the other."

"Air-Hair-Lair," said the candidate.

The colonel got to his feet and shook the candidate warmly by the hand. "Air-Hair-Lair," he said, beaming. "Welcome to the regiment and I'm sure you'll be very happy with us."

Such esoteric speech mannerisms can occasionally have their uses. If someone keen to crash the OBN pretends to have been at one or other of the major public schools it is relatively easy for a genuine old boy to trap the imposter with a few snatches of arcane school slang. Sometimes OBN members have used elements of their shared language to send coded messages. The Victorian general Sir Charles Napier's cryptic, though apocryphal, cable "Peccavi" (to announce his capture of Sind) is an example of this, and for years Latin and Greek were the special prerogative of the public schools. Later the Boer War produced an example of a real OBN code. James Mahon, later the seventh Earl Stanhope, wished to send a secret message to his superior officers, Plumer and Baden-Powell. The message read, "Our numbers are Naval and Military Club multiplied by ten; our guns the number of sons in the Ward family; our supplies the OC 9th Lancers." This apparent gibberish would certainly have bemused the Boers and anyone else not a member of the OBN of the times. The Naval and Military Club was at 94 Piccadilly so Mahon's troops numbered 940; the Ward family consisted of the Earl of Dudley and five brothers so that Mahon had a battery of six guns; and the officer commanding the 9th Lancers was Lieutenant-Colonel Little which meant that he had few supplies. An ingenious code.

Even if it is not actually in that sort of code much network communication goes on in a way which is unfathomable to an outsider. Within the OBN messages are transmitted by a bush telegraph whose workings, like most bush telegraphs, are infinitely mysterious. Rumour and gossip almost invariably get around but they seldom get around in exactly the same way. Julian Mitchell, the playwright, who was at Winchester and Wadham College,

Oxford, has an amusing example of the OBN communication system in his public school based play, *Another Country*.

One of the boys had just committed suicide (couldn't come to terms with his homosexuality – a more common complaint in public school fiction than public school life). The prefects are concerned to hush it up to prevent scandal. "If there's a general scandal," says one, "it won't just be all over the school, it'll be all over England. People won't exactly be enthusiastic when we say we were in Gascoigne's [the name of the house]."

Another boy, a cloddish reactionary, demurs. "It won't get that far," he says.

At which a third chimes in: "It will, you know. Everyone knows everything. Everyone who counts. My pater won't have anyone from Harrow in the firm, because of what he's heard."

Even if scandal like that does not travel in the official non-network way, through newspapers and television or even *Private Eye* – which is almost bush telegraph in print – it will somehow penetrate to the far corners of the network, or at least to that part of the network which cares enough to take an interest. It is done in the classic network manner. A chap bumps into a chap, who happens to say, whereupon the second chap happens to meet a third chap at the club one lunch time and the third is playing golf with a fourth who is having dinner with a fifth who . . . and so on.

At its most refined, network communication is so gnomic that people on the outside are hardly aware that a message has been passed even if they are witness to it. Malcolm Muggeridge told me that he once asked Oliver Lyttelton, Lord Chandos, an archetypal OBN operator, how the OBN worked. Chandos thought for a moment and explained. A chap would call him on the telephone and say, "We're thinking of appointing 'so and so' to 'such and such'" (a directorship at the very least, but possibly a headmastership, a bishopric or a chairmanship). Chandos would answer "Yes" but whether he approved the appointment, or disapproved, and a hundred and one gradations between, would be conveyed entirely by his inflection. Precisely how he said "Yes" (long, short, keen, doubting and so on) would probably determine whether or not the man got the job.

Some of the old institutions which are the traditional breeding grounds for networks of the old school tie variety have a complex and idiosyncratic vocabulary of their own which could, theoretically, lead to network identification. Some Oxford colleges, for example, have one formal name and another for use by members of the university. St. Edmund Hall is Teddy Hall, Christ Church, the House, Brasenose is always BNC. But the language is really only relevant to the institution itself. It describes customs and buildings and even personalities which simply don't crop up in everyday conversation away from the place. Even where public school language describes artefacts which are common in ordinary adult life men seldom seem to go on using them after they leave school. "Wagger" for waste paper basket, or "new boy's privilege" for a tie so loosely knotted that you can see the top button or stud simply aren't used except in schools. So although it should be possible to distinguish a public school boy from his speech it would be very difficult to tell whether he was a Wykehamist or a Harrovian, unless he was actually talking about Winchester or Harrow.

Signs and mannerisms scarcely apply in Britain, perhaps because we are such a notoriously non-tactile people so little given to gesture. Only the masons are alleged to communicate their masonry through their distinctive handshake but I remain dubious about this. Lapsed masons to whom I have spoken claim they were never taught the famous handshake; practising masons tell me that the handshake simply involves pressing on one or other of the fingers to indicate which masonic degree you hold; officially the masons say nothing.

Masonic ritual itself is a positive orgy of sign language but these signs are not used to communicate one's masonic membership to another mason which is the alleged purpose of the handshake. However, masonic lore is certainly full of instances in which masons were somehow able to convey secretly their membership to fellow masons. Unfortunately they are maddeningly inexplicit about how this is done. There was a famous, successful, case in 1776 when a Mohawk chief captured an American army captain named McKisty, had him tied up to a stake with a fire neatly stacked around him, was about to set him alight only to see that his prisoner was making some masonic appeal. Since the chief was a mason himself he had McKisty untied at once and sent him off to the custody of some masons in Quebec.

The ordinary as opposed to masonic handshake is the generally accepted British introductory affirmation of goodwill. Some kiss, though it is highly unusual for men to kiss each other and most Englishmen will simply smile and nod. In OBN circles a great deal of importance is attached to the style of handshake. Public school housemasters traditionally explain to their charges that it is important to shake hands firmly, looking the person whose hand you are shaking steadily in the eyes.

This is actually codified in the Independent Schools Careers Organisation's printed advice on *How to Apply for a Job*. Having told candidates to arrive on time and preferably early the pamphlet continues: "The interviewer will probably shake hands with you (don't offer your own hand first). Cultivate a steady handshake, neither limp nor over-hearty. If you suffer from sweaty palms, dry your hand on your handkerchief in advance. Don't say 'Pleased to meet you'. Say 'How do you do?' or 'It's good of you to see me'."

Limp handshakes, wet handshakes and – most important – wavering stares are all, according to the old school tie almanack, certain indicators that a chap is thoroughly suspect. Alas, one of the troubles with this, as with the old school tie itself, is that any half decent con-man can work the trick quite convincingly. The trouble as well as the attraction of networks is that they tend to take so much on trust.

Members tend to believe that, unless the idea is manifestly preposterous, a man wearing an Old Etonian tie does so because he went to Eton and not because it caught his fancy in the window of the Co-op in Tonypandy. It is precisely this attitude of trust – or gullibility, depending on your point of view – which leads to aberrations like Blunt, Philby, Burgess and Maclean. The ease with which the OBN can be infiltrated was borne in on me by the experience of an old military friend of my father's, a former Parachute colonel dedicated to network principles but with an unusually sceptical disposition. Some years ago this man found himself on a particularly high powered selection committee. The committee was looking for a man to run one of those Kurt Hahn inspired establishments where young men go to be toughened up. The job called for leadership qualities, administrative abilities, physical prowess and absolute moral integrity and when the applications came in one combined all these to a degree which made the competition look ridiculous. This man, the secretary of a county cricket club, had represented the Army at several different sports, had enjoyed a distinguished military career and so on and on. The selection committee which included the then Provost of Eton as well as assorted bishops and generals were almost unanimous. No need to look any further. The only suspicious mind was my father's friend who, unknown to his more credulous colleagues, instigated some discreet enquiries. He checked the army sporting records; he checked with friends who had served in the same regiment and with people who had been at the army staff college in Camberley at the same time; he spoke to one or two cricketers he knew. In other words, he consulted his network.

The day of the interview dawned. The candidate entered. He was clean-limbed, square jawed, stripe tied and as he shook each of the interviewing board firmly by the hand he smiled at them and fixed them with a manly, unflinching stare from his clear blue eyes.

"Tell me," said my father's friend, when everyone was seated comfortably, "you were in the First Blankshires. You must have served under Freddie X?"

"Yes."

"Was that in Malaya or Kenya?"

And so on. Ever so gently the candidate was led up the garden path he had laid until it was revealed that Freddie X had never commanded the Blankshires and they had never served in Malaya *or* Kenya, that the man had never played for the Army at anything. He was a phoney.

Years later my father's friend noticed a small paragraph in the paper which said that a man of the same name, now headmaster of a preparatory school, had been arrested on a charge of interfering with little boys.

The members of the selection committee, each one in his way a trusting believer in the efficacy of the OBN and its symbols, were distressed by the incident. My father's friend was amused at their discomfiture.

"The moral is," he says, "never, ever, trust *anyone* who looks you straight in the eyes and shakes you firmly by the hand."

Had they been less gullible they could have checked the candidate out without even having to telephone their contacts within the relevant chapters of the OBN. For such an elusive institution the OBN is extraordinarily well documented. There are, in effect, cribs for all codebreakers. If you are sceptical, for instance, of a man's claim to have been at Harrow, and Christ Church, it is possible to consult the Harrow School register which lists all Harrovians (all other public schools have similar books) and the Christ Church published register of its former undergraduates. The Oxford and Cambridge Calendars list all their living graduates of those universities. The law list* catalogues qualified lawyers; the

---

* There used to be a publication entitled the Law List, but this has now been superseded by the separate Bar List and Solicitors' Diary and Directory. Nothing is sacred: the latest (1983) edition of Crockford's is the last.

army list, soldiers; Crockford's, the clergy. The aristocracy and gentry may be found in Burke's and Debrett's, and Whitaker's annual Almanack contains most significant institutions and organisations, together with the names of those who run them.

Of all such cribs the best known and most ambitious is *Who's Who*, the fat red annual which supposedly contains the names and biographies of the nation's and the world's top people. Perhaps unsurprisingly, it fails to measure up to its ambitions. It failed, for instance, to list Ronald Reagan until several months *after* he had been elected President of the United States. As that other OBN bible, *The Times*, once remarked, unkindly tongue in cheek, "One of the most influential people in the United Kingdom is clearly the editor of *Who's Who*. But she is not in there." Her name is Margaret Clark and she heads a team of five lady editors. The final decision about who's who and who's not is taken by senior members of its publishers, A. and C. Black under the chairmanship of Charles Black, who is not included in *Who's Who* either. As *The Times* has said, "The trouble with the useful red catalogue of the great and good is that it is overcrowded with extinct volcanoes, and thin on young meteors. Who needs all those superannuated civil servants and ageing baronets who have done nothing but sit in their ancestral acres since they were privately educated before the first war? We do need the men and women at the peaks of their careers, who are taking the big decisions. And they are often not included."

It is alleged that, though understandably hopeless about creative people outside organisations and stuffily pompous about excluding sportsmen and pop stars, the good book is immaculate when it comes to those "people of power in hierarchical organisations". This is much easier because you say, as the *Who's Who* editors appear to, that all soldiers who are promoted to major general are automatically included. Likewise *all* peers of the realm, members of parliament, public school headmasters . . . but even here they are fallible. Why is the headmaster of the Leys, Cambridge, in but not the head of King's, Taunton? And Viscount Stansgate, Tony Benn as we are supposed to call him, was not only allowed to renounce his peerage, but for a while his *Who's Who* entry too. Now, surprisingly, he's back in *Who's Who*, though not yet the House of Lords. The present literary editor of *The Times* (who penned those tart opinions) is in; his two predecessors were not.

The supposed network significance of *Who's Who* is that inclusion is an accolade. Being in *Who's Who* is widely believed to be recognition that you have made it into the higher tiers of the OBN:

it is the OBN's upper sixth. The arrival of the long blue dark sealed envelope inviting you to join is eagerly awaited and much sought after. (Lord Rosebery suggested the design a hundred years ago – he thought they should look as much as possible like the envelopes used for cabinet correspondence!) But the editors are incorruptible and even using your network connections will not get you in. Or so it is said.

For all its obvious faults – perhaps the most glaring of which is that people write their own entries, concealing, omitting and chuntering on apparently unchecked – it is the nearest we have to a definitive list of senior OBN members. And for students of the OBN it can be a rich treasure trove. Dig away at the small print and you can uncover a wealth of unsuspected network connection.

In fact there is an absorbing parlour game to be played with this maddening, if indispensable, volume. It is a sort of networking form of consequences and the object is simply to take a name at random and see how far you can push the connection. For example, Sir Geoffrey Howe (whose various network connections are explored in some detail on pp. 93–4) is married to Elspeth (née Shand) whose brother Bruce is married to Rosalind, sister of Lord Ashcombe, who was married to Virginia, daughter of Lord Carrington. Score four (though you could push the connection further if you had more reference books). Or "Duke" Hussey, former chief executive of Times Newspapers, is married to Lady Susan Hussey, daughter of Lord Waldegrave and sister of Lady Elisabeth Waldegrave who is married to the Hon. John Dewar, who is the son of Forteviot and brother of the Duchess of Fife. Score seven. Or again, Sir John Colville's wife is the sister of the Duke of Sutherland whose first wife, Diana, was a sister of the Duke of Northumberland whose wife is a sister of the Duke of Buccleuch. That would be five unless you are sufficiently snobbish to believe you should score double for dukes. This does not necessarily prove anything, but it is an amusing way of discovering the ramifications of a wide variety of dynastic networks.

On a less facetious level the investigator trying to use *Who's Who* to break some network codes is constantly being reminded that if this is a membership list of the OBN, then there are two very different classes of members. There are those who are born to membership – the Foundationers – and there are those who achieve membership. And the more you thumb the thin and close-packed pages of that big red book, the more you realise that they are not always the same.

3

The Clarendon Nine and the Eton Eight

> You must apply to the world the laws that apply to this
> school. You must abide by those rules; and you must see to
> it that others do the same. In life you will be one of the ones
> who lead the way; it is expected of you and you must fail
> neither yourself nor the School. So you see there is more to
> it all than mere mathematics and Latin.
>
> William Trevor, *The Old Boys*

The evidence of the OBN codes and particularly of the old school
tie suggests that the public schools are at the heart of the network.
But the evidence is not conclusive. Does everybody who ever went
to a public school belong to the OBN? Is it a case of public school
men versus the rest? Or are there public schools and public
schools? The Labour party, with enviable certainty, declares that
"there are 259 of these schools". I wish I shared their assurance. It
seems so much more complicated than that.

The left attacks the public schools as if they were indistinguishable from each other; each one conferring the same advantages –
network and otherwise.

"It is not the alleged inadequacy of the maintained schools,"
said Labour's education spokesman, Neil Kinnock, "which per-
suades people to buy places in public schools. The thousands of
pounds spent on a public school place, whether by parents, local
education authorities, companies or the state, are the membership
fee for a stratum of social status, educational and occupational
access, life opportunities, economic strength and political power
which is passed from generation to generation through the channel
of the private school sector. The maintained schools could (and do)
provide education which rivals and betters anything that the
private system can offer. But they cannot sell guarantees of
admission to particular parts of higher education or elevated
professions, they do not market social cachet and they do not offer
the tribal security of an old boy network."

Mr. Kinnock's notion of "tribal security" is, I think, more apparent from outside than within. I am also sceptical about his apparent belief in an unchanging public school class. When I was at school I was aware that there were old boys' families who sent their sons to the school so that the sons of the sons would go there in their own turn and so on down the generations. These were exceptional. Most of us, it seemed to me, were the sons of upwardly mobile grammar school men or minor public school boys. For them sending a boy to Sherborne was a step up the ladder, just as sending a son to Eton is a step up for an Old Shirburnian. Ever since I have known public school masters, they have said in a sepulchral voice: "Of course, we're getting a very different class of boy these days." This means that the boys' fathers are not public school men (like most public school masters), but successful state educated people intent on consolidating the family's newly enhanced image.

Most public school boys do not (as even Prince Philip has suggested) go to their father's old school. Of thirty-one public schools surveyed in 1981 not a single one had a majority of pupils whose fathers had also been at the school. The average was just over eighteen per cent. Only Eton came near to having a majority of boys whose fathers were Etonians, with forty-seven per cent. Ampleforth and Downside, two of the leading Roman Catholic schools were the only others with more than a third. Gordonstoun, to which one of the most famous old boys, Prince Philip, *did* send his three sons, could only manage five and a half per cent and the bottom of the poll was Westminster. Perhaps it is significant that one of the most famous contemporary Old Westminsters is Lord Stansgate's son, the downwardly mobile Tony Benn, who sent his children (of course) to Holland Park Comprehensive. Only just over four per cent of Westminster pupils had Westminster educated fathers.*

The public schools would like old boys to send their sons there. They encourage them, often by putting forward financial incentives. My old school subsidises the fees of between thirty-five and forty sons of "Old Shirburnian" parents every year and in financial matters, though the pinch is there for them too, schools are often flexible and susceptible to hard luck stories from parents, especially if they are old boys. Nevertheless the schools are no longer in a position to insist on parents producing referees to guarantee respectability, as they used to, let alone bar entry, as was the

* See Appendix VIII.

practice at Harrow, to those who could not produce "Harrow references and connections".*

Mr. Kinnock also seems to think that *all* public schools offer a passport to the OBN and he is much clearer than I am about this and about what public schools are. The public schools are actually much like networks in that they may seem easy to recognise but difficult to define.† The most usually accepted criterion is that a school must be a member of the Headmasters' Conference. This body was first formed in 1869 to protect the public schools from plans to force them into a national system of secondary education (such ideas have a long history). Originally there were twenty-six schools. Today the HMC has several hundred members and as Tim Devlin, director of the Independent Schools Information Service, points out, "There are a few state schools in membership. These include, for example, Watford Grammar School, Worcester College for the Blind and Cranbrook School." Apart from the HMC, there is a smaller body called the Society of Headmasters of Independent Schools. Some of its members belong to another organisation called the Association of Governing Bodies of Public Schools, but this does not include all the members of the Headmasters' Conference. It used to include more than seventy Direct Grant schools before that system of funding was abolished; and it includes a number of other schools of non-existent network significance such as Ackworth of Pontefract, Avonhurst of Bristol and Morrison's Academy of Crieff.

---

* This sort of thing is not, however, confined to the independent sector. The brochure of one over-subscribed Catholic comprehensive in London says that after asking for "Catholicity with Priest Support" and insisting that the school is the pupil's first choice it will also take into account "(a) Sibling connection; (b) Parental connection". But then among English Catholics the sense of network has never been confined to Ampleforth and Downside.

† It may depend on context. A public school may be a public school for some purposes but not for others, as this letter to the *Daily Telegraph* (December 23, 1982) demonstrates: "Sir," wrote M. B. Thomas of Eastbourne. "On behalf of your regular crossword solvers, I protest about the 'public school' clue (25 across, Dec. 11). 'A public school man entering the Civil Service in the coldest part of the year.' The answer is apparently 'Winchester'. Really this won't do. Every regular solver knows that a public school in crosswords is always Eton. Similarly an ancient town is always Ur; a Norfolk town is Diss; a flower is a river and the thing that grows in the garden a bloomer; a party is a do. Tyneside is N.E., and home counties S.E. Some latitude is allowed over doctor which may be Dr., M.O., or M.B.; over ling which may be fish or heather; and over R.A., which may be an artist or a gunner. But public school is *not* in this class.

A word to your compilers, sir."

The most telling and perceptive classification of public schools is unlikely to come from studying these various organisations, let alone from anything the Labour party has to say. The question of school status depends on a number of factors and is almost infinitely subtle and subjective. It is therefore not surprising that the most acute suggestion came from a novelist with a mordant eye for such detail – Evelyn Waugh (Lancing; Hertford College, Oxford; OBN). In *Decline and Fall*, Waugh introduces a character from a thinly disguised Gabbitas–Thring, the teachers' employment agency. "We class schools, you see, into four grades," says this person. "Leading School, First-Rate School, Good School and School. Frankly, School is pretty bad." The first two categories are "major" public schools, key institutions in the OBN. The rest are "minor" public schools whose network value is much more questionable.

When one thinks of the public schools does one think of Ackworth, Avonhurst and Morrison's Academy? I don't; but they seem to be public schools within the meaning of some people's act. Personally I think that there comes a point when a public school becomes such a "minor" public school that it ceases to be "public" and becomes a "private" school. Many people in the public school world nowadays prefer to use the less emotive phrase "independent" school, which means more or less the same thing. In terms of the OBN only comparatively few schools really count – Leading and First-Rate Schools on the Waugh scale. This is a subjective view.* Practically all who were educated at "independent" schools regard themselves as having been at "public" school, but many of them are self-deluding.

If we accept that the public schools, "major" and maybe "minor", are the key to the OBN, do we find a homogeneous family whose members all love and respect one another? We do not.

Working on the rough and ready basis of an average of 500 pupils per school (it's actually slightly more) and a total of about 300 schools with about 150,000 pupils, that would mean about 30,000 public school leavers a year. If we accept a retirement age of sixty-five as average, it looks as if, at any given moment, there are just under one and a half million former public school boys of employable age, even allowing for a reasonable number of deaths. That is rather a large network, so large that it can hardly function in a meaningful way. To be one of a club a million and a half strong

* See Appendix I.

does not, in itself, make one feel part of a very élite élite, nor of a very exclusive club or network. It includes the "Clarendon Schools" (Charterhouse, Eton, Harrow, Merchant Taylors', Rugby, St. Paul's, Shrewsbury, Westminster, Winchester) which were investigated by a nineteenth-century enquiry and are often taken as a sort of super élite to the justifiable irritation of a small number of other Leading Schools; and it also includes many more old country grammar schools or large urban day schools which may be academically sound and operate their own localised networks but which can hardly compete in those terms with the universally known great schools. There is a difference between Eton and Giggleswick, Winchester and St. Bees.

Within the system the pecking order is generally understood and it emerges quite clearly when there is one of the periodic games of musical chairs attendant on the resignation or retirement of the headmaster of one of the major schools. Eton is generally regarded as the top job for a headmaster. It would be unthinkable for an Eton headmaster to resign to go to another school so that, for instance, when Anthony Chenevix-Trench left Eton for Fettes in Edinburgh in 1971 everyone knew that he had not moved entirely of his own free will. It was a step down. His successor, Michael McCrum, had previously been headmaster of Tonbridge, exactly the sort of respectable top of the second division place from which you would expect to poach an Eton headmaster. (Chenevix-Trench had previously been headmaster of Bradfield. His successor there, Michael Hoban, was also poached, in his case by Harrow.) When McCrum left after ten years he moved to Cambridge as master of his old college, Corpus Christi. (*Any* Oxbridge college is a step up from *any* public school.)

"It's like being delivered back into the hands of the true Church," remarked one honorary Fellow of Corpus. He had not cared for McCrum's predecessor, Sir Duncan Wilson, former British ambassador to Moscow and an outsider. Worse still, in this Fellow's eyes, not only an Oxford but a Balliol man.

In the wake of McCrum's departure from Eton and Hoban's from Harrow there was a flood of speculation in the gossipy inbred world of the public school headmasters – a world in which the lines of communication are kept open by any number of informal clubs and liaisons, one or two men who like to regard themselves as well informed "kingmakers", and two large, more or less formal, dining societies, the "Twenty-Seven" and the "Gang", to one or other of which all the key headmasters belong. Most of the appointments were quite predictable not only in terms of the personalities concerned but the status of the schools involved. Eton went to Eric Anderson, a Balliol educated Scot who had come south a decade earlier after being a housemaster at Fettes, where he had been a boy. His first headmastership was Abingdon (Good School on the Waugh scale) – respectable but minor. Five years later he moved to Shrewsbury (near the bottom of Leading), one of the Clarendon schools and alma mater of Michael Heseltine and a peculiarly large number of the *Private Eye* team. Another Shrewsbury product, or Old Salopian, was Princess Margaret's friend, Roddy Llewellyn, who would much rather have gone to Eton (whose entrance exam he failed). "It was a shame because at Eton you make a network of friends to last the rest of your life whereas I have only a couple from Shrewsbury. That place was so priggish, humourless and uncivilised."

Anderson's job at Shrewsbury went to Simon Langdale who had been headmaster at Eastbourne College (Good School like Abingdon, where Anderson had come from). Before Eastbourne Langdale had been a housemaster at Radley (First-Rate School).

The succession to Harrow (Leading School) proceeded along similar grooves at first, with Hoban's job going to a good muscular Christian called Ian Beer who had played rugger for England and had been a housemaster at Marlborough (Leading School), headmaster of Ellesmere (Good School) and headmaster of Lancing (First-Rate School). There was then a surprise when Beer's job at Lancing went to the headmaster of Rugby (Leading School). Rugby is generally thought to be a better school than Lancing, but this move down was explained by the fact that James Woodhouse, the man moving down the ladder was very keen on sailing. Lancing is by the sea, Rugby about as far away from it as you can get.

The Rugby job went to Brian Rees, headmaster of Charterhouse (Leading School). This was a sideways move for Rees, previously headmaster of Merchant Taylors' (Good School), one of the Clarendon Nine which has slipped sharply in the league table since that élite was first recognised. Rees was married to the daughter of an Eton headmaster, Sir Robert Birley (she died in 1978) and had once been master in college at Eton. Eton is as impressive a nursery of public school heads as it is of other public figures. Rees' successor as master in college, Canon Pilkington, became headmaster of King's School, Canterbury (First-Rate School). David Cope, who got his first headmastership (Dover College – Good School) in 1973, while not yet thirty, began his teaching career at

Eton; when in 1974 Sherborne (First-Rate School) suddenly found itself unexpectedly headmasterless it turned for a safe bet to an Eton housemaster named Robin Macnaghten. Before becoming headmaster of Bryanston (First-Rate School) in 1974 David Jones was Eton's chaplain. Roy Giles, the head of Highgate (First-Rate School) since 1974, used to run modern languages at Eton. Indeed for several years until the end of 1982 "the ex-Eton mafia" in the words of Roy Giles, "had north London in its grip". Alan Barker, who retired in 1982 as headmaster of University College School, Hampstead, had taught there in the fifties; and Alastair Graham was an Eton master for over twenty years before becoming headmaster of Mill Hill in 1979. Nor do Eton masters only go on to be headmasters – John Wells, the joint author of *Private Eye*'s Dear Bill diary, and John le Carré both taught at Eton.

It is intriguing to find such networks at the heart of the OBN but the real point of these apparently random headmasters' musical chairs is that they follow easily discernible network patterns. With few exceptions headmasterships remain firmly in the family. Perhaps the most notable exception is Coll Macdonald who became headmaster of Uppingham (First-Rate School) in 1975 after being headmaster of Portsmouth and Maidenhead grammar schools, but he had been a boy at Rugby and an assistant master at Bradfield and Sherborne.

Although the rules are not formally laid down it is no more likely that the Eton headmastership will go to a man who has not already been a public school headmaster than that the Army will have a field marshal who was not previously a general or the Church an archbishop who was not previously a bishop. Still more important, the career structure of the headmasters is a remarkably sure indicator of the status of the schools.

Eric Anderson's progression from Abingdon to Shrewsbury to Eton tells us as much about the schools involved as it does about Anderson. Each job is an improvement on its predecessor and so, as far as its rating within the OBN is concerned, is each school. It cuts more ice to say that you were at Eton than at Shrewsbury and having been at Shrewsbury is more impressive than an education at Abingdon. Ian Beer's career, with a climb from Ellesmere to Lancing to Harrow, makes a similar point. It may technically be correct to bracket old boys of Ellesmere, Lancing and Harrow in one OBN and call them all public school boys but it is very superficial and quite misleading. The differences are at least as great as the similarities. The public schools are not a sort of class based lump in which the individual components are indistinguishable from each other.

Distinctions are, at least tacitly, acknowledged within the schools and inter-school rivalries and snobberies are acute. They also persist into later life. There may be a general recognition that public school men are a superior breed but the prime allegiance is to the individual school, just as the army officer's is to the regiment and not the Army as a whole. At Eton, for example, a poll in the College Chronicle in 1980 revealed that seventy-four per cent of Etonians thought that, "Etonians could be said to have certain features, that for whatever reasons, set them apart from others." (Forty-eight per cent also thought this "undesirable".) "Others" did not simply refer to people who were educated at state schools. It referred to everybody who had not been to Eton, including Harrovians, Wykehamists, Rugbeians, let alone those who had been to "public schools" of which most Etonians have never heard. As the college Boating Song puts it:

> Rugby may be more clever
> Harrow may make more row;
> But we'll row for ever,
> Steady from stroke to bow;
> And nothing in life shall sever
> The chain that is round us now.

As explicit a statement of élitist network philosophy as one is likely to encounter.

It is also "knocking copy". There is nothing in that verse to suggest that Etonians acknowledge any sort of Union of Public School Men. It acknowledges that Rugby may be brighter and Harrow noisier but it denigrates their inferior esprit de corps, their ability to stick together, in short, their particular sense of network.

The solidarity of Etonians has already helped to produce *eighteen* Old Etonian Prime Ministers with a supporting cast to match. It is an Etonian solidarity not a public school solidarity. Also because it is a large and, as one master pointed out to me, "a very decentralised school" its own internal networks are peculiarly complex.

"A leaving boy's strongest links," explained the same master, "are with his Housemaster (which means what it says, not the House) and his Tutor, and not the school." Personal observation leads me to think that Old Etonian loyalties are more clearly focused on friends and acquaintances who happen to have been at the school at the same time rather than the school itself. Etonians often seem to have Etonian friends but they seem to be less given to reminiscence about the "old school" than others.

Close lifelong school-based friendships do sometimes have a lasting significance as the friends help each other up the ladder of life but the true network importance of the great English public schools, led by Eton and Winchester, lies not so much in this formation of "one-to-one" network links, as in the expectations they create both in and outside their networks.

Etonians observe that Harold Macmillan and Sir Alec Douglas-Home are merely the latest in the long line of Etonian Prime Ministers and that Old Etonian cabinet ministers are two a penny. They therefore believe, from their early teens, that politics is a viable option and the top a reasonable possibility. What is more, the world shares this belief.

Wykehamists, likewise, know that Wykehamists do well no matter what they turn their hands to. Even if they follow the comparatively un-Wykehamical path of taking up arms, probably in the Royal Green Jackets, whose regimental headquarters are in town, there is every reason to believe that they can achieve a field marshal's baton like those two very Wykehamist, and in different ways typically intellectual and militarily unorthodox, Winchester products of this century: Field Marshal Lord Wavell, the compiler of that classic anthology *Other Men's Flowers* and the flinty Field Marshal Lord Carver, Chief of the Defence Staff, 1973–6.

Etonians and Wykehamists are curiously dissimilar animals but they do share a boundless self-confidence – rather more shamelessly displayed by the average Wykehamist than his usually smoother Etonian counterpart. Even marginally further down the public school pecking order that self-confidence diminishes, sometimes quite dramatically. By the time you get to my own school, Sherborne, which moves uneasily backwards and forwards from the top of the second to the bottom of the first division in the public school league, rather like a scholastic Queen's Park Rangers, the expectations and in turn the achievements, are quite obviously lower. Famous old boys include David Sheppard, the Bishop of Liverpool; the actor John le Mesurier; Chris Chataway, the athlete and former MP; Nigel Dempster, the gossip columnist; the late Lord Boyd of Merton, who as plain Alan Lennox-Boyd was a not particularly distinguished colonial secretary, but married a Guinness and sent his sons to Eton. These are famous enough men, and no doubt worth praising, but in terms of Eton and Winchester they are small beer. They are lesser icons and the iconolatry is accordingly diluted. Shirburnians who enter politics aspire to be Lennox-Boyds; Etonians hope to be Macmillans. Etonians who go into the Army expect to be field marshals (unless they retire at thirty to manage the family estates); Shirburnians are happy to make brigadier. Some Sherborne boys go into the Foreign Office and become ambassadors but it is not the norm. If there is a Sherborne mafia it is in Chartered Surveying, not All Souls and the Treasury.

A Sherborne education does, however, suggest some sort of OBN membership. It may not be Eton, but it is not a minor (dread indictment in network terms) public school either. For five years I was educated at this conventional, rather hearty public school in a pretty North Dorset town. Oddly enough Evelyn, inventor of the Waugh scale, would have gone to Sherborne himself if his elder brother Alec had not written a thinly disguised fictional auto-biography called *The Loom of Youth* and got himself expelled from the Old Shirburnian Society, the school equivalent of becoming an Orwellian "unperson".* His father resigned in sympathy, explaining, "I could not choose but stand by my son, and follow him into exile." Evelyn went to Lancing instead. In the context of the OBN they both counted.

To be an Old Shirburnian (provided you didn't write a scurrilous novel about the place) automatically conferred membership, and at Sherborne you were even given a form of identity card to prove it. At the end of your time there you were formally enrolled in the "Old Shirburnian Society" and presented with a small stiff document bound in maroon mock leather with the school crest gilded on the front.

Inside mine it says that T. V. Heald who had attended the school between 1957 and 1962 was "enrolled as a Life Member of the Old Shirburnian Society" on 2nd April 1962. On the facing page was a printed message from the headmaster explaining what this meant:

> I hope that you will take a proper pride in being an Old Shirburnian and a member of the O.S. Society. At the same time I would ask you not to let the word "old" bear more than a

* He was reinstated in the early thirties after the intervention of the Old Shirburnian poet Cecil Day-Lewis. Both Alec's sons went to Sherborne and he himself became a regular at the annual Old Shirburnian dinner. So as the former secretary of the society remarks, "the hatchet was well and truly buried".

formal meaning, but to think of yourself always as a Shirburnian. For the School at all times is the centre of a community whose fellowship reaches far beyond the limits of this pleasant place and the people who at any one time live and work in it. Membership of that community is life membership. To you, wherever you go, the School offers help, support, goodwill which you will enjoy the more fully if you are a wholehearted member of the Society. From you it expects an allegiance to its ideals and a due care of its good name. Through you, as through its latest generation, it must thrive, not only for our present benefit, but that it may endure to supply true religion and sound learning in times to come.

Re-reading it after the Blunt revelations it did seem the sort of statement of OBN principles which his interviewers might have had at the back of their minds and which so fatally undermined MI5's recruiting procedures. "Membership of that community is life membership" is a fairly unequivocal phrase and so are those sentiments about "help, support, goodwill". Yet in the twenty odd years since I left the school I really have not been aware of that continuing sense of community. Very few of my friends date from my time at Sherborne and I tend to think of those who do as *Oxford* friends. They, like me, had gone on there and I feel that it was there that I really got to know them properly. My brother, five years younger than myself had been at Sherborne, too, but any bonds between us owed more to having had the same parents than the same housemaster. When I asked him if he considered himself part of an old boy network or of the OBN he was positively scornful. As a teacher in the state educational system he had found that his public school background and, above all, accent, was as often as not a disadvantage – particularly when facing job interviews where the interviewers were non-public-school educated. These people often seemed suspicious, accusing him, by implication at least, of having strayed outside the OBN which *they* apparently recognised even if he didn't. A negative network in fact.

I asked my other surviving Sherborne friends about the OBN and the Old Shirburnian passport.

Only one had the slightest recollection of it. "I seem to remember," he said, "that at Oxford it was the sort of thing one put on one's mantelpiece in one's first year. But I've no idea where it is now. If I'd missed it, I'd have asked for another."

Even more surprisingly, when I wrote to my old headmaster, the author of the passage in the passport, he replied from retirement in the picturesquely named village of Childe Okeford, not far from the school: "I'm afraid I have absolutely no recollection or record of my 'message on Old Shirburnianism'." As a headmaster, he said, "It was easy to be superior and amused by the heightened memories of schooldays, by the sound of shirt studs popping out of starched fronts as the hearts beneath them heaved with emotion; easier still to get hot under the collar when some decent kindly OS implied that there had been a decline in standards. But such things were so occasional and so minor. To know that there was a great bank of goodwill on which one could draw was heartening. It also seemed to me wholesome that men should look back on their boyhood and school with generous affection and sentiment rather than enjoy the bitterness of making school and parents the whipping stocks for all subsequent failures and idiocies." This unexceptionable view seemed something of a climb down from the stirring aspirations of the passport message. I wondered if it was simply a case of old men forgetting or whether the times themselves had changed. Such fervent protestations of old boyishness are out of kilter with the age. Even if you believe in the OBN and consider yourself a member it is no longer politic to say so. You must not let people think that you have got wherever you have on the strength of anything other than your ability. I sensed some support for this when I turned to the small blue booklet which all Old Shirburnians receive every year (except for that distressingly large number whose addresses are no longer known to the authorities and are reported missing in a list at the back). Not much evidence of a flourishing mafia here: trouble raising a quorum for the annual dinner though the golfing and sailing branches thriving; an inaugural dinner in Hong Kong thanks to the Old Shirburnian C-in-C, Far East. Bulawayo branch alive and well. The masonic lodge on its last legs. ("Serious consideration must be given to surrendering the lodge's warrant and bringing it to an end.") The nearest to the sort of network I was looking for seemed to be among Chartered Surveyors (exactly the sort of safe, professional area in which you would expect to find old boys of a leading South of England public school.) The master of the Surveyors' Livery Company and the president of the Institute of Chartered Surveyors were both Sherborne educated – "purely fortuitous" claimed the president.

In fact the coincidence seems more likely to have prompted a formal network than emanated from one, for as a result of it the two men set about trying to start "some form of association". By 1983 they had found over a hundred OS surveyors, which turned out to be just over half the number from Blunt's old school, Marlborough, a traditional rival of Sherborne. This clearly rankled and they were hoping to find more Shirburnian surveyors in order to outdo Marlborough, thus perpetuating, in a genial way, the youthful hostilities of the playing fields. By so doing they seemed bound to highlight the idea within the school that Chartered Surveying is an appropriate career for leavers and at the same time create a feeling within the profession that Sherborne boys are likely candidates for it. This looks like a coming network, fortified by regular formal dinners for OS Chartered Surveyors in Sherborne and London.

If the proof of the OBN is in the eating my own experience looks, from within, rather ambiguous. Journalism, my chosen career, is network prone, but its networks are usually self-created. As Max Hastings, once of Charterhouse, has remarked, "In Fleet Street or at Television Centre, there has never been much call for an Old Carthusian bingo night." True, in a sense, for although the public schools and Oxbridge have produced many journalists, their numbers are not "disproportionate" (the favourite word of the anti-élitist). The trade or profession is so obviously accessible to people with little formal education and no class advantages that it is quite surprising to find that there are still graduate old school journalists at work at all.

There *are* Old Shirburnian journalists – indeed the head of Reuters in New York once beat me for not having a cold bath – but we are no more likely to form a Fleet Street branch of the OS Society than Hastings' Carthusians. We do not function as any sort of journalistic mafia.

On a more general level it is true that most major public schools, do have old boys, arguably a "disproportionate" number, in jobs where their experience and advice may be useful for boys who are about to decide on their own careers. At Sherborne a quarter of a century ago, this pool of well disposed "godfathers" was hardly used, though the Rev. David Sheppard, Old Shirburnian, did come to preach and made a general offer to help anyone he could. On the strength of this I asked him to write a piece for a sixth form magazine I was editing, and got turned down. I tried Alec Waugh as well, and was refused by him too! Nowadays Sherborne adopts a far more professional attitude towards its potentially useful old boys. Every year it asks some of them to attend a Careers Convention for Sixth Formers. I went to one of these and found that boys were being advised on: advertising and sales management, agriculture, architecture, banking, the British Council, broadcasting, Chartered Accountancy, Chartered Surveying, the Civil Service, engineering, industry and management, insurance, journalism, law, medicine, nature conservancy, the police and public relations. This was not a definitive compendium of those jobs thought appropriate for Sherborne's sixth formers, but it was an interesting indication of what the school thought appropriate.

The careers master had also wanted to include the Foreign Office, computing and stockbroking, but had failed to conjure up the appropriate figures. The mix would vary from year to year and although it would take in such new areas as computers and public relations, it looked heavily weighted in favour of the professions. It was also clear that boys' expectations were still geared to the idea that they were of what used to be called "leadership quality". Just as in the old days of national service a Sherborne boy – and anyone from one of the major public schools – would *expect* to be a commissioned officer, so this generation of Shirburnians unquestioningly expected to be the civilian equivalent. In a society which still consisted of those who ordered and those who were ordered it was obvious which side they were on.

Not that there was any sense of security about this – let alone euphoria. I saw about thirty sixth formers in five separate sessions of half an hour each. The most consistent impression I received was a considerable apprehension about the chance of getting a decent job in any circumstances, coupled with a rather touching belief in the power of academic qualification. If they did believe that the fact of having been to Sherborne would in itself benefit them in what was rather quaintly referred to as "life after further education" they were damned if they were going to admit it.

This impression came through even more strongly at the last session of the convention, a brains trust attended by the entire lower sixth.

One of the questions, inserted for my benefit, was, "Is there such a thing as the old boy network?" One boy remarked that on a visit to the stock exchange he had thought there might be some mileage in it* but in general the response was fairly dozy. Then, from the

* Charles Eglington, deputy chairman of the stock exchange, is a keen Old Shirburnian member of a keen Old Shirburnian family but he is, naturally, quick to assure me that it is ability not contacts which count nowadays. The old school tie might still get you an interview but it wouldn't get you in.

back of the hall there came an interruption from the Western Regional Representative of the Independent Broadcasting Authority. He had spent much of his time making determinedly controversial remarks in the hope of getting some sort of reaction. This time he succeeded, earning much the most enthusiastic applause of the session. What he said was: "When you go for an interview don't think you can get in just by wearing your Old Shirburnian tie." This brought forth a storm of clapping and euphoria. He had struck a chord. He and the boys were united in a conscious, self-congratulatory repudiation of the OBN. They were all meritocrats together.

Whether they really believed it is another matter. Whatever the true feelings about the OBN, Sherborne can still put together a formidable network on its own account. In March 1982, a year after that career convention, the school launched an appeal fund (see Appendix IV) for £700,000 to build a new theatre, provide more scholarships (irrespective of Sherborne connection and awarded only on academic grounds) and more bursaries (exclusively for the benefit of Sherborne fathers unable to foot the bills – about sixteen per cent of Sherborne boys have Sherborne educated fathers). The appeal, headed "The Pursuit of Excellence" was presided over by Lord Boyd of Merton. Vice presidents included two MPs, four peers, two field marshals (with supporting generals, lieutenant generals, colonels and so on), two full admirals, a brace of bishops, the masters of two Cambridge colleges, sundry other assorted and, not always lesser, luminaries and the chairmen of three companies (De La Rue, Vosper and Hill Samuel). I have a hunch they, or perhaps I should say we, will get the £700,000. The first £400,000 was in within a year of the launch.

Other public schools can and have put together similarly influential networks to raise money. Other public schools provide similar bonds and connections for their old boys, for Sherborne is nothing if not typical.

If, however, this was "the old boy network heedlessly looking after its own", enrolling its members into MI5 with no questions asked and generally insinuating itself into the corridors of power with a mere flash of the old school tie I was not particularly impressed. It seemed to me that the school itself was much less sure of its place in the world than I remembered, and although obviously there were some "professional" Old Shirburnians who were reluctant to accept the fact that they had ever left school, there were not very many of them, and they were not particularly significant. Most people, it seemed to me, simply spent five years there and moved on to the next stage in their life. As far as tapping old boys for advice or information or help (fair or unfair) they were much more conscious of the possibilities, yet were still sometimes surprisingly unsophisticated. Several of the staff, for instance, seemed unaware that Stanley Johnson, the Euro-MP and novelist, had been at the school. He would have been an obviously interesting OS contact even though (like Lennox-Boyd) he has sent his sons to Eton. And as far as I know no attempts have been made to get my Old Shirburnian journalistic colleagues to go and talk to school leavers, much less find "jobs for the boys".*

In other words, the Sherborne branch of the OBN was clearly alive but could scarcely be said to be kicking. The school was trying to produce an élite of sorts but, publicly and semi-privately at least, this attempt was being sustained by educational excellence and, of course, the funds to support it. Élite maybe, but not much of a network. Networks are concerned to get people in by the back door and Sherborne appeared scrupulous about getting them in by the front. A public posture if not always a private reality which has been adopted by most such schools as an acceptable attitude for the 1980s.

---

* Personally I have found that the pressure to get me to augment a school curriculum by talking to pupils about writing and journalism has been far greater in North America than anywhere in Britain. North American teachers batten on to a writing parent with a relentless flattery not known in the UK. Americans may have fewer and less sophisticated networks but they are keener and less inhibited about using them.

4

Gentlemen Playing the System

"First of all," Brown asked me, sitting back with his hands folded on his waistcoat, "do you happen to know my pupil Timberlake?"

I was puzzled.

"I've spoken to him once or twice," I said. "Isn't he a connection of Sir Horace's?"

"Yes."

"I know the old man slightly," I said. "I met him over a case, two or three years ago."

Brown chuckled.

"Good," he said. "I was almost sure I remembered you saying so. That may be very useful."

"Well," he went on, "he sent young Timberlake to the college – he's a son of Sir Horace's cousin, but his parents died and Sir Horace took responsibility for him. The boy is in his third year, taking Part II in June. I hope to God he gets through. It will shatter everything if he doesn't. He's a perfectly decent lad, but a bit dense."

C. P. Snow, *The Masters*

Just as there are major public schools with a high network profile so, in university education there are some institutions which enhance their students' life chances by conferring network membership. No matter how you look at it, Oxbridge creates high expectations in its own graduates and correspondingly high expectations among potential employers and competitors. Just like the public schools. And Oxbridge also, more than all but the most effective OBN schools, introduces people to friends who tend to remain friends for life and *tend* to prove useful and influential. On paper, the academic qualification you get after three or four years at a Redbrick or provincial university is the same as a degree from Oxford or Cambridge. In practice, however, there is often thought to be a qualitative difference. The "proof" of this is often out-of-date for it is difficult to assess a person's success until he has reached at least middle age. If you say that, for instance, most cabinet members are Oxbridge men, you make a valid point but you are talking about men and women who graduated thirty or so years ago. Maybe life has changed, but we can never really know until it is too late.

You cannot *prove* that Oxbridge will still provide a "disproportionate" number of top people in the year 2,010 but you can assess the relative job prospects of students now graduating from Oxbridge and the rest. In 1978 only 2.2 per cent of all that year's Oxford graduates were unemployed. As the national unemployment rate soared, Oxford's moved to 5.3 per cent in 1981. This was still only half the national average. By this rather fundamental yardstick an Oxford education looks appreciably more life enhancing than any other. And, of course, the critics argue that Oxford is "disproportionately" public school. The standard OBN progression is seen to be from middle class parents to public school to Oxford to a life of riches and worldly success.

Neil Kinnock suggests that public schools can "sell guarantees of admission to particular parts of higher education or elevated professions". "Social cachet" and "the tribal security of an old boy network" are less open to absolute proof, but the idea that the public schools can fudge their pupils into Oxford and Cambridge or the law or medicine or the Civil Service is quite clear cut. It implies that the OBN has got the ancient universities sewn up and has the Inns of Court in its pocket. The view is widespread. In the spring of 1982, Richard Hoggart, warden of Goldsmiths' College, London, author of the seminal *Uses of Literacy* and a leading opponent of the OBN, told a conference of educationalists that he was not going to talk to any more public school sixth forms because it was a waste of time.

He went on to say that, "The links between certain public schools, certain Oxbridge colleges and certain estates of the realm are no weaker now than they ever were." And he supported this by telling the story of the public school boy who wanted to read English at a university other than Oxford or Cambridge and was told by the careers master that he didn't know of any other university which would be suitable. When the boy's father complained, he was told, "It is not the habit of this school to recommend colleges other than those at Oxford and Cambridge." When the parent threatened to withhold his fees if he didn't get a more satisfactory reply he was told, grudgingly, that, "I understand one may read English at King's College, London University."

This was not what I had found when I went back to Sherborne. When I was a boy there clever school leavers had gone to Oxbridge; those who failed went to St. Andrew's in Scotland or Trinity College, Dublin, both of which were judged to be socially acceptable. The rest went to the Services, medicine, law, farming, but almost always into a career fit for gentlemen – or for aspiring gentlemen. It was assumed, I think correctly, that all school leavers would find some sort of employment, however dim and unqualified they might be. Looking back on it, I suppose that this assumption was based at least partly on the efficacy of the OBN, that somehow something would be found through a "chap" who knew a "chap". Now, however, there seemed a clear realisation that unemployment could affect the middle classes too; that the world was a hostile place and that to get on in it you needed a qualification. There still seemed to be an assumption that the *best* qualification of all was an Oxbridge degree. At the same time it was acknowledged that all sorts of other institutions awarded qualifications which might prove relevant and that, whatever else might be the case, one's further education depended on exam results and nothing else. More specifically this meant achieving high grades in 'A' levels. There may have once been links between Sherborne and "certain Oxbridge colleges" and indeed some still existed; but they were not, it seemed to me, the sort of illicit links which could fudge substandard candidates into Oxbridge at the expense of the more able but less privileged.

Oxbridge itself is now scrupulous in its protestations of absolute fairness and impartiality – admitting only the best no matter where they came from. The admissions tutor for one famous college assured me, hand on heart, that the old corrupt days were gone for ever. Oxford places were awarded on merit only. You could no longer fiddle your way in on the OBN much less buy your way in.

The very next week that view was refuted dramatically when it was revealed that Wadham College had just "sold" two undergraduate places for £500,000. The recipients were not, however, the moronic sons of an Old Etonian duke; they were a couple of very rich Hong Kong Chinese. I was told subsequently that the only people who still seem to try to blatantly wangle substandard students into Oxbridge are foreigners. One admissions tutor told me that the worst example he had known came from the supporters of the son of a former Islamic ambassador to London. After he had been failed ("Quite properly – he was way below standard.") the admissions tutor was subjected to an absolute bombardment from

the boy's friends and relations. The first call was from his own
tutor, at an Oxford crammer's. The second from his brother. There
was another from his sister and yet another from his father, by now
his country's ambassador in Moscow. A senior British Foreign
Office official also tried to intervene on the grounds that we had a
responsibility to educate the future leaders of the Third World –
particularly if they were as stupid as this one. The father later stood
this argument on its head by saying that Britain needed the Third
World and threatening to send the boy to a Russian university to
learn how to be anti-British. The admissions tutor was unmoved by
all this and the family turned their attentions to the college's master
who proved equally disinclined to reverse the examiners' judgment. None of the boy's supporters – not even the Foreign Office
man – appeared to believe that the college could not be persuaded
to admit him, and they clearly regarded the dons' protestations
that the boy was not up to academic scratch as an irrelevant sham.
No public school housemaster today could be quite so naïve.

In the old days such behaviour was quite commonplace. Until
the mid-sixties my old college, Balliol, maintained a tradition
whereby the master, as an agreeable sort of "perk" had four places
entirely within his own gift, to be awarded at his discretion. A
shockingly "unfair" procedure no doubt, but it has to be said that
the recipients of the master's generosity were not noticeably more
stupid than other students and usually did more than adequately in
their exams. Elsewhere, network links of the sort Professor Hoggart deplores were formally organised in a widespread system of
"closed scholarships". This meant, for example, that there were
scholarships at New College, Oxford, for which only Winchester
boys were eligible; St. John's, Oxford, scholarships for Merchant
Taylors' boys; even a celebrated one at Keble, Oxford, for sons of
clergymen from the West Riding of Yorkshire.

Harry Judge, now director of the University of Oxford Department of Educational Studies and tutor for admissions at Brasenose
College says: "The gift of admission lay in a small number of plump
hands, often those of the head of a college. Links with particular
schools and skill in manly sports were assiduously cultivated.
Admission arrangements, for system there was none, were of
Byzantine complexity. Closed scholarships protected the status
quo."

All closed scholarships at Oxford and Cambridge are now
abolished, a step so universally recognised as being in the right
direction that I would feel obliged to offer a slight protest even if I

had not been the beneficiary of one myself. My award, the Walter Galpin Scholarship, was restricted to those born in Dorset, educated in Dorset for at least three years and with at least one parent born in Dorset. It was a Balliol scholarship and its principal effect, as far as I could see, was to promote a link between Balliol and Dorset which would not otherwise have existed. Most Galpin Scholars were educated at Poole Grammar School and it was unusual for a privileged public school educated boy like me to get the award because relatively few boys at the main Dorset independent schools had quite such strong Dorset credentials. Balliol, being Balliol, did not award the scholarship to anyone who was not up to their required academic standard and I had already been offered a place at New College. There was no question of my depriving someone else who had better academic qualifications. I was simply being steered into this bizarre academic niche, awarded in memory of a charmingly eccentric Balliol man who had been killed in the Boer War. The senior history tutor of the day was Christopher Hill, whose Marxist credentials are immaculate. He was the man most responsible for giving me the award and I certainly never heard him say anything against it. In fact he became quite angry when I asked if I was entitled, like other scholars, to the rather footling privilege of wearing a long gown. He said that it was a Balliol scholarship like any other, though it wasn't, quite.

The intended effect of abolishing closed awards like the Galpin and the more celebrated Winchester Scholarships at New College is to make the system fairer and to encourage more successful applications from the state educated. It is unlikely to sever the link between New College and Winchester which has existed since the fourteenth century when William of Wykeham founded the two places, or on its own, to make the admission system fairer. Nevertheless, the system has changed. Mr. Judge of Brasenose claims that, "The meritocracy has triumphed." And, "all that [by which he means the old fuddy duddy corrupt closed scholarship and easy admission for rowing hearties system] has now been stood upon its head." He may exaggerate the extent of the revolution and also the corruption of the old ways. At least since the early sixties, *most* Oxford dons have wanted to admit the ablest pupils they could find, wherever they came from.

The old links between schools and colleges were often an easy way of ensuring a regular flow of clever and well educated scholars from the one to the other. Between the sixteenth and nineteenth centuries the headmaster of Westminster was appointed by the dean of Christ Church, Oxford, and the master of Trinity, Cambridge. Every year "electors" from the two colleges would go to Westminster and cream off the ablest pupils. Such a practice today would offend the egalitarian susceptibilities of all but the most reactionary. Yet for the dons of Christ Church and Trinity it meant that they could be certain of getting students whose academic provenance they could trust. Westminster, they believed, attracted able pupils who were well educated along lines they endorsed. Nowadays over thirteen per cent of Westminster's post 'O' level pupils still win Oxford and Cambridge places every year. Since the old custom was abolished they have had to compete along with everyone else, but the results have been much the same because they are still able children well educated. And still Westminster school-leavers go on to Christ Church* and Trinity. "There is a momentum in it," says John Rae, Westminster's headmaster, who is far from being a dyed in the wool traditionalist and is in fact regarded by fiercer colleagues as a dangerous leftie, "There's enough folk memory in a school like this to sustain links." But those special relationships are already weaker and may ultimately die. However their death won't prevent clever Westminster pupils continuing to get into Oxford and Cambridge for the forseeable future. So, although the method may be different, the result in this case is not dissimilar. Proof, if proof were needed, that scholarship boys at the best public schools are very clever. And that, at its best, public school teaching is very good. These are two facts which only a fool would deny but they complicate the network theory. The latest move – a Cambridge one – is the abolition of *all* entrance scholarships. Oxford will probably follow suit. The view is that almost any discrimination in entrance exams is likely to benefit pupils from independent schools. And this is no longer fashionable.

The result of Oxbridge's attempts to break free from the shackles of the OBN bonds between itself and the public schools has been that some of the public schools feel they are being actively discriminated against. "Dons," claim Harry Judge, "now prowl the countryside like medieval friars searching for brains while sixth formers from comprehensive schools are welcomed on visits and reassured of the accessibility and normality of the place." (This last can be a problem, and it is not helped by remarks like Hoggart's

* For a list of distinguished Old Westminsters who went to Christ Church see Appendix VIII.

which have much the same self-fulfilling qualities as Enoch Powell's about "rivers of blood". If, as Hoggart suggests, there is an unbroken umbilical chord between the public schools and Oxbridge, then it follows that Oxbridge is irredeemably snobbish and that any self-respecting working class lad would be better off in Leeds, which seems to be one university where Etonians don't go.) Because there are many more applicants than places and because the university has retained more control over its admissions than most places, the procedure often looks arbitrary. Some Oxford colleges still insist only on the minimum two 'A' levels with 'E' grades and they set great store by the interview.

Often those who fail entrance believe that they have failed on "class grounds". A letter writer in the *Daily Telegraph* at about the same time as Professor Hoggart's speech complained that, despite six 'A' levels, including two 'A's, two 'B's and an 'A' in general studies, he had been turned down by Oxford because these grades "were of course only secondary to other considerations. Would I fit in with college life and play rugger? Indeed before going to the interview I was advised to greet the interviewing panel warmly, as they would choose those candidates whom they would enjoy teaching." This unsuccessful candidate thought the "socially divisive system" should be ended forthwith. His letter elicited a reply from a state educated eleven-plus failure who got in after an interview "centred almost entirely upon the subjects I proposed to read and [which] did not touch at all on educational background, my father's profession or even my ambitions." For every complaint that a state educated working class boy was discriminated against by right wing, public school educated dons I met another alleging that a public school boy had been turned down by left wing, state educated tutors. "Some might think our boys are discriminated against, rather than for," says Eton's careers master. "I doubt that, but can see no evidence that we are favoured." Certainly, he says, Etonians get no preferential treatment from King's, Cambridge, though the situation is not as extreme as it was ten years ago when, despite the fact that Eton and King's are sister foundations (1440 and 1441), no boys went from the one to the other. ("Their wish not ours," says the Eton man laconically.) If I were Oxbridge, I should be well pleased with this situation which puts it in the same admirable position as the BBC, a whipping boy for left *and* right.

The problems confronting those admissions tutors at the old universities who want to destroy any vestige of the public school/ Oxbridge network is that many public schools are extremely adroit in preparing their pupils for the Oxbridge entrance exams. It is perfectly simple to prevent the obviously outrageous abuse that used, allegedly, to go on when rowing mad dons would telephone headmasters of famous rowing schools like Radley or Shrewsbury and offer to admit their eight en masse. But it is much more difficult to distinguish between the genuinely clever applicant who would benefit from three years of university and the relatively ordinary one who has been "coached" or "crammed" to an artificial level he won't be able to sustain. The schools that some dons are most suspicious of are not the grand, traditional old style ones whose "pull" or "connection" is no longer strong, but the Oxbridge oriented hot-house which has a reputation for being able, almost at will, to get large numbers into Oxford and Cambridge. It is significant in this context that in 1980 Harrow only achieved twenty-six places (including scholarships) at Oxbridge – less than half the number achieved by St. Paul's and fewer than several other "socially inferior" schools such as King Edward's Birmingham, Dulwich, Latymer, the Royal Grammar School, Newcastle, Bradford Grammar School, and Haberdashers'.

These, and other schools like them, maintain large, well taught sixth forms with an established tradition of Oxbridge entrance. The new generation of Oxbridge dons are anxious to find bright candidates from outside that relatively new, relatively meritocratic network as much as the old one. Colin Lucas, a history tutor at Balliol who was also at school at Sherborne (a connection he is scrupulous about not exploiting) echoes the contemporary attitude by saying that he doesn't believe candidates should be penalised for their school. It is not their fault that they went to a very expensive, very well staffed public school, nor is it their fault that they went to a very dim comprehensive in a remote part of the country where they were the only person attempting the Oxford exam. But without penalising either category, argues Lucas, you must in all fairness interview in a different way and draw intelligent and often differing conclusions.

He cited two cases from a recent year. Candidate one was from one of the modern élite schools. He seemed to be highly intelligent and he had obviously been scrupulously well prepared.

At this level the really sophisticated school will use its network to find out who the interviewers will be, what they have written, what they are like, what prejudices they suffer and so on. It can be invaluable. Years ago when I was doing the rounds of the Oxford colleges as a candidate, I was asked questions arising from an essay

I had written about the British Labour party. The chairman glanced down the table and asked if I had read the works of his colleague at the far end of the room, Henry Pelling, then a Fellow of Queen's. I hadn't, nor had I anticipated he would be there, since I hadn't applied for Queen's. But had the network been shrewdly operated, and had I been interested in Queen's, I would have read every word Pelling ever wrote and been able to make a rather better showing than I did.

The first candidate Lucas mentioned had obviously been briefed in just such a way. He had read all the right books, he held all the right opinions. He was astonishingly up-to-date. So up-to-date that when he was writing about Catherine the Great of Russia he quoted from a book by Isabel de Madariaga which was so recently published it had scarcely been reviewed. Reading the essay, Lucas smelled a rat. Funny, he thought, that book was only published in October and it's November now. He *can't* have read it. At the interview, Lucas asked him point blank. No, the boy conceded, he had not actually read it, but their history master had read the reviews and prepared an abstract for him to swot up before the papers. The boy was admitted because the examiners thought he was clever. But they also felt that he and his school had been trying to work a form of academic confidence trick.

The second candidate Lucas used to illustrate the problem came from a comprehensive in the Midlands which none of the interviewers knew anything about at all. Not the remotest network connection. His papers were solid enough but not very interesting. During the interview it emerged that he was the only person in the school studying history for university entrance. This immediately put a different perspective on the otherwise unalleviated "beta"s of his papers, and Lucas became interested. The boy had quoted Voltaire in one of his essays. Where had that quote come from, Lucas wanted to know. He mentioned one or two standard text books. No, replied the candidate, mildly affronted. It came direct from *Candide*. He had come across references to Voltaire in the course of his studies and had gone down to the town library and read all the works of Voltaire he could lay his hands on. Same with Montesquieu.

In the end, of course, he too was given a place, not because of his written papers which on their own would probably not have been thought good enough but because he had shown that he was keen and resourceful and likely, therefore, to benefit from the teaching Oxford could offer. None of that would have emerged without an interview, let alone from a sort of computerised analysis of 'A' level results. Balliol was looking for genuine potential and motivation as much as well drilled and organised knowledge; but the former is much more difficult to find than the latter. Even if the old networks are dead there must always be a tendency to create new ones. To build a system which really effectively discovers genuine talent among all potential university candidates in all schools throughout the country is probably impossible. There will always be a bias towards the well taught and it will always be difficult to find the clever but neglected boys like the one who went to the library to discover Voltaire for himself. It is an uncomfortable fact of life for the left, but academic powerhouses like the scholars' houses at Eton and Winchester do attract some of the cleverest twelve and thirteen year olds in Britain and do educate them intensively and cleverly. When they emerge five years later they are almost invariably first class university fodder and it would be wrong for any university with meritocratic aspirations to ignore them. By the same token, when institutions like the Civil Service examine candidates they are still likely to admit a "disproportionate" number of men and women from Oxford and Cambridge because – they would argue – Oxford and Cambridge try hard to attract the ablest candidates available and then educate them better than any other university. It is impossible to prove this objectively but it is what many people believe.

If this is so, it is crucial to one's understanding of the OBN. A public school education suggests many things about a man but it tells you only one for certain: that someone, probably his father, paid a considerable amount of money for his education. A public school education is a privilege, but an Oxbridge degree is a qualification. It does not tell you anything about the graduate's father's wealth but it does suggest that the graduate is a high flier with enough brain to qualify for arguably the best university education the country has to offer, and enough motivation to take advantage of it. A public school background on its own is a dubious advantage. It only really comes into its own when married to Oxbridge. Blunt, Burgess, Maclean and Philby were all public school men but it was at Cambridge that they met and as the result of Cambridge that they were talent spotted. It is not the public schools which are at the heart of the OBN but the public schools *and* Oxbridge. The link between the two is still strong but it is weaker than it was and new ones are slowly being forged: on the one hand between Oxbridge and different sorts of school; and on the other between the public schools and different sorts of university.

The head of careers at Eton writes that, "Polytechnics are beginning to be considered, and non-Oxbridge universities are now recognised as being not necessarily inferior (this has been recognised for a long time by OEs at university, but only recently by Etonians still at school)." The headmaster of Harrow says that, "A far greater number of pupils are going into engineering and other technical subjects," and that while the brightest still wish to go to Oxford and Cambridge the links between Harrow and individual colleges are based not so much on long-standing tradition as on "having successful ex-pupils in those colleges".

The statistics demonstrate a gradual tilt towards the maintained and especially the comprehensive schools. Some comprehensive pupils are admitted without an exam (a fairly astonishing piece of reverse discrimination) and of 2,836 undergraduates who went up to Oxford in 1981 fifty per cent were from maintained schools. The figure was forty-four per cent in 1975 and forty per cent in 1965, so there is a perceptible, if gradual, move away from privilege and the old network. Enough to cause some parallel changes in the public schools and also a certain sense of grievance. One public school master referred to "Oxbridge's recent policy of wooing the maintained sector" but just as often there is a sense of marginal disenchantment with Oxbridge which parallels the same perceptible though still marginal feeling about the public schools within Oxford and Cambridge. "Of course," said one public school's Adviser on Universities and Polytechnics (how impossible such a title would have been in the days of privilege and closed awards!), "there is a tendency for the able to aim at Oxbridge, though I find there is an increasing tendency to question the wisdom of such a choice."

My findings, based on questions put, formally and informally, to schoolmasters and to dons are that the old patterns are changing. The public schools are looking at universities other than those which were once acceptable, and Oxford and Cambridge are looking at schools which would once have been thought unfertile ground. New links are sometimes manifested in quite comical ways. Sitting among the potted plants and gilt of the drawing room at the Ritz (well you couldn't call it a lounge) Peter Townend, the social editor of the *Tatler*, suddenly assured me that when it came to assessing the social acceptability of a "debs' delight", "Exeter is all right."

"Exeter?!"

"Oh yes. Exeter is a gentlemen's university these days."

And on closer inspection – and if you happen to believe in such an idea – he turns out to be absolutely right. More Etonians go to Exeter than to London. It has become a popular choice at Marlborough, whose 1981 leavers went to twenty-seven different universities, and Cheltenham, where in the last five years, "We have sent 225 boys to fifty-nine universities and fifty-two boys to polytechnics."

One public school which would probably notch a First-Rate on the Waugh scale told me that in 1981 it had "at least" five boys who could have aimed for Oxbridge with a realistic chance of success but chose not to. The reasons were usually based on precisely the sort of up-to-date first-hand research that the school cited by Professor Hoggart was so lamentably unable to produce. Parents, whose inclinations were probably snobbish and whose information outdated, were sometimes upset, but an aspirant engineer at this particular school would be able to make an intelligent comparison between, for example, Brunel's special engineering course and reading engineering at Cambridge, and might (in fact did) decide on the former. (Brunel may not be a gentleman's university but it did admit three Etonians between 1967 and 1974!)

This school – which asked for obvious reasons to remain anonymous – willingly conceded that they played the network for all it was worth, though it was a network born of personal friendships and experience rather than long-standing school/college relationships. What they wanted to know was the "up-to-date and sometimes libellous information which may never get into the prospectus on which to base advice to the customer – the state of the application market, the acceptability of unusual qualifications, the success or otherwise of recent changes of staff or syllabus, the probable effect of cuts in government spending, the truth behind newspaper rumours, etc." The man in charge of this remarks candidly that, "It is my job to be as well informed as possible." And that, obviously, "I will be better informed by university men I know and who know me than by complete strangers." He concedes that links exist with Oxbridge colleges as well as other universities and that he and his colleagues might make particular recommendations (Pembroke, Cambridge, for engineering – Worcester, Oxford, for law were two examples he quoted). But, he adds, "This is based on our assessment of whether a candidate is likely to appeal to known likes, and on the comments of Old Boys who have been through the mill. Again, there is no assumption of preferential treatment. Oxbridge colleges are looking for the best they can get and who can blame them? We play the system to the best of our collective knowledge and ability, and see it as our job to do so."

This man is clearly one of nature's networkers but he is playing a network game which is available to any comprehensive head who wants to compete. It may be true that the average public school has better contacts because it has a tradition of sending boys to Oxbridge and because it has more Oxbridge graduates on its staff. But, increasingly, Oxbridge admissions tutors allow for that. On the face of it, it seems improbable that such a high proportion of able and clever candidates should come from places where the main requirement is simply that you should have rich parents. But Oxbridge is different, and becoming more so. Entry is highly competitive and open to all. The reputation of Oxford and Cambridge is such that they are likely to attract the cleverest students and the cleverest teachers. That is certainly what they aspire to and, although there are exceptions, there is some evidence for thinking that that is what they do. If so, and Oxbridge is a sort of civilian equivalent of the army's staff college, then surely it is reasonable to expect Oxbridge graduates to be of a higher calibre than others. And, if so, to protest that the Establishment contains too many Oxford and Cambridge men is a little like complaining that the England football team contains too many players from Liverpool and Ipswich and not enough from Scunthorpe United and Crewe Alexandra.

Neil Kinnock suggests that the public schools offer "the tribal security of an old boy network", but that is not the essence of the problem. What makes the public schools "unfair" is that they select pupils on the basis of parental wealth and educate them to a level at which the education – cramming to use a more pejorative word – makes some of them appear cleverer and better qualified than more naturally talented children who are less well or intensively taught in state schools. That is wasteful as well as unfair – "a barbarity" in R. H. Tawney's words – but it does not mean that the schools constitute a gigantic network which fiddles substandard products into Oxbridge under the old pals act.

"Fiddlers" networks may once have been the benefit of a public school education, but the schools, just as the Shirburnians at the careers convention implied, are increasingly conscious of the need for qualifications. The Independent Schools Careers Organisation, which had a membership of 261 schools on August 31, 1980, shows that eighty-four per cent of girls and seventy-four per cent of boys go on to further education* and that, for boys, the four leading categories were engineering, economics or business studies, science and languages. Reports from individual schools confirm this. Marlborough, for instance, now sends over seventy per cent of its leavers on to degree courses, whereas in the early 1960s it was under half.

The case for there being an OBN conspiracy between the public schools and Oxbridge has become incomparably less convincing over the past ten to fifteen years. On one level it was very much the sort of network that the Kinnock–Hoggart school allege. Certain schools expected, and got, preferential treatment from particular colleges – a preferential treatment that was enshrined in statutes. Like-minded, friendly chaps met for dinner or at their clubs and arranged for dim rowing men and heads of school to take their place at Oxbridge while a blind eye was turned to their frightful 'A' level results. That sort of networking now scarcely exists.

There is, however, another sort of network, a network born of expectation. A boy from one of the great public schools believes that he has a better than even chance of going to Oxford or Cambridge because his predecessors have gone there for generations. He is taught by men who are Oxbridge graduates themselves. Going to Oxbridge is no very big deal. Someone at a comprehensive in the countryside has no such expectations and can make no such assumptions. There is no such tradition. Few, if any, of the staff will have been to Oxbridge which will not seem, as it does to the Wykehamist or Etonian, a quite ordinary institution much like his own. For the comprehensive school pupil to even think of Oxford and Cambridge will seem presumptuous, its atmosphere rarified, its standards unattainable. Conversely, Oxbridge dons expect the great public schools to produce able and well qualified candidates for admission. They have done so in the past; their standards have not faltered. They can make no such expectation of the small comprehensive of which they have never heard.

That network of expectation is far more difficult to change than the cruder network of the smoke filled room; but it is far more insidious.

The Oxbridge division of the OBN, like the public school one, is a mosaic. Oxbridge and public school men have exerted a huge

---

* 1979 figures, but the trend is consistent.

75

influence on British life and continue to do so, but there are too many of them for the overall network to have the cosy cohesion of the networks in which everyone knows everyone else at least by reputation and in which the link between the alumnus and alma mater is close enough to become really sentimental.

This is different abroad where Oxbridge and more particularly Oxford men are often a recognised élite. In New Mexico, for example, that élite is so tiny that the state Oxbridge Society could only muster sixteen for its 1983 dinner in Santa Fe – including wives. But the rarity of New Mexico Oxbridge graduates does give them strong network potential: it is possible for them all to know one another personally. Even where (in Australia, Canada and the United States) the domestic universities are quite respectable it is still chic to be a Rhodes Scholar. I recently watched a TV broadcast of an American football game between the University of New Mexico and the Air Force Academy at Colorado Springs. One of the two commentators had been a Rhodes Scholar at Oxford. His less academic colleague reminded viewers of this throughout the game and kept asking the Oxford man to correct his English. Even on ABC-TV in Colorado the notion of Oxford conveyed an impression of class and clout.

The all-embracing Oxbridge network is more plausible than the all-embracing public school one, but just as some individual school networks are more powerful so there are small networks within Oxbridge which operate more effectively than the unwieldy Oxbridge one.

The intimate Oxbridge networks are based on units within the universities which may be clubs like the Bullingdon or the Hawks, or debating societies like the Union, or theatrical organisations like the OUDS or the Footlights. Most often they are the colleges themselves. Of these the one which is most widely supposed to have networking down to a fine art is Balliol, home of the art of assiduously cultivated effortless superiority. The sun, in Oxford, rises over Wadham, I once heard Harold Macmillan tell a Balliol audience, and sets over Worcester. Which is a Balliol man's way of saying that it shines on Balliol. Anthony Sampson, a Christ Church man, conceded in his 1971 *New Anatomy of Britain* that "for worldly success, the most formidable college is *still* Balliol", quoting the late Lord Samuel's remark that, "Life is one Balliol man after another."

Hilaire Belloc, a Balliol man, wrote some lines to "The Balliol

men still in Africa"* which gives some idea of the place's cultish-
ness:†

> Balliol made me, Balliol fed me
> Whatever I had she gave me again.
> And the best of Balliol loved and led me,
> God be with you, Balliol men.

Balliol men, even myself, make unreliable witnesses on this
subject but the evidence is interestingly contrary. When I asked Sir
Ian Gilmour, at the time the only Balliol man in the cabinet (and
after *he* went in 1981 there were none), for his views on the subject,
he said, "I don't think there is anything in the Balliol network."
Yet just three days earlier I had had a letter from a young television
director trying to get himself some publicity. I had never met him
but our mutual Balliolity was clearly, as far as he was concerned,
recommendation in itself. "Balliol supplied me with your address,
in fact. As we both went to that college, and as I remember you
interviewed Charles Sturridge of *Brideshead*,†† I was hoping you
might take some interest in my more modest achievement of
directing a *Playhouse* for BBC 2."

The coincidence of our both being Balliol men was sufficient
introduction for him to write the letter. It gave him the necessary
handle and, if not a guarantee, it provided at least a suspicion that
he would be rewarded with a "warm response". Had I been at
another Oxford college he could theoretically have written, "As
we both went to that university," but it would have been a thin
pretext. Oxford men are not particularly interested in other Oxford men per se. They do not feel an immediate empathy and,
almost invariably, their first question will not be, "What did you
read?" but, "Which college were you at?"

Just as I was writing those words, I had them questioned in the

* Reprinted by permission of A. D. Peters Ltd.
† Balliol is the most popular college in Oxford with foreign applicants and in
1982 had students of thirty-one different nationalities, thus sowing the seeds of a
wide-ranging international network of the future. Unfortunately government
policies have led to foreign students being charged "full cost economic fees". This
has made the cost of a Balliol education half as much again as that offered by an
American Ivy League university like Yale or Harvard. This, in turn, has meant
that the number of overseas students coming to Oxford has been falling by ten per
cent a year. The obvious networking possibilities of educating a high proportion
of the world's leaders alongside our own is thus being gratuitously squandered.
†† For the *Telegraph Sunday Magazine*.

oddest way. A letter arrived from a prisoner in Wormwood Scrubs. It came entirely out of the blue because he had happened across a crime novel of mine in the prison library. In it I had, quite unwittingly, described a murder which bore a striking similarity to one in which he had been involved. At his original trial his theories about it had been dismissed as far-fetched but in his appeal he wanted to quote my fictional description to demonstrate that other people could develop similar theories. I wrote, naturally, to say that he could make any use of the passage that he wanted. As far as network was concerned, what really made me stop and think was one almost thrown away sentence which began, "I had wondered, you being a Balliol man (I was at Pembroke)." It seemed that the man might have been at Oxford around the same time as me; that we might have had mutual friends or at least acquaintances. I could not help experiencing a strange "There but for the grace of God go I" empathy. That might have been stronger if he had said he too was a Balliol man, but even so, the allusion to his time at Pembroke College was enough to evoke a definite and rather eerie feeling that we were, however remotely, part of the same old boy network. But generally it is the college and not the university which exerts the tighter pull, seeks to create loyalty to itself and one's fellow members, and tries to build the close network typical of some individual schools.

Being at the same college does not necessarily typecast you and set you in the same mould as other members even though in some cases, particularly Balliol, outsiders assume it does. At a recent annual dinner of the Balliol Society, one of my fellow guests was Bryan Magee, the Labour (later Social Democrat) MP for Leyton. Magee is a Keble and All Souls man whom I had met at Mount Pleasant, a curiously little known retreat for writers, artists and musicians which has an eclectic network all its own. Magee's only connection with Balliol was that he had taught philosophy there for a year a decade earlier, so he was at the dinner almost as an outsider – more because he was part of the philosophers' network along with the master of Balliol, Anthony Kenny. Gazing around at the assembled graduates as they drank beer in the senior common room after dinner he expressed himself astonished. "These men," he said, "have absolutely nothing in common with each other except Balliol." His argument was that if you made them change out of their dinner jackets and set them down in the street they would have no recognisable similarities. He found this all the more surprising because, as he said, "Balliol man" means something in the English vocabulary; it conjures up an image in the way that "Etonian" does (though the image is very different).

The man who habitually returns to annual reunion dinners is, of course, a particular breed and not, probably, a sound basis for sociological observation but it has always seemed to me that the college had a stronger sense of identity and apartness than most of its rivals and a more diverse social and national mix. It also had a strong and widely resented sense of superiority, not necessarily effortless, which does, I think, transmit itself to most Balliol men. Balliol men tend to think of themselves as better for being Balliol men and are not always good at concealing it.

The luckier Balliol men are introduced early to the potential of the Balliol network thanks to the generosity of one of Balliol's richer sons, Bill Coolidge, now an honorary fellow of the college. A handful of Balliol undergraduates are, in effect, given a paid holiday in the United States. They are split into pairs, provided with spending money and sent, quite literally, from one Balliol man to another across the width and depth of the USA. The network link is Balliol. One of my contemporaries who held such a Pathfinder Scholarship is now a successful international banker who quite deliberately tailors his jet-setting to coincide with Balliol friends around the world (though he has failed to get himself to the New Hebrides where one of our contemporaries has been drafting their constitution).

Presumably there are Balliol men who hated the place and would not respond to the opening gambit of shared Balliolity but my impression is that it is a more effective link than most. And the tradition of diverse and sometimes spectacular success (and notoriety) makes its potential considerable. In his latest "Anatomy", Anthony Sampson remarks that compared with the past "younger Balliol men show less evidence of driving ambition". This I doubt. As my generation nears forty, I note that should I need access to power and influence there are MPs I was at Balliol with in all three of the traditional parties and that I have a Balliol contemporary in the US senate as well. Two are directors of publishing houses. There are Balliol bankers and civil servants, a few soldiers, and even one contemporary who featured as the star in one of the biggest drug smuggling cases of recent years. He also claimed to have worked as a spy for British intelligence – a job he got, of course, through a Balliol connection.

In a formal sense, Oxbridge colleges operate their networks much like public schools. An annual report records news of old boys, a run down on the college's academic, sporting and extra-curricular activities and a statement of the accounts of old members' society or association – membership of which is automatic. There are bursaries to subsidise certain educations.

Once a year, the old boys dine. For this they pay, though Oxbridge colleges also have regular reunions, called Gaudies, for the alumni of particular years which are free and to which everyone is invited. One of these was the basis for Michael Frayn's play *Donkey's Years* which was both amusing and true (Frayn was at Emmanuel College, Cambridge) except for one flaw. As far as I could see none of the men returning to the scene of their salad days had kept in touch with any of their peers, so that their present day appearance, success, marital status and general character were all, more or less, a cause of amazement and merriment. Yet Frayn began his professional life on the *Guardian* and the *Observer* and belonged to a Cambridge generation which included Jocelyn Stevens, Mark Boxer, Nicholas Tomalin and others who have over the years made parts of Fleet Street look like a permanent Gaudy. If Frayn had been aiming for total veracity, some at least of his characters would have "kept in touch", almost certainly to their mutual benefit and quite possibly without being able to avoid it.

But there is a feeling throughout the play that the power of the OBN, at least in this college, is not what it once was. As one character remarks to another, "I sometimes look at the present generation of undergraduates and I wonder if we are still turning out a credible oppressor class."

The "above the counter" get-togethers are buttressed by a host of other semi-official occasions – boat club reunions, anniversary celebrations for self-consciously eccentric dining clubs, even, in the case of worldly success orientated Balliol, a regular dinner for the Balliol men in parliament.

At none of these will you encounter the same almost tangible sense of family loyalty that you would find at, say, a regimental dinner. Balliol men tend to come from a variety of different backgrounds and even countries, and when they depart they pursue widely different careers. It is one of the few institutions which seems consistently able to accommodate foreign royalty, Old Etonian peers, and Marxists and revolutionaries from home and abroad. The Balliol politicians, like those who attended my Balliol Society dinner, often have nothing in common but Balliol. Of the older generation, Denis Healey, Roy Jenkins, Edward Heath and Jo Grimond are all Balliol men.

The younger generation retains this catholic representation of the political spectrum. It includes Lord James Douglas-Hamilton, a Tory whip in Mrs. Thatcher's government; Chris Patten, a leading Conservative "wet"; Alan Beith, the Liberal whip; and Stuart Holland, a Labour party ideologue of the Bennite persuasion. (Three of the country's surviving Prime Ministers have Balliol connections; Heath and Macmillan were educated there; Harold Wilson was an undergraduate at Jesus and a don at University College but his son, Robin, went to Balliol where he is now a don. Of the rest, Margaret Thatcher and Alec Douglas-Home were at Oxford – Somerville and Christ Church – and James Callaghan did not go to university. The last Cambridge Prime Minister was Baldwin.)

With this sort of disparity it is hardly surprising that Balliol dinners do not always have quite the cosy camaraderie of dinner in the officers' mess.

In my experience, that comes across most clearly on the melancholy occasion of a memorial service when, in the case of someone who taught several generations of undergraduates and was a member of the senior common room for years, the atmosphere is precisely that of a family funeral.

Both sorts of function can provide excellent opportunities for network behaviour as well as an uncomplicated wallow in nostalgia. At several of them I have had business cards pressed into my hands by people who might one day be useful or to whom I might be useful, but nothing much has come of it. At one I watched an exhausted member of parliament being lobbied mercilessly by several other diners, notably a don from the University of the West Indies complaining about the government's policy towards foreign students. His protestations were counter-productive. The MP wanted to relax and gossip and was, in any case, opposed to that particular policy. But having one's ear bent is a permanent hazard of the life political.

Obviously these occasions can be used like this, though as in some West End clubs, there is a prejudice against talking shop or doing business when, as the MP believed, the purpose of the gathering is simply to have a good time. And of course the very diversity of the career patterns followed by men from a successful Oxbridge college can render a potential network useless. One such high-powered Oxford cell consisted of a QC, an Oxford medievalist, a pop music producer and a lecturer at the Royal Military Academy, Sandhurst. They had been close friends at university, they had been close friends ever since. They would have done anything for each other, a fact which was reaffirmed at their reunions, formal and informal. Yet there was no way in which they could see themselves being of mutual benefit. It was a source of constant irritation: an unconsummated network in search of a common cause.

Other colleges, other networks. Some flamboyantly wealthy and aristocratic, others already devoted to the cause of Marxist revolution and the final overthrow of the former; some a tiny cell of close friends; others, quite loose associations bound together by a common interest in anything from rugby football to Zen. All of them component parts of the massive OBN which dominates British society, their accession to positions of power and prosperity and influence merely a matter of time. Or were they? The more I thought about the OBN the more fragmented it seemed to become. There seemed to be networks everywhere. Being a member of a good one *seemed* to help. But which was cause and which effect? Did the Balliol members of parliament become members of parliament because they were Balliol men? Or did Balliol just happen to attract aspiring MPs? Were all public school/Oxbridge people members of the OBN? I was still unsure. And were there members of the OBN who had risen through the ranks? Could you get in from outside? I thought back to Blunt. Would he have become a spy if he were not a member of the OBN? Or Surveyor of the Queen's Pictures? Would he have been treated so deferentially in the boardroom of *The Times* if he had not been Sir Anthony Blunt (KCVO), Marlborough and Trinity, Cambridge? Was he a member of the OBN because he was born to it and educated into it? Or was he a member of the OBN because he was a worldly success and a member of the Establishment?

5

Players Establishing their Status

In the mid-1970s, of external Administration Trainee
candidates who finally passed the Final Selection Board,
more than half came from public schools, almost two-thirds
came from Oxbridge, and most were arts graduates. In all
probability that will closely resemble the mix of Permanent
Secretaries in thirty years' time.

Peter Kellner and Lord Crowther-Hunt,
The Civil Servants

Another way of looking at the OBN is to define membership in
terms of actual achievement rather than privileged qualification.
Such members would be, as it were, "elected" to, rather than
"appointed" like our foundation members – the public school and
Oxbridge men. By these criteria, OBN membership would be
automatically conferred on the editor and proprietor of *The Times*,
the cabinet, senior civil servants, the law lords, captains of industry, and others of that ilk. Logically, it should contain trades union
leaders, some of whom, particularly after leaving office and moving on to the House of Lords, have looked the very self-made
model of Foundation OBN members. There is a case for saying
that Clive Jenkins and Arthur Scargill are, de facto, ex officio
"elected" members of the OBN, even though they might not think
so. Appearances in this Establishment OBN are often deceptive.

During Blunt's interview at *The Times*, the spectre of the OBN
was raised and dismissed with such world weary confidence. It was,
was it not, a classic piece of OBN cover-up? The distinguished, but
discomfited, OBN professor chatting with the apparently OBN
gentleman from *The Times*. The rest of Fleet Street, excluded from
the conversation, affected great outrage. John Junor, editor of the
Sunday Express, his Establishment OBN membership now formally acknowledged with a knighthood from Mrs. Thatcher, said
Professor Blunt would not have been offered a stale kipper at the
Express. What really offended him was the idea that the "press

conference" was for "decent chaps only". But the irony of the situation was that the "decent chap" from *The Times*, Louis Heren, was a man who had been educated quite perfunctorily at a London state school, had no further education and joined the paper as an office boy in his teens. He had risen through the ranks to become deputy editor and, after the 1981 departure of William Rees-Mogg (Charterhouse, Balliol, Oxford, fully paid up member of the OBN in both senses), was a candidate for the editorship. He was defeated by the editor of the *Sunday Times*, Harold, or Harry, Evans (St. Mary's Road Central School, Manchester, and Durham University, non-OBN Foundation member). Evans lasted only a few months before being succeeded by another OBN foundationer, Charles Douglas-Home, Etonian nephew of the former Prime Minister Sir Alec, who compensated for his lack of Oxbridge by having served in a smart Scots regiment (the Royal Scots Greys) and as ADC to the Governor of Kenya.

In network terms, the more you look at the recent history of *The Times*, the more complicated and fascinating it becomes. Until the mid-sixties it had been owned by the Astor family (OBN foundationers) and edited by Sir William Haley, revered today by old *Times* hands as a keeper of the *Times* tradition and yet really an OBN member only by election or assimilation. He had been a boy at a minor public school, Victoria College, Jersey, and had no further education until joining the *Manchester Evening News* in his early twenties.

Haley moved upstairs in 1966 when Roy Thomson (now Lord Thomson of Fleet) purchased the paper. Thomson could not have come from further outside the British OBN, being a self-made tycoon from small-town Ontario. He was, however, intent on becoming an elected member and in due course succeeded, in becoming a widely enjoyed if curious British institution.*

Thomson made Rees-Mogg editor of *The Times* and also made Denis Hamilton, previously editor of the *Sunday Times*, editor-in-chief of the combined papers. Hamilton, with his officer class manner and moustache could easily have passed as a foundationer OBN member. In fact he was educated at Middlesbrough High

---

* His son Ken, blessed with the OBN (quasi-Colonial) passports of Upper Canada College, the best known Canadian version of a public school, and Cambridge (England!), sold the paper, hardly used his title and returned to Toronto where he consolidated his pre-eminence in the *Canadian* OBN by buying the Hudson's Bay Company and building an unrivalled collection of pictures by the early Canadian painter Cornelius Krieghof.

School and joined the Middlesbrough *Evening Gazette* straight from school. Oddly enough, another Middlesbrough High School boy, Sir Edward Pickering, was installed as the resident éminence grise after the paper was bought in 1981 by Colonial OBN member, Rupert Murdoch. Like Hamilton, Pickering, a former editor of the *Daily Express* and supremo at the *Mirror* group, had assumed, during a successful lifetime, many of the characteristics (club, country house, good contacts with Buckingham Palace, dapper dark suits) usually associated with OBN foundationers.

The Times is the one newspaper more than any other associated with the OBN. It is supposed to serve as a noticeboard for judges, bishops, ministers and other top people. Yet for years it appears to have been infiltrated, if not dominated, by people who came from outside the public school/Oxbridge Foundation OBN. The elected, or assimilated, OBN members were virtually indistinguishable from the foundationers. Sometimes they even appeared to change sides so that non-foundationers, Sir William Haley and Sir Denis Hamilton, appeared as *Times* traditionalists, whereas a foundationer such as Anthony Holden (Oundle, Merton, Oxford, and biographer of Prince Charles) was brought in as a reforming features editor by Harold Evans.

Were other parts of the Established OBN similarly infiltrated by non-foundationers?

We already know that public school headmasterships, the absolute kernel of the foundationer OBN, are kept quite strictly in the family; that a successful headmaster tends to move from an assistant mastership at First-Rate School to headmastership at School and back up through Good School and Leading School to First-Rate School. It is clear that a teaching job at Eton gives you a head start and membership of a small élite network, but are the heads who are ex-officio "elected" members also foundationer members?

My own headmaster, the author of the "Old Shirburnian passport", was not a foundationer – he came from Bristol Grammar School, though Christ Church, Oxford, had given him a deceptively OBN manner.

Returning to that list of headmasters involved in the musical chairs sparked off by Michael McCrum's departure from Eton to Cambridge, we find that they are all Oxbridge men, but only one – Hoban of Harrow who had been a boy at Charterhouse – was from an indisputably major public school. His successor, Ian Beer, was at Whitgift; Anderson of Eton at George Watson's, the Edinburgh day school.

The headmaster who in many ways is the senior member of the elective Established OBN is from right outside the Foundation OBN. Brian Rees had been master in college at Eton where he married the headmaster's daughter. He is the only current headmaster to have been head of three of the old Clarendon Nine – Merchant Taylors', Charterhouse and Rugby, but he himself is an old boy of Bede Grammar School, Sunderland.

It is perhaps not entirely surprising that Eton which, like Balliol, has a tendency to put excellence above all things, should provide a starting point for a Welsh grammar school boy intent on penetrating the supposedly impenetrable. Rees is not the only Eton master to have a similar provenance. Another is Raymond Parry, for years a housemaster at Eton, though he never made the break to become a headmaster elsewhere. He is, however, married to Margaret Parry, headmistress of one of the country's leading girls' public schools, Heathfield. By a piquant coincidence Mr. Parry is an alumnus of Lewis School, Pengam, whose most famous old boy is Neil Kinnock, as Labour's education spokesman a shrill arch-enemy of the OBN in both its manifestations. If Mr. Parry's experience is anything to go by, there is nothing in Mr. Kinnock's educational antecedents to prevent him teaching at Eton and marrying the headmistress of a girls' public school!

Mr. Kinnock implies that a public school education, the first prerequisite for membership of the Foundation OBN, is essential for success. The Labour party's discussion document in the "Socialism in the 80s" series, which deals with "Private Schools" claims that, "Attendance at a private school means something far more than an education. In Britain it is the basic requirement for membership of the hierarchy which still dominates so many positions of power and influence." This document then goes on to produce statistics illustrating the "disproportionate" number of ex-public school boys who are senior civil servants, diplomats, judges, officers in the armed forces, bishops and directors of the clearing banks.

The writers of the document do not, however, refer to a small survey conducted just before he died in 1977 by David Malbert, city editor of the *Evening Standard*. Malbert took as his sample the chief executives of the thirty companies whose shares are quoted in the *Financial Times* index and he found that eighteen of the thirty came from "middle- or working-class homes with no large inherited wealth or family strings to draw them upwards". Some of these were public school products but among them were some interesting state educated exceptions.

The head of Courtaulds, whose father was a porter at King's Cross, attended Tottenham County School.

The chairman and chief executive of Boots, whose father was a lathe operator, was at Long Eaton Grammar School.

The boss of GEC (and in effect its creator) was a council school boy whose first job was as a junior administrative officer at the Admiralty.

The head of Glaxo, whose father was a gardener, went to the County School, Acton.

Hawker Siddeley's chairman and managing director was at Alsop High School.

The chairman of ICI was at High Pavement Grammar School.

The chairman of Vickers was at a Manchester secondary school.

The chairman of Grand Metropolitan Hotels was at a London grammar school.

The chief executive of Tube Investments, a schoolmaster's son, was at Manchester Grammar School.

The top man at Lucas Industries was at Bishop Vesey's Grammar School, Birmingham.

Beecham's boss was at Yeovil Grammar.

The executive head of EMI was at Brighton, Hove and Sussex Grammar School.

Even those whom Malbert identified as "silver spooners" – men who had some sort of family connection or other parental advantage – were not all public school men. Marcus Sieff, of Marks and Spencer, was at Manchester Grammar (though he did later go to St. Paul's and send his son to Repton). The head of United Drapery Stores, who had been part of a family firm taken over by UDS, was at Leeds Grammar School.

Nor does the Labour party document mention a 1981 survey conducted for the executive search agency (alias head hunters), Korn Ferry by the London Business School. This found that a majority of top directors in Britain (fifty-one per cent) had been to grammar school. Five per cent were at secondary moderns, three at comprehensives and two at technical schools. Only thirty-eight per cent were privately educated.

Captains of industry are obviously members of the Establishment OBN, though, as we now see, not necessarily members of the public school/Oxbridge or Foundation OBN. Cabinet ministers even more obviously belong to the first OBN though not automatically to the second. They are likely, also, to belong to another much smaller and more exclusive network. As part of a team appointed by a Prime Minister on his or her own initiative, they presumably belong to that person's personal network of confidants and followers. In Britain most cabinet ministers have to be elected MPs, a constraint which is particularly British. In other countries the leader is able to put in a personal network of followers whose only qualification is their loyalty and compatibility. It happens, shamelessly, in American politics when every four years a new mafia takes over the White House, unelected and unanswerable: Camelot and Cape Cod; the Watergate Conspirators; the Georgians and now the Californians and the men from Bechtel. All of them friends of the President no less, and in some cases not much more.

The obvious outsider in President Reagan's team was Secretary of State Alexander Haig, who was chosen on grounds of supposed ability rather than compatibility. After his sudden resignation in June 1982 a *New York Times* article commented that, "Mr. Reagan was at last free to construct a corral of cordiality around the Oval Office. Its main stanchions are four easygoing Westerners – counsellor Edwin Meese 3rd, chief of staff James A. Baker 3rd, deputy chief of staff Michael K. Deaver and national security adviser William P. Clark. The ascent of these three Californians and a lone Texan, Mr. Baker, shows that, for better or worse, Mr. Reagan intends to surround himself with advisers who make him feel comfortable." Haig's successor as Secretary of State was George Schultz, president of the Californian based Bechtel Corporation where a colleague of his had once been Reagan's Defence Secretary, Caspar Weinberger. At his first conference Schultz introduced himself with the words, "I'm George Schultz. I'm from California." Enough said! everyone agreed.

In Rumania at the beginning of the eighties President Ceausescu imposed a network government unprecedented in any system which has pretensions to election or competition. Ceausescu was President, Secretary General of the party, Supreme Commander of the armed forces and head of the Permanent Bureau of the party's Political Executive Committee which actually runs the country.

His wife Elena was first deputy Prime Minister and his brother-in-law, Ilie Verdet, Prime Minister, a job in which he succeeded another brother-in-law, Manea Manescu. Ceausescu's son, Nicu, was Secretary of the Union of Communist Youth; his brother, General Ilie Ceausescu, deputy Defence Minister; a second brother, Ion, deputy Minister of Agriculture and a third, Martin, director of the Rumanian economic agency in Vienna. Their sister, Florea, was the regime's public relations person. And to complete this cosy family picture there were two presidential nephews in the hierarchy – the Minister of Foreign Trade and another deputy Prime Minister.

In Britain we do things differently.

During this century several Prime Ministers have made a minor fetish of promoting men from within their own branch of the OBN. In 1923, Stanley Baldwin told the Old Harrovian Association: "I remember how in previous governments there had been four, perhaps five Harrovians and I determined to have six . . . I managed to make my six by keeping the post of Chancellor of the Exchequer for myself."*

Many a true word . . . , though a love of such associations has never been confined to Baldwin, Harrovians or even Conservatives. Clement Attlee was very proud of his old college, University, Oxford, where Harold Wilson was praelector in economics and domestic bursar. In 1947 Attlee made Wilson President of the Board of Trade, thus creating the youngest cabinet minister since Pitt. Wilson was just thirty-one years old and had only been an MP for two years. The Prime Minister was an even prouder Old Haileyburian. Haileybury which had then been in existence for less than a century had scarcely had time to build a political tradition. Even though the Labour party was full of public school men (Cripps, Dalton, Gaitskell, Crossman, even Michael Foot) no other Haileybury men were senior enough to be put into the cabinet. Luckily, however, there were some in more junior echelons of the party. "Other things being equal I didn't see why I should not select someone from my own school," said Attlee. Other things being equal, he therefore made Sir Geoffrey de Freitas, Old Haileyburian, his PPS. De Freitas was, naturally,

---

* The decline of Harrow, historically the most successful political nursery after Eton, has been remarkable. The last Harrovian Prime Minister, Churchill, seemed to prefer family to school chums and his sons-in-law Duncan Sandys and Christopher Soames were both at Eton. The only Harrovian given cabinet rank by Mrs. Thatcher has been Sir Keith Joseph.

quite clear that he would not have got the job if he hadn't been up to it thus reinforcing a fundamental point about *modern* networking: the network connection is seldom enough on its own. Attlee could not and would not have appointed *any* old Haileyburian but having found one who was appropriately qualified and whom he liked he was delighted to appoint him. "Other things" must be equal, and even more important, seen to be equal. Another Haileyburian, Julian Snow, later Lord Burntwood, became a junior whip, a source of extra delight to Attlee. Because Snow was an officer in the Gunners, he was entitled to wear his uniform in parliament. Snow, who was extremely tall and imposing – and the grandson of a baronet – was exactly the sort of figure the Conservatives would have liked as a junior whip themselves, visible evidence that Labour were indeed the masters now. This appealed to Attlee's sense of humour.

His third Haileyburian appointment was Christopher, now Lord, Mayhew who went to the Foreign Office to work for Ernest Bevin.

"Clem Attlee was undoubtedly a very loyal Old Haileyburian," says Mayhew, "and when appointing me parliamentary under secretary at the Foreign Office in 1946, he made a joke that he enjoyed promoting Haileyburians – mentioning Geoffrey de Freitas and an air marshal (presumably Slessor). But it was, of course, just a joke – certainly in my case, because Bevin had asked for me specifically and Attlee merely agreed."

Mrs. Thatcher is not much given to jokes and certainly not to that kind of joke. Being a woman, though in many ways a remarkably virile one, she is naturally excluded from many of the traditional all-male OBN stamping grounds. Her first Foreign Secretary, Lord Carrington, a fine specimen of clubbable man is a member of the Turf, Pratt's, White's and the Carlton. Mrs. Thatcher is a member of the Carlton by virtue of her leadership of the party but her sex excludes her from the others. She is emphatically from outside the old Tory "magic circle". She was not at Eton, nor did she serve in the Guards. She was at Oxford but Somerville, impressive forcing ground for lady politicians though it is (Mrs. Gandhi and Shirley Williams are other Somerville women), is not Balliol or Christ Church. Her style, like Mr. Heath's, is abrasive and brisk. The least apposite adjective you could use of her would be genial. (Odd that the Tories should have chosen two such essentially un-OBN loners as leaders while the Labour party should have elected, in Wilson, Callaghan and Foot, three networkers who cultivated – or at least acquired – an image of almost extravagant agreeableness and sociability.)

Mrs. Thatcher took office in 1979 with a reputation for being very much her own woman. Like all Prime Ministers she had, in theory, a free hand in the appointment of her ministers and yet only three of them had not served in some previous Conservative government. Unlike American or Rumanian cabinet members they come from a party network rather than a personal one. These included two who were not destined to serve long in her cabinet, Norman St. John-Stevas and Angus Maude, neither of whom seemed to be a very obvious expression of the new Prime Minister's personality. The third was John Biffen, who looked more characteristically Thatcherite, with apparently similar views on monetary policy and a state school and Oxbridge education. Otherwise they did not look like her men at all. Many looked like Heath's men, notably Peter Walker, and for a time it seemed she would even be obliged to find a place for Mr. Heath himself. Some had much longer pedigrees. She even brought back Sir Winston Churchill's son-in-law, Lord Soames. After almost a decade away in Paris and Brussels he had been put out to grass in spectacularly lush pastures as a director of the National Westminster Bank and N. M. Rothschild and Sons (where his son Nicholas was also employed). He certainly wasn't part of her network. "As I first entered politics in the House of Commons in 1950 – twenty-nine years before the first cabinet of the present government was formed," he says, "it is obvious that I would have a number of friends and acquaintances in the political world particularly among the present more senior members of the Conservative party in the House who had been in or near government as I was, between '51 and '64; notably Quintin Hailsham, William Whitelaw and Peter Carrington. I think I am right in saying that, of the '79 cabinet, only Hailsham and myself had been in the '59–'64 cabinet. As I had been abroad from '68 to '77, I did not serve either in the Heath cabinet or in Mrs. Thatcher's shadow cabinet. So though I had met Mrs. Thatcher perhaps a handful of times before she formed her cabinet in 1979, I did not know her at all well."

The first cabinet of the daughter of the former chairman of Grantham Rotary Club was twenty-two strong. It contained six Etonians (half the number appointed by Edward Heath, the same as Harold Macmillan and only two less than Neville Chamberlain before the war); three Wykehamists and only four who had not been to public school. Six ministers had served with the Brigade of

Guards and eighteen had been at Oxbridge, though even here the Prime Minister had not chosen in her own image. There were eleven Cantabridgians against only eight Oxonians (the extra man is Norman St. John-Stevas who, rather excessively, attended both Oxford *and* Cambridge). It was a very traditional old-fashioned looking cabinet, apart from its leader, even down to boasting a hereditary baron (the sixth of that name since the barony was created at the end of the eighteenth century) as Foreign Secretary.

Could it, since it was so manifestly not a reflection of Mrs. Thatcher's personality, be described as a ministry of all the talents? Were they simply the best men for the job? That is not an argument to which any reasonable person would readily subscribe. It does not fit with the facts of life as known to the network theorist.

Allowing for a certain number of wild cards who always seem to crop up in a team – Mrs. Thatcher herself being the most obvious example – that cabinet contained two identifiable groups. The first is the old school of Tories epitomised by Lord Soames. Soames himself mentions Hailsham, Whitelaw and Carrington. In their response to my questions, Mr. Whitelaw and Lord Carrington both singled out each other and mentioned their main extra-political link. "Peter Carrington and I were both in the Brigade of Guards during the War, he in the Grenadiers and I in the Scots Guards," says Mr. Whitelaw. Though he adds that, "Our paths did not cross much during the War although we knew each other at that time." Lord Carrington also mentioned Lord Hailsham as "a particularly valued friend outside politics" adding with characteristic urbanity (and political caution), "For the rest, they are all friends."

In the course of Mrs. Thatcher's Prime Ministership this group has suffered severely. Three Guards officers (Soames, Gilmour and Carrington) had gone by early 1982. Their departure also meant that the number of Etonians had been halved and Eton suffered further with the exit of Lord Thorneycroft, the party chairman and his replacement by Cecil Parkinson of the Royal Grammar School, Lancaster, and Cambridge. The already "disproportionate" number of Cambridge men increased and the team acquired its most recognisable Thatcherite member, the aggressively tough talking (in a thoroughly un-OBN accent) Norman Tebbit of Edmonton County Grammar School.

By 1983 Mrs. Thatcher's self-confidence had grown to such an extent that her enemies were referring to her appointments as "ruthlessly partisan". After her final pre-election cabinet reshuffle in January 1983 the Cabinet casualties were Carrington, Soames,

Gilmour, Stevas, Atkins, Carlisle and Nott. Their successors were visibly more Thatcherite in style and political attitude. Of Tebbit, Lawson, Fowler, Brittan, Parkinson, King and Lady Young only Lawson and King had been to a major public school (Westminster and Rugby), though Lady Young was, like Lady Antonia Fraser, one of those rare females to attend the Dragon School, Oxford, arguably Britain's leading "network" prep school (see footnote to p. 141). Oxbridge gained. Six of the new were Oxbridge graduates, against only two of the old, but the complexion of the cabinet was now unprecedently light blue, Cambridge leading by a score of thirteen to eight. But, most important, the cabinet looked much less like a product of traditional Tory party networks and much more like Mrs. Thatcher's own.

When you examine the network fine print there are some odd details. Unexpected, for instance, to find that both Tom King and Cecil Parkinson were at Emmanuel College, Cambridge – not a place with traditionally impressive network credentials.

Sir Geoffrey Howe, who obviously understands networking,* revealed some interesting points of detail such as that between 1963 and 1966 he and John Biffen shared a constituency house together at Malpas, Cheshire, when he was MP for Bebington, to the north, and Biffen represented Oswestry, to the south. There is also a long standing link between Sir Geoffrey and Patrick Jenkin.

The two men, says Howe, "came down from Cambridge at the same time, and studied for and passed our Bar Final examinations together, while sharing a flat at 28, Denning Road, NW3 – for which we paid the princely rent of three guineas a week inclusive. Our feeding arrangements during that still rationed era were guided by a book called *Cookery for Brides, Bachelors and Beginners*. We were the founder members, indeed the only active members of the Denning Road Parliamentarians Club, of which the president was our landlady, Miss Alexander." The Denning Road parliamentarians are obviously a key mini-network of our times.

More seriously Howe points to the Bow Group, which is a focus for the second mini-network group. He was chairman in 1955. Ten

---

* "If you want a different link," he says, "I was at school at Bryntirion School, Bridgend, with John Stradling Thomas (MP for Monmouth and deputy chief whip). Both he and I were at one time Conservative candidates for Aberavon – so too were at least three other Conservative MPs."

"I hope," he adds, "that this lays enough further false trails for you to follow."

Bow Group members including himself were destined to become Mrs. Thatcher's ministers: Michael Heseltine, Nicholas Edwards, Patrick Jenkin, John Biffen, David Howell, Mark Carlisle, Norman St. John-Stevas, Norman Fowler and Keith Joseph. Another was Leon Brittan who joined the cabinet in 1981 and is described by Howe as "a very close friend of ours for many years".

The majority of these men were at Cambridge and this seems to have been more than just coincidence. It was a network based on personal links not just a common background.* John Nott told me that David Howell and he were contemporaries and friends – though not debating partners and that Nicholas Edwards, the Secretary of State for Wales, was in the same college, Trinity, at the same time. Leon Brittan and Norman Fowler, Minister of Transport, were his immediate successors as President of the Cambridge Union. John Biffen, Geoffrey Howe and Cecil Parkinson had only just left and were still very much a part of recent memory.

Howe, pointing to the preponderance of Cambridge men in the Bow Group of the mid-fifties, says that although it was "only a political association" it was "a very close one in some cases". It is a necessary reminder that politics itself is a great network breeder and that the nature of the House of Commons, in particular, and of the MP's life, in general, lends itself to the formation of cliques and cabals and groups which may be initially based on realpolitik but which often come to have as much to do with friendship and a pleasure in each other's company as with particular views on the Common Market's agricultural policy or the advisability of purchasing Trident.

At first I thought it was flannel – a way of trying to explain to an outsider that politics was simply about politics and not to be sullied with considerations of family, education or network of any kind – but after a while the protestations that political friendships were formed *within* the House of Commons *after* arrival began to convince me. Humphrey Atkins, who, like his boss Lord Carrington, was a victim of the Falklands affair, said that he had never met a single one of his cabinet colleagues before entering the House in

---

* William Whitelaw points out that, "Various members of it (the cabinet) were at Winchester," but that his fellow Wykehamists, Geoffrey Howe and George Younger "are both much younger than I am". And there are a crucial five years between the two younger men as well. A shared alma mater, therefore, but no personal friendships.

1955* (he was at Wellington, and was the cabinet's only naval officer). "Since then, of course," he told me, "I have got to know all of them socially, but the main contact has been that of politics." Francis Pym also told me that "my friendships with colleagues have grown up during my time in politics", and even though John Nott pointed out the newly dominant Cambridge mafia he also said it hadn't been possible to get to know senior colleagues really well until he became an MP in 1966. Remember, too, Lord Soames on his thirty years of political life since he first entered the House: "It is obvious that I would have a number of friends and acquaintances in the political world." Obvious? When you think about it, it *is* obvious but it wouldn't be obvious everywhere, even in places which are thought of as similarly cliquish. "As I first entered the Board of Trade in 1950." Much less . . . "as I first entered ICI or Tube Investments . . ."

Some careers are conducive to the forming of friendships and networks. Others are not.

The cabinet ministers were saying that, whether or not they were members of the Foundation OBN, they had spent much of their time in politics building a set of friends and acquaintances who might in time become useful to them. Most of them had acquired a personal political network which transcended the unwieldy OBN. At the same time, many of those who came from outside the Foundation OBN had been at obvious pains to acquire the superficial characteristics of the traditional old boys. This meant that they were virtually indistinguishable from the genuine article and stood a better chance of being assimilated by them than if they preserved the class image with which they were born. The top brass of the Labour Party, much less Oxford than in the Harold Wilson era, obviously promote a folksier image even when they are public school men such as Michael Foot and Tony Benn. But they too have PPNs acquired in their time in parliament and if they are not, for the most part, OBN foundationers they are, ex officio, OBN establishmentarians.

To the untutored eye, Cecil Parkinson looks the very model of an old school tie Tory chairman, just as much a part of the OBN as, say, the Old Etonian Francis Pym, which was why, perhaps, he seemed to appear so often on American television putting the

*. The only other minister to make the same claim, Angus Maude (Paymaster-General in Mrs. Thatcher's first cabinet), was at Rugby and Oriel, Oxford, and served in the RASC.

government case on the Falklands crisis. Mr. Parkinson has jumped a class or so. Nothing wrong with this except that it complicates the Kinnock type view of the OBN as something fixed and self-perpetuating.

The links between the Establishment OBN and the Foundation OBN certainly exist, in the sense that a high proportion of the latter are members of the former, but there are large numbers of OBN foundationers who do not make it into the Establishment OBN; and a significant number of Establishment OBN members who graduate from outside. And, very often, small personal networks like the Cambridge/Bow Group connection or the Eton College staff room can be infinitely more valuable than membership of the large impersonal Foundation OBN.

Politics is not an exact science. One does not take a written exam before becoming a member of parliament. It is essentially a matter of wheeling and dealing, winning people's confidence, returning favours scrupulously and judiciously: a matter of networking; likewise journalism, even at *The Times*, and still more so climbing to the top of a big business or making the career leaps from one headmastership to another. But somewhere in life there must be places where all that counts is absolute merit and ability in the abstract. In social institutions where clubbability is the main criterion it is obvious that electors, usually the other members, will tend to vote for those who are in their own image. In the Army, as we see later, officers for certain regiments are chosen because of their associations (always allowing for the fact that they have gained their commission in the normal way by passing out of Sandhurst). Most people assessing someone for a job will take into account factors other than paper qualifications. (I always remember how Reuters conducted their recruiting at Oxford twenty years ago. Most of it was geared to the mechanics of news gathering. Then, after various exams and cross-examinations had been conducted, candidates were shown into a room where David Chipp, now editor in chief of the Press Association, gave you a drink and set out to see whether or not you were the sort of chap with whom the correspondent of *The Times* might be prepared to go into the jungle. In the light of the ensuing years in journalism it has seemed the only bit of the exam which made any real sense.)

There are times, however, when appointments must be made or distinctions conferred entirely on the basis of objectively assessed merit, and it would be thought quite scandalous by all concerned if any question of personality entered into it. Yet even when procedures seem most rigorous, and impartiality most scrupulously maintained, a sense of network has a persistent habit of creeping in to complicate the issue.

There was an interesting example of this in January 1982 when Dr. Herbert Eisener conducted an analysis of the elections to Fellowships of the Royal Society. Since 1660 the society's members have generally been acknowledged to be the most distinguished scientists in Britain. Dr. Eisener had done a similar survey ten years before in which he found that six times as many Fellows "could claim Cambridge as their alma mater than the distribution among UK universities of science undergraduates of the period warranted".

In this earlier analysis most of the Fellows were men who had taken their first degrees before and during the second world war. In the second he was dealing with a post-war generation educated during the "great expansion of university education and its opening up of Oxbridge to a much wider stratum of school leavers". Obviously, one would think, the Royal Society would reflect this expansion and the Cambridge pre-eminence would be diminished if not demolished. Not a bit of it. Thirty-three per cent of all the Fellows elected between 1971 and 1980 were Cambridge men. In roughly the same period those born since 1928, 1930 and 1932 were respectively thirty-nine, forty-three and forty-six per cent of Cambridge men. Of the twenty presumably brilliantly precocious Fellows who were under forty at the time of their election during these years, half were at Cambridge, with five from London, two from Oxford and three from the rest of the country.

There were too many elections under consideration for this to be some sort of statistical quirk – about 300 – so there has to be an explanation. Dr. Eisener suggests that the "disproportion" between Oxbridge and the rest may be due to the fact that the ancient universities creamed off the best teachers and students leaving the others as "also-rans". "The league table of British universities so hotly denied by the occupants of Redbrick chairs, yet avidly courted when it comes to placing their own offspring, is a reality," he insists, in a spiritedly contentious phrase. But he refuses to accept that Cambridge is ahead of Oxford in that league table. Entrance exam, he avers, every bit as stiff, rejection ratios for aspiring undergraduates equally discouraging, teaching staffs just as eminent. No reason for Cambridge to have more FRS than Oxford.

Eisener does not believe that the answer to this disproportion lies in the universities themselves. No amount of such study could explain why, in 1981, there were more than three times as many Cambridge Fellows as Oxford ones. He suggests looking at the way in which the Royal Society (and other societies) "propagate and perpetuate themselves," and the best way to do this, obviously, is to examine the society's election procedures. These, it turns out, are arcane but meticulous. The only overt favouritism is for the benefit of the royal family, Britain's leading network. The relevant statute says that, "Any one of Her Majesty's subjects who is a Prince of the Blood Royal may be proposed at one of the Ordinary Meetings of the Society by any Fellow, and may be put to the vote for election on the same day, provided public notice of such proposal shall have been given by the proposer at the preceding Meeting of the Society."

There are no such instant short cuts for the unroyal. Candidates must be proposed by at least six existing Fellows, and every year recommendations are made from a list "not exceeding forty". This list is drawn up by the council on the recommendations of a variety of specialist sectional committees with the capacity to advise on scientists in particular fields. (Committee number eight, for instance, is composed of experts in "biochemistry, molecular biophysics and chemical microbiology".) The idea is that these Fellows, "from their connexion with other societies and otherwise, are specially qualified to advise the Council". Of the six proposers three must "certify their recommendation from *personal knowledge* [my italics]." Moreover, two of those who have "personal knowledge" act as proposer and seconder "in so far that all communications on the subject of the candidature shall take place with one of these".

This insistence on "personal knowledge" and specialised committees is presumably designed to make sure that the scrutiny of candidates is expert and well informed; but an inevitable side effect is that recommendations are made and enquiry conducted by scientists who are certainly acquaintances and, in all probability, friends of the candidates. It is statistically most likely that this "personal knowledge" will be most widespread where there is the highest concentration of Fellows of the Society and, by corollary, that it will be much more difficult for a scientist, however brilliant, to be personally known to his peers if he is carrying on his work in a university where there are no Fellows and which is geographically far away. (International conferences and learned journals compensate for this but nothing can quite substitute for daily propin-

98

quity.) Of course, electors would plead objectivity, and insist that personal feelings don't come into it; that they are assessing candidates on their work alone. But the statistics and the regulations suggest otherwise. Elections to the Royal Society are not (of course not), rigged by a Cambridge dominated mafia but the rules of election surely make the continued Cambridge "disproportion" likely if not inevitable, and it is, actually, difficult to conceive of a rigorous and expert system which did not have that effect. The network – or the appearance of network – has become almost impregnable. Cambridge Fellows elect Cambridge Fellows. They have become a self-perpetuating tradition, combining many of the characteristics of both élite and network.

Another example of the meritocracy in action – you would have thought – is the Civil Service. Rigorous and impartial exam procedures govern admission. Only the clever need apply.

In their book on *The Civil Servants*, Peter Kellner and Lord Crowther-Hunt demonstrate that even in the late seventies the Civil Service was still admitting a "disproportionately" high number of Oxbridge candidates. Given the huge expansion in university education that took place in the sixties, they argue, this is wrong. "The 'output of the educational system'," they say, "has changed markedly during the last thirty years: the great majority of graduates are now non-Oxbridge, non-public school and non-arts and humanities. If the results of the administrative qualifying tests are taken as an objective reflection of the calibre of the candidates; and if it is thought important that the Civil Service should attract a cross-section of Britain's brightest graduates – then, quite simply, the Civil Service is attracting the wrong candidates."

From the point of view of social engineering they have a case, obviously, when they talk about public schools, but perhaps that does not apply with the same force to Oxbridge which, as we have seen, is generally seeking to establish itself as the academically rather than socially élite part of the university system. The Oxbridge view, and evidently that of the Civil Service mandarins, is that Kingsley Amis was correct in his gloomy prognostications about the university explosion of the sixties and that "more" has meant "worse"; or at least that "more" has not interfered with Oxbridge's pre-eminence. In fact by creating genuine alternatives for the marginal public school candidates who previously made up the lumpen-proletariat of Oxbridge's "good college men" it may have actually enhanced Oxbridge's academic pre-eminence.

The Kellner–Crowther Hunt argument is, essentially, that while the Civil Service exam is, superficially, both fair and rigorous, it is actually a procedure designed by Oxbridge educated civil servants for the benefit of men in their own mould.

"So why?" they complain, "do the statistics repeatedly show such biases towards public school and Oxbridge-educated candidates?" The answer is that old bugbear of the self-perpetuating élite: the OBN looking after its own. "However unwittingly," they argue, "most assessors are likely to look for the qualities they think they have (or should have) in themselves. And since most assessors are themselves past products of similar recruitment exercises it would scarcely be surprising if they seek to recruit in their own image. To do otherwise would be to confess that the Civil Service might have been wrong to choose people like themselves in the past."

They point out elsewhere in their book that there has been a quite dramatic decrease in the number of top civil servants who went to public schools anyone has heard of (The Clarendon Nine and a few others). It has gone from about a third in 1950 to one in eight. The three wise men, Robert Cox, Douglas Wass and Ian Bancroft, who entered together in 1946 and ascended the ladder together to become Sir Robert, Sir Douglas and Sir Ian, head of the government's Property Services Agency, the Treasury and the Home Civil Service were each at Oxford or Cambridge. None, however, was at a well known public school. Only Sir Douglas Wass was at a school which belongs to the Headmasters' Conference and that was Nottingham High School, now a fee paying day school.

Part of the complaint about them and their kind is that they are "generalists". This is a product in which Oxford particularly takes pride and pleasure. There *is* something OBN-ish about the idea of the brilliant unspecialist mind, able in some mysterious way to adopt a more uncluttered, Olympian over-view than any mere specialist blinkered by his own idea of expertise. But as we have seen, the men like them who get to the top tend to come from schools low on the Waugh scale and consequently lacking in "network" properties. The final part of the complaint is that they come from Oxbridge, the implication being that because there are now so many universities in the United Kingdom (over forty), it would somehow be better or more representative if more civil servants came from them.

A disproportionate number of people from a common background invariably raises the spectre of the mafia and the cabal, and the plea that what they have in common is excellence is likely to be met with derision and disbelief. Outsiders don't like to admit that Oxbridge graduates have anything in common except their Oxbridge degrees; just as outsiders are reluctant to concede that Liverpool footballers have anything in common except their red shirts.

Not that all insiders approve of the selection procedures and their Oxbridge oriented results. In non-literary life the novelist William Cooper, author of *Scenes from Provincial Life*, is Harry Hoff, a retired civil servant who for two years in the mid-seventies was assistant director of the Civil Service Selection Board. He is a state educated Cambridge graduate, which is par for the senior civil servant course, but like his old Cambridge friend, C. P. Snow, he has an untypically amused eye for the intricacies of personal politics.

Snow himself appreciated the tendency for a certain type of person to perpetuate himself, even when the rules of election or selection are apparently scrupulously fair and well ordered. In an early scene of *The Masters*, his novel of intrigue in a Cambridge college, the dying master is talking to Snow's narrator Lewis Eliot about college elections. "Some of our friends," he says, "show a singular instinct for preferring mediocrity. Like elects like, of course. Or between you and me," he whispered, "dull men elect dull men."

Hoff says that "of course" examiners tend to look for the answers that they would give themselves, just as [is this the novelist ruefully speaking from experience?] fiction editors look for the novels they would have written themselves." He does, however, disagree "that the self-perpetuators are anywhere near as aware, or rather as calculating, as Kellner and Crowther-Hunt make out. It just comes to them like the air they breathe – the air they first breathed in Oxford?" Like them, however, and like his old friend Snow, he is sceptical about the generalist concept "which enthrals so many of the people at the top of the Civil Service," and resuscitates Snow's "Two Cultures" idea which he thinks as useful and valid now as it was thirty years ago. "As I see it, the nearer you are to the 'literary' pole, the dearer to your heart the concept of the 'generalist'; the nearer to the scientific/technological pole the dearer that of the 'professional'. The division of feeling between the two is just as powerful as ever, albeit unrecognised (that's why people are so annoyed when it's pointed out to them)."

101

This worship of the generalist does tend to favour Oxbridge, or more accurately Oxford. (Hoff dislikes the word Oxbridge, believing that the two older universities are quire unlike each other.) "I feel," he says, "that the Civil Service Selection Board tests favour a capacity for literary expression on paper and in discussion which flourishes more strongly in Oxford than in Cambridge, and in those two together than in most of the other universities each taken as a whole."

Certainly all the figures show that Oxford and Cambridge graduates are more successful, especially in the early stages of the Civil Service's exam procedures. There is also some evidence to suggest that Oxford people are more successful than Cambridge, though it seems also to be true that more Oxford people apply.

Hoff remembers that when he was examining for the Civil Service the Oxford candidates had a generally higher expectation of success. "I seem to recall," he says, "that the level of self-confidence of our Oxford interviewees was higher than that of the others. 'Very Oxford,' we used to say, when some highly self-confident young man went out – especially if it wasn't justified."

Even if you accept all this, however, there remains the uncomfortable possibility that the Oxford or Oxbridge candidates tend to be what the results suggest. Namely better. "Given that Oxford and Cambridge have a reputation that attracts a higher proportion of the cream of the school leavers – the cream: the brightest, if it's permissible nowadays to refer to people as bright – I don't see how that fact is to be got round by any kind of written examination."

You could do it by introducing some form of quota system to ensure that the successful candidates were drawn from a representative cross section of universities and disciplines. But that could mean that in the interests of an arguably bogus principle you were simply lowering standards. When they used to discuss this, Snow and Hoff sometimes came up with the radical solution of abolishing Oxford and Cambridge as undergraduate universities altogether. "He and I used to propose playfully the means of abolishing this awful dichotomy by turning Oxford and Cambridge into post-graduate institutions making everybody graduate at one of the other universities first of all."

I bet Mr. Kinnock would like that idea.

The key word is "disproportion". Critics argue that the Oxbridge stranglehold is a form of conspiracy. Apologists say that it is meritocracy at work. All are agreed that the Foundation OBN, particularly its Oxbridge half, continues to provide a "disprop-ortionate" number of Establishment OBN members (even though "disproportionate" seldom means much more than "too many for my taste"). The trouble is that the Foundation OBN is able to make such a persuasive case for the excellence of its members and therefore to claim, with some conviction, that they are not so much a network as an élite. If we were to abolish the public schools and genuinely equalise the universities might not that same élite still be dominant?

As Jonathan Gathorne-Hardy has pointed out in his book, *The Public School Phenomenon*, the French, whose best and smartest schools are the lycées and colleges which are not fee paying, have very much the same sort of élites. Their system is open to all and is highly competitive, yet the results do not seem to be any more "democratic" or "egalitarian" than our own. "Not one person," claims Gathorne-Hardy of the French, "whose father was either a skilled or unskilled worker has ever entered the *Inspection des Finances*. About sixty per cent of all top civil servants in France come from the prosperous upper middle class. In one study of a group of 440 top civil servants studied between 1946 and 1969, 28.4 per cent – an astonishing figure – came from just three famous lycées in expensive middle class areas of Paris, as it might be from Westminster, St. Paul's and Dulwich."

One of the innumerable paradoxes in all this is that the public school and Oxbridge influence seems to be strongest in those areas where the rules are laid down strictly and where entrance is apparently fair and competitive. The Civil Service is OBN domin-ated and yet it is virtually by definition bureaucratic and governed by strict rules of impartiality, promotion and selection by merit alone. Elsewhere, where the rules are less clearly defined and the laws are, essentially, those of the jungle, the OBN stranglehold is less marked. Journalism and industry are full of outsiders (even if they become insiders with the passage of time and the increase in their power and influence). If "networking" is a way to the top this suggests that the art can be successfully practised by those who are non-Foundation members of the OBN as well.

Indeed if networking is the art of exploiting connections, anyone can practise it. Success will depend partly on the skill with which you do it and partly on the effectiveness of your network and your fellow members. By the time someone reaches adulthood he or she will have acquired the educational network connections we have discussed, but these in turn will depend on your family. Will the

103

family send you to public school? Will it advise you to go to university? Will it provide support? Encouragement? Finance? Will it act as your first and most reliable network – an association based on kith and kin and ties of blood? Is it, ultimately, as important to have a particular sort of family as it is to have been to a particular sort of school or a particular university? Is it more significant that Blunt was a Marlburian? Or a Cambridge man?

Or a Blunt?

6

Happy Families

It is certainly of service to a man to know who were his
grandfathers and who were his grandmothers if he entertain an ambition to move in the upper circles of society, and
also of service to be able to speak of them as persons who
were themselves somebodies in their time.

Anthony Trollope, *The Prime Minister*

Everyone, the world over, has an obsession with "placing" people,
with trying to relate them to some recognisable landmark. In most
parts of the world the opening gambits will be "Where are you
from?" and "What do you do?" In Britain, particularly in the
OBN, among the upper and middle classes, we use family and
school to give us that basic information. Family naturally gives a
more precise social map reading than school but most of us do not
come from families which are widely recognised networks. In my
case, a fairly unusual surname has meant that people to whom I am
introduced almost invariably relate it to the one relatively famous
Heald, namely the late Sir Lionel, a Conservative politician and
lawyer who was once Winston Churchill's Attorney-General.

"Any relation to Sir Lionel?" they enquire, hoping for the
answer "Yes" and almost always looking mildly crestfallen to
receive the answer "No". Only once did not belonging to that
particular Heald network act to my advantage. In 1965 I was being
interviewed for a part time research job by Winston's son, Randolph. There were other members of the Churchill équipe present
at Randolph's home in East Bergholt as well as outside guests.
Before lunch he and I remained in the drawing room for a moment
while the others walked through to the dining room. Randolph,
inevitably, popped the question: "Any relation of Sir Lionel?" On
receiving a negative response he said nothing.

We too walked through to the dining room where the assembled
company was contemplating soup.

Randolph looked round triumphantly. "I have good news for

105

you all," he said. "Our young friend here is no relation of Sir Lionel Heald."

Generally speaking, not being related to Sir Lionel seems to have proved a minor handicap in life though I cannot think that being related to him would have yielded any very substantial benefit. It would probably (I guess) have produced much the same sort of network expectation in others as having been to a top of the second division public school, although obviously it would have meant more to older generations of Tories than to younger generations of socialists. Sir Lionel's son Mervyn is, incidentally, a QC like his father before him, but went to Eton rather than Charterhouse and Magdalene, Cambridge, rather than Christ Church, Oxford. In network terms, Mervyn got a greater school but a lesser college than his father.

Of all the social cements, blood is the strongest. The family network is indissoluble and, impossible to conceal. It is also ubiquitous. We may not belong to a very numerous or even a very distinguished family; we may not care much for our relations, we may have lost all touch with them, we may not even know who they are, but we are, like it or not, our father's sons and our mother's daughters. Cain, Oedipus and others notwithstanding, all the evidence is that the family does regard itself as a network, that it is permeated with team spirit and inclined to close ranks against the outside world. The genealogist Hugh Montgomery-Massingberd suggests that there are some "500 significant and historically important English and Welsh families which have continued to produce men and women of prominence and achievement – not just an individual celebrity – over a considerable period of time." Belonging to this "Massingberd 500" (see Appendix IX) can still mean an automatic place in a family business or the acquisition of hereditary estates and titles, or an inheritance of the family beauty or brilliance. In all cases, however, it means automatic membership of a powerful mutual support system: the nucleus of a really effective personal private network – or PPN.

The success of the family as a network depends on its size and its closeness. Rothschilds and Guinnesses operate highly successful family networks based on family companies. The Pakenhams (Lord and Lady Longford, their children Tom, Antonia Fraser/Pinter, Rachel Billington) look, at least to the outsider, like a superlatively well drilled literary mafia. There are military and naval families, like the Hill-Nortons; ecclesiastical families like the Bickersteths; legal families like the Hoggs and Havers; rowing families like the Clays; cricketing families like the Edriches. Belonging to such families creates expectations and supports of particular kinds. The success they engender makes them highly visible. They are models. All families emulate them to some extent and so do other networks. All networks are an attempt, conscious or not, to imitate sibling and filial loyalties. Like families they buck the system, they open the way to making arrangements through informal contact rather than "through the usual channels".

For most families their relations may not seem to have very obvious network potential. We live in an age when the nuclear family is, apparently, "the normal household unit in Britain". For most of us, therefore, this particular network option looks limited. A close mutually beneficial relationship with a single brother or sister may technically constitute a sibling network but it is, obviously, too small to develop the numerous tentacles associated with the idea of a network. However, even if one lacks the opportunities for realising the network potential of numerous siblings and of the cousins, aunts, uncles and other kith and kin which the great network families of Britain boast in such prodigious quantities, one must not neglect the vertical network which stretches back into the past.

Ancestors create expectations and demands just as much as brothers and sisters; fathers most particularly. In fact, genetics apart, parentage has an even greater effect on career than school or university. Being the son of an OBN father does not automatically confer membership of either the Foundation or Establishment OBN according to conventional thinking, but in practice it may. To take an extreme example, the eldest child of the monarch might be educated by tutors and not go to Oxbridge, but he or she would still become King or Queen. The present Queen had just such an upbringing and in those terms is not a Foundation member of the OBN, though in practice she is patron of both branches. Sceptical though I am of statistical methods to "prove" such theories, two researchers who did a complex and exhaustive survey of the old boys of a single school, Winchester, did come up with one table which seemed to prove that who your father was was more significant than where you went to school. They found that:

"It was a very highly significant 'advantage', statistically speaking, to have had a father who reached the career élite himself. Thus a Wykehamist whose father was a judge or a colonel seemed to have, statistically, a much better chance of reaching the élite than another Wykehamist whose father was a magistrate or a major."

In Britain we retain a strong sense of family even if our idea of the ideal family size diminishes that family's network potential. We are helped in this by the fact that our keynote institution, the monarchy, is the most effective and powerful family network in the world.

Thirty years ago in the early fifties the royal family looked wan and flimsy. The former King Edward VIII was exiled and childless; his brother George VI died in 1952; another brother, the Duke of Kent, was killed during the war. At the core of this fashionably nuclear family there were only the Queen Mother, the Queen and Prince Philip and her unmarried sister Margaret. The Queen herself was much younger then than Prince Charles now, and not as well prepared for the job nor as temperamentally well suited. The Queen Mother was newly widowed. Prince Philip was quite untrained for life as Prince Consort and enjoyed an ambivalent relationship with press and public, as did Princess Margaret. There were a few others on the fringe – Princess Marina, the Duke of Kent's widow, who had style and charisma; the Duke of Gloucester, the Queen's uncle, who could not honestly be said to have either, well meaning and dutiful though he was.

Since then the family has married and procreated and in the case of the Queen Mother and Lord Mountbatten (who became a much more identifiably quasi-regal figure with the advancing years) survived into a sprightly old age. The family firm has grown from a corner shop threatened with bankruptcy to a thriving chain store in which those members who have comparatively little taste or aptitude for public life can be virtually pensioned off and allowed to pursue their own lives. There are plenty of newcomers like the Princess of Wales or Princess Michael of Kent who have genuine if variable star quality. They have turned themselves into a formidable network.

Underpinning this family network at the centre of the British stage is a hereditary peerage, a network of often interconnected families who still share, by right, in the parliamentary process – and get paid for doing so. In 1959 Evelyn Waugh taking stock of *Brideshead Revisited*, his wartime lament for the lost ancestral seats of England and for those who sat in them, conceded that he had "piled it on rather, with passionate sincerity".

He added, with a combination of regret and satisfaction at being proved so agreeably wrong, that, "The English aristocracy has maintained its identity to a degree that then seemed impossible." More than twenty years later the survival, through a period in which there was more often a Labour government than not, seems just as remarkable. Measured by those ancestral seats Waugh so loved, the aristocracy is virtually intact. There are no longer Roseberys at Mentmore, or Brookes at Warwick, or Astors at Hever but most of the really great houses are still owned by the great families who have owned them for generations. In many cases a transition has been effected from that generation whose estates death duties were to have killed off, through to another which most prophets thought could never succeed. Since Waugh reassessed the verdict of Brideshead there has been a new Duke of Marlborough at Blenheim; the Marquess of Tavistock has succeeded his father the Duke of Bedford at Woburn; the Marquess of Hartington now runs Chatsworth instead of his father, the Duke of Devonshire. All these great houses remain in the family. And the young Duke of Westminster is so rich that he does not have to bother to open any of his houses to the public at all. The dukes and other peers still sit, if they wish, in the House of Lords.

These aristocratic and royal families have vertical and horizontal ramifications. Their family trees extend vertically into the past and horizontally across the present. The past is often as potent a network as the present. It creates expectations and traditions which – with the exception of a few renunciations such as Lord Stansgate (Tony Benn) and Lord Altrincham (John Grigg) and a single abdication – are absolute. The heir to the throne becomes the monarch. The heir to the dukedom becomes the duke. Even a baronet's eldest son becomes Sir Somebody Something. It is inevitable and obvious and visible and it breeds imitation.

Some of the most interesting of these imitations surround the Crown itself. When it comes to an important position in the court network it pays to be at the bottom of your own relevant vertical or hereditary one. Prince Charles' first private secretary and mentor was willed on him by Prince Philip when Charles was still a Gordonstoun school boy. David Checketts, later knighted for his services to the royal family, was a grammar school product and former squadron leader in the Royal Air Force. He was from well outside the royal family's preferred OBN recruiting ground. In fact he was an obvious example of Prince Philip's typically Mountbatten efforts to bring a little middle class breeziness into stuffy Buckingham Palace life.

Eventually the time came for Checketts to leave. No real evidence of hard feelings emerged but there were rumours that Prince Charles was feeling the need to assert himself more, to establish his independence, to create his own secretariat with men of his own choosing. Checketts was more of a father figure than a chum. When the teenage Charles had been sent away to Timbertop in Australia far away from home and family it was Checketts who had gone along "in loco parentis". In a sense this uneasy artificial father–son legacy dogged their relationship. So after Prince Charles left the Navy and became a full time prince, Checketts went off to public relations and Prince Charles chose his own man as substitute.

"His own man" turned out to be Edward Adeane, a bachelor barrister, born nine years earlier than Prince Charles, and keen on shooting and fishing. Adeane was the latest in a vertical family network which had royal links going back to the late nineteenth century. After the Prince Imperial was killed in 1879 Queen Victoria transferred Colonel Arthur Bigge to her own staff as a secretary. Bigge remained at court until his death in 1931 by which time he had become one of the most influential royal bureaucrats since Burghley and Walsingham, better known to historians as Lord Stamfordham and described by his employer King George V as "the most loyal friend I ever had". Bigge's daughter Victoria married, along sound OBN lines, a Coldstream Guards officer named Adeane. Their son, Michael, worked for George VI and became private secretary to the Queen in 1953, a job he held until 1972. His son, of course, is Edward who will, unless things go badly wrong, one day become the number one courtier just like his father and great-grandfather before him. They form their own vertical family network, shadowing royalty through the ages.

Hugo Vickers, the author and royalty buff, who knows more about the royal family than is quite decent, maintains that many of the secrets of the royal networks may be found in George VI's game book. Lord Adeane, he points out, was once one of the twenty best shots in the country. He often shot at Sandringham with the King. So did Sir William Fellowes who from 1936 to 1964 was land agent at Sandringham. *His* son Robert is now one of the Queen's secretaries and, in a further network ramification, married to the Princess of Wales' elder sister, Jane, herself once touted as a suitable bride for the prince.

The choice of Lady Diana as his bride was the final flourish to Prince Charles' assertion of independence. Yet, while not wishing to deny the importance of the heart in the matter, it is interesting to look at the decision in terms of network. If you accept Vickers' claim that the old King's game book (see all those Leghs, Lascelles,

110

Penns and Cokes) is the key to the cipher you will be pleased to find that Lady Diana's father, Earl Spencer, was a member of the party when George VI shot his thousandth woodcock!

Quite apart from having been present at this landmark slaying, Earl Spencer was also equerry to him and Queen Elizabeth later. No less than six senior members of Lady Diana's family have been members of the Queen Mother's court. Indeed if one is to consider the match in network terms it can be considered as a victory for the King's game book/Clarence House connection over a Mountbatten/Prince Philip faction which might have been expected to favour a union with one of the European royal houses (Princess Marie-Astrid was the best known example) or even one of Lord Mountbatten's grand-daughters. But, of course, nowadays marriages, even royal ones, are never "arranged" – they merely take place.

A few court appointments, like Checketts', have been made from outside the magic circle. Group Captain Peter Townsend, who came near to marrying Princess Margaret in the early fifties, was made an equerry during the war, because of a high level decision that such appointments, which were traditionally made from within the OBN, should in future be based on fighting record. Townsend was gallant and had a DSO and a DFC and bar. William Heseltine, the Queen's deputy secretary and heir apparent to the top job, came to the Palace from Australia as a press secretary and transferred. Prince Philip's private secretary from 1957–70, James Orr, was recruited from the Kenya police. But it was a network appointment: Orr was head boy when he and Prince Philip were at Gordonstoun together. There is a formula for bringing in non-network courtiers to the press office at Buckingham Palace on temporary secondment, usually from Commonwealth diplomatic corps. The main press office job has also been farmed out to people from unconventional – in royal terms – walks of life, including business (Robin Ludlow) and sports broadcasting (Ronald Allison). And for years a balance was preserved by having one press officer who really was an insider. Mrs. Anne Wall has retired after many years in the press office with the valedictory title of Dame Commander of the Royal Victorian Order. She is a niece of the Dowager Duchess of Gloucester.

Royal press officers may come from outside the courtiers' network but there are written "understandings" about other jobs. Buckingham Palace's official wording on, for instance, the Mistress of the Robes is that she "is the senior lady of the Queen's

Household and is usually a Duchess". The two Ladies of the Bedchamber are "usually the wives of Earls". These people are, naturally, chosen by Her Majesty but her choice is limited by written convention. There are not so many duchesses and countesses in Debretts.

None of this is any longer very significant when it comes to the exercise of power. "Through many reigns" comments the Palace about the Mistress of the Robes, "the appointment was entirely political, and at one time these ladies were an important factor in the politics of the country. Today the appointment is of no political significance and Her Majesty names whom she pleases" (provided she is a duchess). This is fair comment, but in other ways the royal family and its attendant fleet of pilot fish, are important. On a fairly narrow plane they remain a focus for what used to be called "society", and on a much wider one they are, still, the standard bearers for middle England: decent, God fearing, conventional, family people who dislike change and enjoy having people to look up to and an example to follow. Part of that example and of the lesson that monarchy and aristocracy has for the country as a whole is that dynasty works, that families have an enviable solidarity, continuing traditions, and present a strength which derives from their past as well as present members.

This means that while we may baulk at the idea of "nepotism" we are attracted by the idea of "family" and family connections, especially in those areas with which the royal family is most closely identified: the aristocracy, the Church, and the armed services.

There was a time when the younger sons of the aristocracy followed careers that were as automatic as the eldest's. One of those was the Church. Today, the idea that the family living is an appropriate destination for such young men has vanished. The Church of England is no longer an officer-class OBN establishment, although the very senior men are still demonstrably upper or middle class. Archbishop Runcie was a Scots Guards officer during the war and the man who is supposed to have almost got the job instead of him was an Etonian, Habgood of Durham. But the coming men just behind them have the common touch – men like Bishop Westwood of Edmonton (Grove Park Grammar, Wrexham) or Bishop Cross of Blackburn (Royal Grammar School, Lancaster).

For a generation now, the Church has not insisted that its new priests must be graduates. This is a part of the growing trend away from the traditional Oxbridge and Durham based theological colleges (with Trinity Hall, Bristol, and St. John's, Nottingham, making up the "Redbrick" contingent) towards community based ordination schemes: nowadays an increasing number of priests come from bible colleges which do not restrict membership to the cloth and are run on similar lines to the polytechnic. Almost imperceptibly, the clergyman has changed from a parsonical leader figure, in cahoots with the squire, to a servant of the community who wants to identify with his flock rather than dominate it.

This should have meant, one would have thought, that the old ecclesiastical dynasties would have died out, yet alongside the new men in the Church there are still a number of representatives of families which have in some cases been associated with the Church for over 200 years. In 1982 at least three Church of England bishops belonged to ecclesiastical family networks. The first, Simon Burrows, the Bishop of Buckingham, is the son of Hedley Burrows, who was Dean of Hereford. His line goes back to the Reverend John Burrows, Vicar of St. Clement Danes, who was born in 1733, and had Dr. Johnson as his churchwarden. "The general feeling in the family," remarks the present bishop wryly, "was that if you could survive that, you could survive anything." The second, Freddy Temple, signs himself Freddy Malmesbury, being the suffragan bishop of that place, and is the only bishop to be descended from two Archbishops of Canterbury. The Temples have tended to marry into other ecclesiastical families – a common characteristic of the great Church dynasties, though the Bishop of Malmesbury's grandfather, Archbishop Frederick, married a Devonshire, Beatrice Lascelles, and used to remark that before marriage he treated those in the House of Lords with respect and after marriage he treated them as cousins. When Freddy Temple went to Hong Kong as dean he found himself moving into another sphere of family reputation the moment he passed Suez. His maternal grandfather, Reginald Copplestone, was "the Boy Bishop of Colombo" – appointed at the age of only thirty before moving on to be Metropolitan of Calcutta. The Boy Bishop was succeeded in Colombo by a younger brother and the Copplestone reign in Ceylon lasted more than fifty years.

But arguably the most remarkable of the Church's family networks is the Bickersteths'. John Bickersteth, Bishop of Bath and Wells, is the fourth Bickersteth bishop in the last hundred years. Other Bickersteths have been head of the Community of the Resurrection at Mirfield, Dean of Lichfield, Chaplain to the King and Chairman of the Mission to Seamen. Even those who did not

113

become clergymen were strong churchmen and Christians. Henry Bickersteth, who was a doctor in Kirkby Lonsdale at the beginning of the eighteenth century, wrote a useful volume called *Medical Hints to Clergymen*. In the long family tree of the Bickersteths I counted sixteen Bickersteth priests. Eight of the Bickersteth women married clergy. And rummaging through the Bickersteth family tree, I completely lost count of the male Bickersteths who married the daughters of clergymen.

If it wasn't for a bequest from Ada Bickersteth, the diocese of Polynesia might not exist; and if it wasn't for the Right Reverend Edward Bickersteth, Bishop of Exeter, we would not be able to sing the hymn "Peace, Perfect Peace". As well as ecclesiastical Bickersteths there are medical Bickersteths and Bickersteths who made money from shipping in Liverpool but the crucial thing about Bickersteths is their Bickerstethishness. A few years ago they had a family get-together for Bishop John's father's ninetieth birthday, a joint celebration with Sybil Thorndike's family (she was an old family friend). It was packed with Bickersteths. Not many men are close friends with their fifth cousins. The bishop is.

As well as the vertical network of ancestors, there is a surviving horizontal network. Apart from John Bath and Wells, there is a fourth cousin who is also an ordained priest and has turned the large house in Sussex he inherited from his mother's side into a Christian Trust. His twenty-six-year-old nephew was recently ordained, though none of his own three boys show any inclination for holy orders as yet. All three were at Blunt's old school, Marlborough, (concessionary rates for the sons of clergy), thanks largely to the generosity of his bachelor uncles – another example of Bickersteth cohesion.

Oddly enough, all three of these bishops protest that the family tradition, and the weight of the past, either had nothing to do with their becoming ordained in the first place or was a positive disincentive. The Bishop of Buckingham says that, "As to my own vocation, it was others, not my family, who suggested I should be ordained. In a sense I was dragged kicking and screaming to ordination. But ever since I was priested, I have always adored my work."

Freddy Temple echoes this. "Coming of such an ecclesiastical family I had a period when it was the last thing in the world I wanted to be [ordained] but I grew out of that during the war in which I was a pacifist working with the Friends Ambulance Unit. This caused a good deal of consternation in my own close family but was entirely supported by William* which made it respectable to the rest. This was even though he supported the war strongly. He had died before the war ended and before I was released for ordination and so I have never felt his reputation as a burden hanging over one, but have always had a great affection and love for him, knowing him better than one knows most uncles because my father was a sanitary engineer in India and so Christmas holidays were often spent at Bishopsthorpe."

Bishop Bickersteth says that he, like his father before him, is remaining scrupulously neutral about his offspring taking up an ordained career. He is a fourth generation cleric who became a priest despite rather than because of his father. He told me that he recently looked out some old letters to his father to check that his memory was correct. He quite definitely wanted to be a farmer, but the man who changed his mind was his wartime padre (he was commissioned in the Buffs), who said to him towards the end of the war, "Why don't you stop fighting against what you really want to do?" He was forced to admit that the padre was right.

Once in the Church, being a Bickersteth was an advantage in several ways. He knew his way around. Having been brought up in the Church he had no irrational fears and the Church held no great mystery for him. He felt at home. He also ("no point in denying it") knew a lot of people, but as far as becoming a bishop is concerned he says he had no expectations himself, nor did he feel that others expected it of him. Certainly not because he was a Bickersteth. When he first became a bishop, as a suffragan at Warrington, his father said to him, "Well, that's one thing that never crossed either of our minds." He does not know if it is literally true of his father but says it certainly was of him.

What got him into the episcopacy had nothing – at least overtly – to do with the Bickersteth connection. When he was vicar of St. Stephen's, Chatham, the Bishop of Rochester asked him to take on the chairmanship of the missionary and ecumenical council. This meant that he gravitated to a larger stage, began attending conferences at home and abroad, making speeches and generally getting noticed. This, he assumes, led to his being put on the "preferment lists" which are kept at Lambeth Palace and 10 Downing Street and which only diocesan bishops are allowed to see. He might never have graduated from that list but for the fact that one of the canons of Rochester and the head of the local

* Archbishop of Canterbury during World War II.

theological college was Stuart Blanch, later to become Archbishop of York. Blanch was promoted to Bishop of Liverpool and, over lunch at the Royal Commonwealth Society, asked if Bickersteth would like to join his team as Suffragan Bishop of Warrington.

Suffragan bishoprics are ninety-five per cent in the gift of the diocesan bishop, so the trick here was knowing Stuart Blanch. Most diocesan bishops come from the ranks of the suffragans even though the appointment process (involving two days of deliberation by the Crown Appointments Commission and the submission of two names to the Prime Minister) is extremely careful and involves lots of "soundings".

Bishops, by the way, first learn of their appointment at breakfast. The letter arrives in the morning post with one envelope inside another for greater security – "rather like pass the parcel".

The original effect of these family backgrounds, therefore, seems to have been superficially negative. It may be dangerous to generalise on the evidence of only three bishops, but all three seem to have had a strong vocation which was initially over-ruled or at least threatened by the weight of the past. No parent, clerical or not, seems to have brought pressure to bear on a son to enter the ministry. Perhaps it is not the sort of thing a priest would do. Army or naval officers might; so, assuredly, would a man who runs an old-established family business. But the Church poses different sorts of questions.

"What has characterised the family in each generation," says Simon Burrows of Buckingham, "has been a passionate interest in people, and a certain distaste for central structures and ecclesiastical politics." That passionate interest, passed down through the genes, reinforced by the example of generation after generation of like minded fathers, obviously produced a high proportion of clerics. It's the same with the Temples and the Bickersteths. There is, argues John Bickersteth of Bath and Wells, a clear, demonstrable attraction to the Church throughout the Bickersteth family in all branches and all generations, but it may not be a dedication to the Church itself so much as a continuing and strong conception of service to the community. There are Bickersteth doctors, too – not as strong a strain as the clerics but enough to be statistically remarkable – and there is another group of Bickersteths who, over the years, have gone abroad to serve the Empire, several dying overseas, often young.

Such family networks are certainly not universal within the Church of England – Archbishop Fisher, for example, had six sons not one of whom went into the Church, though at least two became, like him, public school headmasters. And such dynastic tradition is not a phenomenon shared by the Roman Catholics. The one point not often made in the argument about the celibacy of the Catholic priesthood is that it precludes the creation of a truly hereditary caste of clerics – or, if you like, Roman Catholic counterparts to Burrowses, Temples and Bickersteths.

The family traditions of the Armed Services are even stronger than the Church's. The social revolution which has taken place in the Church has scarcely transformed the military, and whereas my bishops seemed to fight against the notion of following in family footsteps, the sons of fighting men seem positively to relish it. "You cannot discount a certain glamour that attaches to a father as far as a son is concerned," says Admiral of the Fleet Lord Hill-Norton, explaining, partially, how it is that his son entered the Navy like him, and became, like him, its youngest captain. The admiral's naval ancestry goes back to the son of the rector of Lerwick, born in 1665, and in nine subsequent generations only one has not included a naval officer. This is, understandably, a matter of considerable family pride but although the Navy has its old naval families (including most notably the royal family itself) its family allegiances are significantly different. The Hill-Norton vertical network* is an extraordinary example of continuing loyalty but it is a loyalty to the Navy as a whole not to an individual part of it. Men develop a loyalty to each other and to their ship when they are part of its company, but it is a passing thing. Ships' names are perpetuated over the centuries but the ships themselves are not. Ships' companies themselves change regularly. But a regiment has a continuing life all its own. When a regiment has won battle honours with, say, Clive in India or Wellesley in the Peninsula it is recalled, honoured and celebrated almost as if the honours had been won by the present members of the regiment themselves. As often as not they are the direct heirs of those men in the family as well as a regimental sense. One man who did his national service in the Royal Scots Greys told me that he had compared the officers' list during his time in the regiment with that of 1815 when the regiment fought at Waterloo. It was almost identical. Commissions had passed from father to son ever since.

"Family regiments" such as this still survive in the British Army. They are double networks, attracting the allegiance of families and

* See Appendix XIV.

117

others who have some network connection with them, and building on such associations to develop a family feeling of their own. They are "family regiments" both because they attract the continuing allegiance of a small number of regimental families and also because they develop a sense of family for themselves, exuding just that sense of being an exclusive unit against the rest of the world which is a pre-requisite of the network. A feeling of "contra mundum" is essential to networks, but it does not make the network popular with outsiders and this is as true of the old family regiments of Britain as of any other exclusive network.

At the end of 1961, when the country was contemplating another of the periodic post-war cuts in defence spending, a small committee of senior officers was formed to draft the 1962 Defence White Paper for the Minister. This committee consisted of a serving rear admiral, a serving air vice marshal, an under secretary of state and the recently retired Chief of the Imperial General Staff, Field Marshal Sir Francis Festing. Festing had moved to Northumbria whence he interrupted his hunting to journey south on occasional forays, mainly, it was said with a touch of affectionate malice, to visit his tailor (he was always having new riding breeches made, which he habitually wore to his office until they were comfortable), and to attend to his remarkable collection of Japanese swords. Most of the donkey work on this committee was therefore done by the admiral and the air marshal but they were outranked by the field marshal (field marshals, by tradition, never retire) and everything had to be passed by him. This was usually done "on the nod". Festing trusted his small team and rarely argued.

In the course of their deliberations it became clear to the naval and air force men that much the most effective way of saving uniformed manpower, and hence a great deal of money, would be to abolish the old army regiments and replace them with different, larger, streamlined units. In particular, there should be one unified Corps of Infantry. That way, argued the two men, as many as 20,000 jobs could be saved. It was so simple, so obvious, so right that the two were hopeful that the field marshal might rubber-stamp it without too much question. He was, however, an infantry soldier above all, and colonel commandant of two line regiments, so some resistance was likely.

The day came. Field Marshal Festing arrived from the country, read the proposals and nodded.

"Quite right," he agreed. And then, "But can't be done, by me."

As that story suggests, the Army's network devotion to its

118

regiments arouses great irritation in the other two services. One retired air marshal who said his thoughts on the matter were so "unkind" that he would rather remain anonymous remembered working on "requirements" in Whitehall where the internecine battles within the Army were quite astonishing. "It was fascinating," he says, "to see how the Gunners wanted a bigger gun and the Sappers a better bridge and no one considered how to win the next war. If the CIGS, was an ex-Gunner they got a bigger gun. The regimental system is one of the most extravagant things the Army has left."

He adds that, "Many years ago, a very senior officer of the Royal Air Force (now dead) said to me that the greatest strength of the Air Force was that everyone in it was an airman. Not a fusilier, a gunner, a guardsman or in the Suffolks, in the 60th or in one of the fractional cavalry regiments who were unwillingly being made to take 'iron horses'. The same advantage is held by the Navy where everyone is a sailor. With the added advantage at that time that if the ship sank the admiral drowned with the rest. A great incentive to float."

The primary allegiance of soldiers is not to the Army but to the regiment. Lord Hill-Norton, casting a beady nautical eye on his army colleagues, remarks, "In soldiers' families constant pressure is put on sons to 'go into the regiment'." For many the regiment is more of a family than family itself. One family he knows has an association with the Inniskillings. "Well," he says, "for them, becoming colonel of the 'Skins' is not *quite* like getting the Garter but almost."

Despite being emphatically un-military I understand a little of what he means at first hand, because after being commissioned during the war my father served with the Dorset Regiment, until 1957. No pressure was ever put on *me* to go into the regiment but some of my earliest memories are of khaki and parade grounds; shining cap badges with the motto Primus in Indis; a regimental band playing "The Farmer's Boy" as they beat retreat in the grounds of the Schönbrunn Palace in Vienna; those olive green packing cases which heralded yet another foreign posting.

There are very few of the old English county regiments left in the Army. Once every county had its regiment, garrisoned in its county town, drawing its members from within its borders, relying on local allegiances and traditions for its continuing strength. Cuts and amalgamations have reduced them so that of fifty-six regular battalions in the modern Army only seven are old style English county regiments as such. They are in order of seniority: the Devon

119

and Dorsets, the Cheshires, the Glo'sters, the Worcesters and Foresters, the Queen's Lancashires, the Royal Hampshires and the Staffords. There are also still Scottish regiments such as the Argyll and Sutherland Highlanders who come into a similar category. When it was threatened with disbandment various interested parties, such as General Sir Gordon Macmillan of Macmillan (a former colonel of the regiment), George Younger MP (who had served in the Argylls in Korea) and Margaret Duchess of Argyll, mounted a campaign to save the regiment. A petition with over a million signatures on it was presented to parliament and the regiment still survives.

South of the border there are other regiments with county associations but they are not recognisable from their everyday title. Thus The Prince of Wales' Own Regiment of Yorkshire only reveals its connection in this full title and is invariably known simply as The Prince of Wales' Own. The Duke of Edinburgh's Own is actually the county regiment of Wiltshire and Berkshire but not many inhabitants of Reading or Devizes would know. The Second Royal Anglians are associated with Lincolnshire, Leicestershire and Northamptonshire but you would hardly guess from the title. Nor that the Green Howards and the Duke of Wellington's are famous infantry regiments from Yorkshire. Believers in the special nature of the seven "proper" county regiments argue forcefully that in order to be effective and meaningful the relationship between county and regiment has to be as clear to the civilians of the county as it is to the soldiers. In these cases it is simply not apparent to the layman and the county association is correspondingly diminished.

The Devon and Dorsets are, obviously, an amalgamation of the Devonshire Regiment and the Dorset Regiment and they in turn of yet older ones (the Dorsets were originally the 39th and 54th foot). The combined battle honours include Plassey, Dettingen (the last occasion an English king led his men into battle), Marabout and Salamanca, the Relief of Ladysmith, Mons, the Somme, Passchendaele, Arnhem, Imphal, Kohima and Mandalay. Every five years men of the old Dorsets return to Arnhem and Nijmegen to commemorate their actions there. Shortly after I saw Brigadier "Speedy" Bredin, the former colonel of the regiment, he was taking a group of Old Comrades to Normandy to commemorate the liberation of a small town there in 1944. Every year there is a Dorset regimental wreath-laying at the Cenotaph in Whitehall and a religious service conducted by the old padre – educated, like many Dorset officers, at Sherborne School and with a son now serving in the Devon and Dorsets.

Their commanding officer when I visited them at their barracks in Colchester was Lieutenant Colonel John Wilsey who had been a boy at Sherborne just before I went there. He was in the same house under a housemaster Hugh Holmes who had himself held a wartime commission in the Dorsets and he was succeeded as CO a little later by another Lyon House, Sherborne, product, "Paddy" King-Fretts.

Wilsey's father had also been a Dorset (ending his career as a general) and it would have been remarkable had he not chosen this regiment. He is, in fact the first CO of the combined regiment to have spent his whole military career with them – all his predecessors had originally served with the old Dorsets or Devons. Had he not opted for the regiment it would have been regarded as a serious slight. Loyalty in this instance is two-sided. The regiment expects its old comrades' sons to join them, just as much as they expect to join the regiment.

The colonel was at pains to point out that anyone who passes out from the Royal Military Academy at Sandhurst and gets a commission is free to apply to the Devon and Dorsets. He may be accepted. He and his brother officers are interested in quality and if a man is not up to standard he won't be taken on, no matter how many colonels of the regiment he may have among his ancestors. During Wilsey's command four of his regimental colleagues – including Colonel "H" Jones*, who won a posthumous Victoria Cross at Goose Green in the Falklands – were commanding battalions of other regiments. The regiment which, historically, has had to endure a certain amount of chaff about its rural origins and supposedly yokellish performance is now a unit of pride and distinction. Even Guards and Green Jacket officers who have some difficulty in not seeming to patronise all other regiments, were *quite* enthusiastic when asked about the Devon and Dorsets. Partly because of this, Wilsey told me, they have many more applicants than they can take. Therefore, he says, "We won't accept people who put us down as a second choice." In the nature of things most people won't put them down as a first choice unless they have good

---

* "H" Jones was Wilsey's greatest friend in the regiment (joint godparents and so forth). Wilsey says: "His eldest son, David, who is in Lyon House, has just been awarded an army scholarship and is heading for the regiment; another illustration of the influence of family on the choices one makes. H's fame stems from his command of 2 Para, but his family was still his old regiment."

reason to do so. And the good reason is usually a family or geographical connection.

In practice most potential officers will start making enquiries in their teens, and will be encouraged to spend some time with the battalion on secondment, as it were, from their school cadet force. This gives the boy a good chance to find out about the regiment and – quite as important – gives the regiment a good chance to find out about the boy. That final selection is made on merit but it remains a fact that of thirty-two serving Devon and Dorset officers in 1981 all had lived in the counties, been educated in them or had a relation who served with the regiment. Of these no fewer than eight were the sons of fathers who served with the regiment or its ancestors, and another nine serving officers came into the same category, though at the time that the regiment conducted the survey on which these findings are based they were detached to other units or were on the staff of various headquarters.

The other ranks are just as traditional and "rooted" as their officers. Of 608 Devon and Dorset soldiers questioned in 1981, 256 or forty-two per cent had some family connection with the regiment. A third of these were the sons of regimental fathers, a third were brothers and the final third were more distantly related to other Devon and Dorset soldiers. And 478, or almost eighty per cent, of the men lived in one or other of the counties.

There are quite as many great regimental families below the regimental salt as there are above, and just as strong a sense of local allegiance. One of the more impressive is that of Sergeant Janes*, who "popped up to Exeter on my motorbike" from his butcher's job in Okehampton one day in the mid-sixties, and took the Queen's shilling because, "It was a natural assumption. Because, coming from Devon, we were Devonshire people." And his sort of Devonshire people joined the regiment. His father served with the Devons in the second world war; one brother became a corporal in the regiment, another, now retired, a sergeant. A sister married Private Lomax, a Devon/Dorset who has a considerable extended regimental family of his own, mainly cousins. Another of Sergeant Janes' sisters married Corporal Rixon, one of three Rixon brothers serving with the regiment.

The customs and practices of a regiment are, to an outsider, largely unfathomable but visiting the Devon and Dorsets it is clear that the

* See Appendix X.

unit functions as a family group in which a particular sort of loyalty is a necessary ingredient. The knowledge that you may one day be called upon, quite literally, to die for your fellow soldier both demands and creates strong social cement. I met a number of family groups among the soldiers of the Devon and Dorsets: Bissets, Edgcumbs, Janeses and others. They seemed a jolly lot with thick West Country accents, wide grins and an attitude to their officers which, while certainly not disrespectful, was markedly unservile. They do, of course, live their lives in each other's pockets to a degree unknown in civilian life. The regiment is most soldiers' permanent home and therefore the men and their officers have got to know each other over a long period of time. Sometimes their careers run parallel. The man who was Colonel Wilsey's orderly when he joined the battalion in 1960 was his regimental sergeant major twenty years later. Just like the royal family and the Adeanes.

The men's attitudes seemed almost always to be virtually identical. "We've always done the same thing, ever since school," was one recurring reason for having joined the regiment together with brothers and cousins and mates. One man had a brother-in-law in the Gunners, a much larger organisation than the single battalion Devon and Dorsets. He shook his head pityingly. That, he said, was a soulless organisation. Nobody knew anybody else. Nobody had anything in common. In the Devon and Dorsets, he thought, "We need each other more, and we help each other more." Another man said it was just like being at home, a third thought it gave you more confidence. It certainly made initiation far easier. They all said that it meant from the very first that there were people to show you the ropes. There was none of that terrible fear and unfamiliarity that most people experience on entering a strange new organisation.

"No one's got anything to prove," said one of the Edgcumbs. "You don't have to make any friends." This is only partially true for bad reputations can precede one just as much as good. Unpopular elder brothers or even fathers are not forgotten and take time to forgive. Their transgressions are sometimes paid for by those who come after. "You don't want an uncle who was a provost," said someone with feeling. Or even a relation with memorable looks. "Uncle Raymond" was mentioned by one young soldier. "Ah, yes," said an officer, thoughtfully. "The ugly one."

It would be difficult to prove that the particularly inbred qual-

123

ities of this regiment make it necessarily better or worse than any other. Devons and Dorsets think it improves it, but then they would. Colonel Wilsey says that even when the Army as a whole was having the "manning difficulties from which it periodically suffers" the Devon and Dorsets were one of the few infantry battalions in the Army with four full rifle companies and a complete support company. They have no recruiting problem. This may be because the regiment is uniquely appealing to those who hail from Devon and Dorset; it may also have something to do with unemployment and the drift from the land in two almost exclusively agricultural counties. "We're a quite friendly regiment," said one of the men. "But I wouldn't like to cross us." "We work together well," said another. "You know each other's quirks. You can look in a chap's face and know whether he's in a bad mood. We know where to draw the line."

Comradeship, maturity, team work, binding together: all these were cited as particularly strong in the Devon and Dorsets. The regiment seemed to be regarded by its members as a particularly warm and friendly place. "In some units," said Sergeant Janes, "it can take you four or five years to make yourself known. I've not seen any regiment where you're so welcome. And we have a much more relaxed form of discipline. We can afford to."

Colonel Wilsey once spent six months with the United States Army in which everything is done, as Field Marshal Festing's colleagues would have liked, by numbers. Units draw their men from all over the States and the sort of geographical family and educational ties which characterise the Devon and Dorsets are quite unknown. As far as he is concerned, the American system, for all its apparent efficiency, equality of opportunity and general logic, is far less cohesive than the British one in which you belong to a regiment because of who you are and where you come from and – about twenty-five per cent of the time – because of who your father was.

But there is more to this regiment and any regiment than time present and time past. Soldiers have a future too. Army officers and soldiers – field marshals apart – retire long before their civilian counterparts. More often than not they still have the time and the inclination to do something else, and more often than not they fall on their feet. Even though the Devon and Dorsets are not normally thought of as a very grand or influential regiment their alumni still manage to secure some plum jobs. General Sir John Archer, for instance, one of the most successful Dorsets of recent years, is now in charge of the extravagantly grand race course in Hong Kong where he was once the commander-in-chief. But it is not only officers who crop up in grand surroundings. For years RSM Webber, formerly of the 1st Battalion of the Dorsets, could be found at the Tower of London, resplendent in the uniform of a yeoman warder. Anyone visiting Lord's cricket ground and observing the splendidly garish striped blazer sported by the man who rings the bell at the pavilion gate to announce the imminent resumption of play should know that it is not the network symbol of some exotic cricket club, but the regimental blazer of the Dorsets. Its owner is RSM Webber's old friend and comrade, Dorset Regiment veteran, John Conlon.

Jobs like these do not come about through "the usual channels". They happen because people "have a word" with people. They happen because someone recommends someone. And if you have served with the right regiment that becomes, in the right circles, recommendation in itself.

Colonel Michael Bullock*, Colonel of the Devonshire and Dorset Regiment (Devon*shire* is the formal title though it is colloquially always just "Devon" – Dorset, on the other hand, is *never* Dorset*shire*) confirms that the network extends well beyond life actually in the regiment. "For many men," he says, "be they officers or soldiers, once they have served in the Regiment, they are committed to a brotherhood, club, freemasonry for life and this extends throughout their lives, long after they have left the Regiment."

For example, a "distinguished solicitor in Devon" provides free legal services for anything to do with the regimental trust. Every year every man in the regiment gives one day's full pay to the Regimental Association's welfare fund. Those funds, now substantial, help run "regimental cottages". Both the original regiments bought cottages in the counties soon after the first world war. The Dorsets have given theirs over to the Forces Help Society though they have first call on any that become empty. The Devons still have three. An architect in Devon gives his services free for any repair or renovation, a plumber gives big discounts and they are run entirely for the benefit of former members of the regiment who have fallen on hard times. "An extremely pleasant semi-detached largish cottage home for worthy Old Comrades," says Colonel

* A great-nephew of Lieutenant General Sir George Bullock, Colonel of the Devons, 1910–21.

Bullock, "where they live for the very reasonable sum of five pounds a month all in."

Regimental after-life comes in a variety of forms: charitable, sociable, job getting, and, unlike some networkers who try to deny that there are networks in their walk of life, soldiers have a habit of enthusing about the efficacy of their networks. The regimental networks are a by-product not an end. Colonel Bullock, however, is very proud of his. "In almost every walk of life," he says, "newspapers, accountants, the clergy, local government, MPs, members of the House of Lords, we have contacts with ex-members of the regiment to whom we can turn for help and advice. Throughout the regimental area there are branches of the Old Comrades Association who provide a wonderful reporting system for Old Comrades or their dependants, who due to age, infirmity, misfortune or human weakness may be in need; this is fed to regimental headquarters where our welfare committees do all they can to help. Wherever an ex-member of the regiment may be in the world (and we are pretty far-flung like other regiments) it is an accepted custom, certainly among ex-officers, that they welcome another member of the regiment and entertain him, whether they have ever met or served together or not."

As far as job getting is concerned, "There is a certain amount of low key patronage whereby officers of the regiment are able to help specific Old Comrades to find employment. Equally, from time to time RHQ receives letters from people looking for grooms, chauffeurs etc. and we occasionally help people find jobs in that way." A more orthodox job agency operates through the formal all-Service Regular Forces Employment Association which has offices in Salisbury, Exeter and Plymouth. In addition, there is what the colonel calls "quasi-military employment such as executive officers or even the county commandants of the Army Cadet Force". The Devon and Dorsets think they can lobby pretty effectively in this area too.

Other family regiments – a term regimental officers use without apparent irony or affectation – operate in much the same way, though if they don't, like the old county regiments, have that strong geographical base then one strand in the family network is obviously removed or diminished. Other regiments have different but similar loyalties, traditions, friendships and the networks which are their inevitable outcome. They are families like the Devon and Dorsets, all unique and yet all instantly recognisable. It

126

is not easy to quite understand that sense of family even if, like me, you have lived on the fringes of it.

The Devon and Dorset Regimental Journal calls it, "The sense of loyalty and comradeship which binds us all together." Adding, without self-consciousness, "Good regiments thrive on the basis of this sort of family spirit and 'togetherness'." I almost caught its elusive quality one raw winter's day when I drove over to Dorchester, town of my birth, where in the remains of what was once the regimental depot and now appears to have been acquired by the Post Office, an officers' lunch was taking place. It's a regular happening: beer and sandwiches and reminiscence. One or two Devons had motored over from Exeter and the West; there was a young subaltern excited about a posting to Hong Kong; the deputy Colonel, a sharp newly promoted brigadier, speculating on those labyrinthine relationships of families like the Janeses and the Rixons on the one hand, and the Wilseys and Gayes and Archers on the other. There was a clutch of "regimental widows", a term used in such a military manner that it becomes almost as official sounding as regimental sergeant major or regimental headquarters, and some faces from my childhood, brother officers of my father (brother officer – there's a network concept for you). These were a little creased with age, men gnarled and tweeded and wearing their rather hideous though to me evocative Dorset ties, red and yellow and green. It was scarcely an exciting occasion, but effectively nostalgic: a twilight network still finding comfort and pleasure in each other's company, and a pride in the regiment. Later, high in the keep which looks like a child's fort and which houses the Dorset regimental museum, (a rather sad collection of old uniforms and medals and flags), Brigadier "Speedy" Bredin rehearsed the activities of the Old Comrades; the regimental tea and the regimental dinner and the interbranch shooting competition and the fortnightly welfare committee and everyone, from the brigadier down, "keeping an eye open" for an old soldier who needs work or cash or simply helpful advice or a spot of company.

The brigadier was small and military with a little moustache and an enormous, shapeless and obviously very warm coat. Somehow he gave an impression of both timelessness and certainty, as if he had always been a brigadier and always would be. A pivotal figure in an enduring martial tribe, a crucial person in a mysterious organic network that has a continuing life of its own. He looked thoughtful for a moment. "Once you've joined the regiment," he said, "you never really leave."

Other units in the Army are undeniably grander, though none are more typical or more English. Certainly none exploit the idea of family network more effectively. In network terms the most impressive of these are, equally undeniably, the Guards and the Green Jackets. Both are talked of with such bated breath that there are occasions on which the reputation outstrips reality.

The Guards are supposed to have various pockets of employment sewn up. This is not so much at the officer level where the network is deceptively multi-stranded (family, school, sometimes university also playing their part) but the Guardsmen themselves.

One pocket of Guards influence is often alleged to be the doorkeepers at the House of Commons. Guards officers said that they understood that all, or practically all, the doorkeepers were Guardsmen, implying that the prestigious nature of the job, the absolute loyalty required, together with the necessity for the men to be immaculately turned out, meant that when all was said and done, nothing but a Guardsman would do.

One former MP (not a Guards officer) even assured me that he remembered the question being raised during his time in the House, during the late forties or early fifties. His recollection was that a Labour backbencher, conducting a personal witch hunt against privilege and corruption, rose to complain about the disgraceful way in which the Brigade was able to monopolise the doorkeepers. "I have evidence to prove it," he said, and proceeded to read from a list: "Smith – Coldstream Guards; Bloggs – Grenadier Guards; O'Reilly – Irish Guards; McAvity – Scots Guards; Jones – Welsh Guards." And then, "Brown – Green Howards". At which a fruity voice from the Conservative benches could be heard enquiring: "How the hell did he get in?"

The truth, alas, is more prosaic. Officials at the Palace of Westminster, like Lieutenant General Sir David House (formerly of the King's Royal Rifle Corps and the Green Jackets), Gentleman Usher of the Black Rod (there *are* jobs in parliament for retired officers as well as men!) conceded that it was a nice story, but no one seemed to know it. In 1954 a select committee on House of Commons accommodation, etc.* (the etcetera was not speci-

---

* The committee was clearly alive to the possibilities of family networking as well as military. Another section of the memorandum concerns: "Degrees of relationship existing between persons shown on the nominal roll of the staff of the Sergeant at Arms' Department." It is a nice example of the pervasiveness of family networks and also some people's concern about it. It was found that: (a) Mr. C. W. Swepson, Senior Attendant, is the husband of Mrs. E. Swepson,

fied!) was given a complete breakdown. There turned out to be nine from the Navy, six from the Foot Guards, five from the Royal Marines, four each from the Household Cavalry and the King's Royal Rifle Corps, two from the Queen's and one each from the Inniskillings, the Hussars, the Rifle Brigade and – unexpectedly – REME. Almost thirty years later it was the Navy and the Royal Marines who had tightened their grip on the élite squad of House of Commons doorkeepers and the breakdown in 1982, for the forty-five men – eleven more than in 1954 – was as follows:

Royal Navy   19
Royal Marines   15
Blues and Royals   1
Coldstream Guards   2
Welsh Guards   1
The King's Royal Rifle Corps   2
14/20th King's Hussars   1
Light Infantry   1
Royal Artillery/Special Air Service   1
Royal Army Service Corps   1
Royal Electrical and Mechanical Engineers   1

So much for that myth, though it is worth noting that even now every single one of the doorkeepers had done military service. Jobs like this may not make it a formal essential but it *is* an actual prerequisite.

The Guards are an élite and a network with a strong sense of family. They operate in very much the same way as a county regiment such as the Devon and Dorsets, but they operate at a national and London level whereas the Devon and Dorsets and other county regiments are, essentially, more localised. They are also, as far as officers are concerned, more aristocratic. A keen student of such matters can recognise the difference the second he steps into the officers' mess. It is the difference between Swansea City and Manchester United, between Sherborne and Eton, be-

---

Woman Cleaner. (b) Mr. W. G. E. Chandler, Senior Attendant, is the husband of Mrs. E. A. Chandler, Woman Cleaner. (c) Mr. K. F. Barnes, Attendant, is the son of Mr. F. J. Barnes, Night Watchman. (d) Mr. S. St. J. Coulbert, Members' Hairdresser is the nephew by marriage of Mrs. K. Coulbert, Woman Cleaner. (e) Mrs. F. C. Randall, Woman Cleaner, is a sister-in-law of Mrs. E. F. Crump, Woman Cleaner. History does not reveal what action was taken to dismantle the Swepson–Crump family networks and prevent further instances of nepotism.

tween men who feel they have something to prove and men who don't. You, demonstrably, need connections to become an officer in the Devon and Dorsets. To become a Guards officer you need connections *and* to be put down at birth. Or so they say. Every time a son is born to a Guards officer, the father gets an application form from Regimental HQ. But if he neglects to fill it in there and then, it scarcely matters. In essence, however, the typical Guards officer uses the network to get in, and he uses the network once he is out.

John Buchanan, later a pioneering headmaster of Oakham School (and once briefly my English master at Sherborne), told me how he got into the Grenadiers at the beginning of the war (when, of course, circumstances were different and chance and the network played an even greater part in life than now).

Buchanan was keen to serve with the Grenadiers because it had been his father's own regiment. "My father had a distinguished career in the Grenadiers," he says, "in World War I (DSO, MC) and as a result when I enquired at Regimental HQ about the 'Supplementary Reserve' (direct commission) the password was simply 'I'm Tiny's boy.' No further questions!" His father, like him, was prodigiously tall, hence the nickname. In the Grenadiers he found it a positive advantage to have been at Stowe, a school of which most of his fellow Eton educated Guards officers had barely heard. "I was one of comparatively few officers who had not been some other officer's fag or fag-master," he says. He was also one of the very few officers with a clean character sheet and no out-of-school stories for people to gossip about. Throughout the war the regimental adjutant was Arthur Penn*, his father's best man. As Buchanan says laconically, "This, again, did no harm for 'Tiny's boy'." In 1946, having had what military men refer to as "a good war" he sought civilian employment. Sitting one day in the Guards Club he encountered a fellow Grenadier, Edward Ford (later Sir Edward Ford, assistant private secretary to the Queen). Ford said that there was a job going at the United Nations as private secretary to Sir Alexander Cadogan, UK representative on the UN. If Buchanan would like the job it was his. He did and it was.

The Green Jackets, the "Black Mafia" of the Army, are the antithesis of the Guards, with whom they maintain a friendly but nonetheless keen rivalry. The Guards have always lost a relatively high proportion of their brightest officers to a premature civvy

---

* Later private secretary to Queen Elizabeth, the Queen Mother.

street; the Green Jackets have produced more generals. Over the last few years the regiment has been astonishingly successful in terms of Green Jackets making it to senior positions in the Army. A bright, progressive and highly regarded general told me that he had actually suffered from this and would have been given a more interesting general's job if (he thought, but could not prove) the then Chief of the General Staff had not been himself a Green Jacket and sensitive to suggestions of favouritism. (Guards officers, incidentally, like to pretend that the days of Green Jacket supremacy are over and that they have been rumbled. Green Jackets say smugly, "Excellence breeds excellence.")

Although the Green Jackets, who have their headquarters in Winchester, tend to recruit their officers from that and other southern England public schools they are not socially grand in the same way as the Guards or the Cavalry. Their élitism is essentially professional. They want the best no matter who he is or where he comes from. They don't believe in fancy drill or flashy turnout; they don't shout their commands, they speak softly. My Green Jacket general told me with pride and amusement about one Green Jacket who had been promoted from the ranks. He was a rough diamond, dropped aitches all over the place, didn't know how to hold a knife and fork and so on, but was a tremendously effective soldier. He commanded a company, and each one of his four platoon commanders was an Etonian. They all ate out of his hand. And so on.

In which case one might have expected the Green Jackets to recruit from outside the network of regimental connections. If their attitude really is that they should get the best at all costs, then surely they should go outside their conventional public school recruiting grounds and look for the best from the state schools? The Green Jacket general nodded and agreed that this was a perfectly fair point. When he had been in charge of regimental recruiting he had made a strenuous attempt to recruit young officers from state schools. "Of course we know perfectly well that there are jolly bright chaps at Manchester Grammar School and places like that," he said. The problem was not that the Green Jackets weren't attracted to them. The young men were not attracted to the Green Jackets. This could partly be attributed – perhaps – to a pacifist tendency among the intelligent state edu-cated young. One *might* suppose that there is a greater degree of bellicosity among public school sixth formers but the general did not seem particularly convinced by this. He thought it more likely

131

that it was a general prejudice against the army officer image. In the same way as, encouraged by teachers and parents, a Comprehensive school boy might decide that Oxford or Cambridge were not for him, so he might be against the idea of the officers' mess and the "Air Hair Lair" style with which he associated it. The general had tried to encourage high flying state school applicants and had got nowhere. They didn't want entry into the family because it looked too posh. So he had to make do with Winchester and Marlborough where there was always a proportion of bright school leavers only too happy to join the regiment.

Negative prejudices among outsiders such as this can do almost as much to preserve networks as the positive prejudices of network members. Even if the Army was genuinely concerned to democratise itself and take on a more classless image it can only accept what it is offered. Becoming a Guards or Cavalry officer or even a Green Jacket is not yet something which often occurs to people outside those aristocratic regimental families. Even if, as the Green Jacket general would have us believe, his particular network *was* vulnerable to infiltration the idea of vulnerability had not been effectively enough communicated. Or it simply didn't seem attractive. It would no doubt come as a great blow to its members but most people actually don't want to belong to Whites or go away to boarding school, let alone Eton.

One of the complications of assessing the real reasons for the effectiveness of a family military network as it operates in civvy street is that the experience of serving in the Army does equip people for a particular sort of job. At the regimental headquarters of the Irish Guards I was shown an advertisement sent to them along with (I guessed) the other Guards regiments. It was headed "City Livery Company requires Beadle and Housekeeper".

Another request was a note from the British ambassador at the Hague, who wanted a butler. The Duke of Marlborough, once a captain in the Life Guards, wanted a gatekeeper. Prince Charles, too, was in the market for a butler.

Obviously there is a network operating here, and a very efficient and well organised one it is too. Until the mid-seventies it was actually called the Guards Employment Agency and was centralised at Brigade HQ. Since then Guards Employment has been organised on a regimental basis. Requests come in to Regimental HQ at Wellington barracks, in Birdcage Walk. The usual form is that the request is then circulated to the other regimental adjutants and their assistants with a note also to Major "Rags" Courage, the public relations man at London District. Many of these jobs will be filled from within the Brigade without a whisper going outside.

In numerous cases it will be a question of keeping it in the family. A rich city broker or Lloyds underwriter who served with the Guards likes the idea of having an ex-Guardsman as his chauffeur cum valet simply because the man is part of that Guards family. They share an experience and an allegiance. Equally, twenty years service in the Guards, especially if the man has spent some time working in the officers' mess, is about as good a training for a British ambassador's butler as you could possibly hope for. The successful candidate is likely to have "loyalty", "integrity", a willingness to work at all hours without putting in for overtime, and all the other virtues which Service people maintain are in short supply in civilian life. He will have the bearing and demeanour of a Guardsman. He will know how to treat ladies, gentlemen and, quite probably, royalty. And – the one qualification which few totally civilian butlers are likely to possess – he will be a more than useful man to have around if the ambassadorial dinner is disturbed by armed men with stockings over their heads. So, as the assistant adjutant at the Irish Guards told me: "If he's been in the Guards *and* he's got something between his left ear and his right, then he'll be OK."

There *are* Guardsmen who manifestly don't have anything between their ears and they end up digging holes in the road. Membership of the network is not all that counts. In this as in most really effective ones you have to be able, particularly these days, to deliver the goods. In the case of any regimental network there are particular organisations which habitually use the regiment as a recruiting ground. With the Guards, the Diamond Company in Hatton Garden is one regular customer. With the Irish Guards there is a continuing association, as you might expect, with some leading Irish companies.

Waterford Glass and Guinness are two favourites of the Irish Guards, but this is not charity. The companies expect to get good men from the Guards and the Guards know it. HQ wouldn't send them anyone they couldn't vouch for. As the assistant adjutant, a commissioned quartermaster with a colourful turn of phrase, puts it: "I'd rather put someone in when I know his face and his character. If Guinness wanted someone and he turned out to be pie-eyed after half a dozen bottles of the stuff and a sniff of the barmaid's apron strings, then I'd be ruined."

Even Guardsmen aren't always able to pick and choose. HQ will do all they can to help but the network is not always large enough to embrace all who want to benefit. A typical letter came in from a man in Liverpool who had lost his job at the Royal Ordnance Factory. Chris Corrigan, who runs the Irish Guards North of England Association, had endorsed the man with a note saying he was "a good reliable chap and a good old comrade". He also had a Heavy Goods Vehicle Licence. Headquarters got out his file and discovered that his "P" (for Personal) file has "v.good" on it. Also that the man once acted as driver for the C-in-C Middle East. On the strength of this, five letters of recommendation go out to five possible employers in the man's neighbourhood. These may help, but there are no guarantees. The letter on headed writing paper from the headquarters of a Guards regiment is a potent recommendation but it is going out to a handful of unknown personnel directors, men whose prejudices, social background and network memberships are unknown. They are not part of the family.

It is best, therefore, to operate within the known boundaries of the network, where having been in the Guards is a recommendation in itself and where, sometimes, the good Guards NCO *can* at least pick and choose. All school cadet corps, for instance, hanker after a cracking Guards drill sergeant as their RSM. The Guards know this but, being Guards brought up in an environment where their officers come only from a handful of the most socially exclusive schools, they themselves are only interested in the same places. All schools hanker after a good Guards NCO. Good Guards NCOs only hanker after Eton and Harrow.

For the man with a reasonably distinguished record in the Guards there is always a job, even though that job is necessarily of a particular kind, sometimes almost an extension of military life (one Guardsman is reputed to have left Hatton Garden recently because he found the regime there "too military"). The reputation of the Brigade is such that, when it comes to hiring commissionaires, or security guards, or drivers, or butlers or tipstaffs for circuit judges, there are still many who will write, poker face, to Wellington barracks, and say (I've seen the letters): "Obviously we would prefer to employ a Guardsman."

The Guards and other regiments make no bones about their sense of family. On the contrary, they use families and family networks in their recruiting and they create a family feeling among their soldiers to build esprit de corps. In life after military service that dual sense of family is used to form a network which ensures that their old soldiers fade away in style and comfort. Few but the military would parade their family preference so shamelessly that they would say, "Obviously we would prefer to employ a Guardsman." Even if God believes it He would never actually commit Himself to the public admission, "Obviously We would prefer to employ a Bickersteth."

7

Family Business

A family firm – I think that probably puts it right. I suppose in the sense that we're all doing the same job, it is a co-ordinating influence. I like to think us more as a family than a firm. It's a great help to have a lot of people all doing the same thing because you can go and talk to them about it, and you can learn a lot from each other.

The Prince of Wales, television interview, 1969

It is in the "family business" that the family network flourishes most overtly and flourishes still. Such companies as John Murray, the publishers, or Guinness, the brewers, have benefited the nation by publishing poets from Byron to Betjeman, and making the world's best stout. But they have benefited Murrays and Guinnesses even more, creating an interesting and lucrative career (allowing that there is more money in alcohol than literature) for members of their families for hundreds of years. Murrays still run Murray and Guinnesses are still around at Guinness, even though the size of that clan and its fortune has meant that many Guinnesses have had little or nothing to do with the best known family brewery in the world.

Considering the increased competitiveness of the business and commercial world, the resilience of the family business over the last 200 years or so has been every bit as remarkable as the hereditary aristocracy at whose survival Evelyn Waugh so marvelled. Some have died. The short-lived Beaverbrook newspaper dynasty collapsed primarily because the first baron, Max Aitken, was a brilliant newspaperman (though not such an impressive businessman) who failed to pass on his genius or even his enthusiasm to his son. There are still Spinks at Spink and Son, the medallists, but they no longer own the company which suffered an astounding collapse of family network. It looked set as a proper family firm until the end of time. Sam Spink who ran the company from 1875 to 1939 had no less than twelve sons. Unaccountably they failed to preserve it as their own. Anthony Spink, whose father was one of the twelve sons who did not work for the company, is now the only Spink on the board though he thinks he probably has some fifty cousins who, under different circumstances, might have comprised the entire population of the firm.

Elsewhere the reverse has happened and companies which long ago ceased to bear their names are still dominated by families who have been there several generations. At Barclays Bank, no less, which was formed in a merger of twenty regional banks at the end of the nineteenth century, the same seven families – Tukes, Bevans, Gurneys, Bolithos, Trittons, Birkbecks and Peases – who dominated the bank then still dominate it at the beginning of the eighties, holding two of the six top jobs and seven of twenty-nine directorships. The huge Pearson Group which owns among other things the *Financial Times*, Penguin, seventy-nine per cent of Lazards, the whole of Madame Tussauds and over half Chateau Latour, a decade after going public in 1969 had four Pearson family members on the board (Lord Cowdray, his successor as chairman, Lord Gibson; Michael Hare, the deputy chairman and chief executive; and M. W. Burrell). At the same time there were almost a hundred family shareholders.

There may have been a time when such companies, first given life by a dynamic, able businessman, became safe havens for layabout scions. There are still those on, say, the Guinness pay roll, who would be unlikely candidates for any businessman of the year award, but generally speaking those who do not have the aptitude for carrying on the family business opt out. Their directorships, if they have them, are nominal and dormant. At Rothschilds, one of the more successful family enterprises which still employs five Rothschilds, I was told by one senior non-family man that the bank had undergone a quiet revolution in, he thought, about the late sixties. With the exception of one or two old style mandarins like Lord Soames, a director between '77 and '79 who joined the board after his son Nicholas started to work for the bank, most people were formally interviewed for jobs and got in on merit alone. "We don't take Noddies any more," said my informant. But what about family? "We don't even take Rothschild Noddies," he said patiently.

Rothschild's chairman, Evelyn, is fond of saying what a meritocracy the bank is. He himself left Trinity, Cambridge, without a degree, but the latest Rothschild family recruit took a first.

At least they have not resorted to the practice of their rivals,

Warburg's. That bank's founder, the late Sir Siegmund, used to insist that all applicants submit to a handwriting test which was sent away to a Swiss expert for analysis!

A problem with family firms in an age when the hereditary principle is intellectually unfashionable is that they are disinclined to beat the drum and explain the secrets of their success. Family firms are inclined, like Rothschilds, to emphasise that family members are only admitted on merit, that they have to undergo all the same experiences, training, and general "roughing it" as those from outside the family. The same Pearson Group report which concedes that their chief executive, Michael Hare, is a member of the family, also has a little paragraph telling us that he has worked "in a number of group companies over the last eighteen years. Starting work in Lazards . . .". This is clearly designed to give the impression of a man who has worked his way up from the bottom, almost as if being a member of the family were just a coincidence.

Not only is his mother a Pearson; he married his cousin Marcia and his uncle and father-in-law Alan Hare became managing director and chairman of the Pearson-owned *Financial Times*. This surely is family networking with a vengeance.

One or two families, however, have no compunction about proclaiming the virtues of combining business and kinship and of admitting that membership of the family network is an essential pre-requisite. Sir Geoffrey Agnew, chairman of Thomas Agnew and Sons Ltd., is one of four managing directors of the company. The others are his son Julian, his cousin, Richard Kingzett, and Evelyn Joll who "having had the good sense to marry one of William (Agnew)'s great-grand-daughters, joined the firm in 1949". Sir Geoffrey is extremely proud of having kept the business in the family, where it has been since 1817.

"There are," he writes in the book that commemorates the company's first 150 years, "art dealers older than Agnew's; but they no longer have a Christie, a Sotheby, a Colnaghi working for them. Our record of six generations, father to son, is something of which we are very proud."

Sir Geoffrey makes the point that, "Buying and selling works of art is a very personal business, so it helps if there is a strong family connection." Over the years Agnew's have had some notable clients. Pierpont Morgan bought from Agnew's. So did Sir E. C. Guinness, who bought a Boucher and a Cuyp from them in 1887 and hardly bought anything from anyone else thereafter. When Lord Iveagh left Kenwood House and its pictures to the nation, no

less than sixty-two of them turned out to have been bought at
Agnew's. The remaining one was said to have been bought from a
Polish countess over the dinner table. It was also said to be a
Romney but eventually found not to be by Romney at all. Listen-
ing to Sir Geoffrey talk about clients – notably his old friend Sir
John Heathcoat-Amory, whose post-war collection was formed
entirely on Agnew's help and advice – I began to realise that the
personal relationship with a loyal client is as much a part of the
business as the pictures themselves. Without that, half the fun, and
half Agnew's effectiveness, is lost. He himself quotes the verdict of
a rival dealer "noted for his intelligence and malice" who
apparently once remarked: "Isn't it strange how some people
remain faithful to Agnew's all their collecting lives? They don't
even seem to enjoy buying a picture from anyone else."

This loyalty also breeds continuity, not only of clients but also,
sometimes, of pictures. A family that was rich a century ago may
have bought a picture from Agnew's and now, in straitened
circumstances, compelled to sell it, will return once more to the
respected family house where it first bought the picture. When I
called at Agnew's there was just such a painting upstairs: a Turner,
purchased from Agnew's in May 1881 by Sir Charles Tennant, had
come back and was waiting to be sold once more.

Of all these long standing associations the most remarkable is
that between Agnew's and the Ashton family. It began in 1826
when Thomas Ashton was a cotton manufacturer in Hyde, and
Agnew's were still based in Manchester. And it prospered as both
family's fortunes grew. In the mid-nineteenth century Samuel
Ashton bought the Constable painting of Salisbury and in 1891 the
family bought another famous picture, "Tabley" by Wilson.
Whenever these two pictures are lent to exhibitions around the
world the head of the Ashton family, long since elevated to the
peerage as Lord Ashton of Hyde, stipulates that they should be
moved and cared for, as they always have been, by Agnew's. The
connection persists in the younger Ashton generations and when
Agnew's celebrated its 150th anniversary Lord Ashton wrote that,
"It is rather like having a golden wedding in the family."

Sir Geoffrey sees disadvantages in running the firm along family
lines. The need for capital has increased vastly and injections of
cash from outside would often have been welcome. Also, he
believes that it is a fallacy to suppose that members of the same
family will necessarily get on. "I was lucky," he says, "I was the
only one of my generation to join." (He has been with the firm

since 1932, a year before it became a limited company, though times were so bad that he seriously considered an alternative offer to teach at Eton.) Fathers and sons, and cousins work well together in his experience, but not necessarily brothers.

Before 1932 there had been two non-Agnew partners but they had proved less than satisfactory. One hit the bottle and the other went off and set up his own opposition gallery elsewhere. "We've been a little bit shy of non-family partners since then," he says. Not that the family have always been entirely satisfactory either. "We did once get a member of the family proving unfaithful after death," says Sir Geoffrey. This was his great-uncle Lockett who died without issue in 1918 and left his entire capital in the firm to a nephew who promptly withdrew it. A successful rescue operation was mounted by Sir Geoffrey's grandfather Morland but the memory still rankles. "It was a dastardly thing to do," he says. "It was Agnew money."

Not all Agnews, even those who make a career in the art world, go into the family business. At the turn of the century two of William Agnew's sons, Morland and Lockett, were running Agnew's so that the other two sought employment elsewhere. One became managing director of *Punch* (Bradbury, Agnew, then *Punch*'s proprietors, was another Agnew family creation) and another became a director of Christie's. From the late fifties to the seventies the chairman of Christie's, with whom Sir Geoffrey had been at Eton, was his cousin, Ivan Chance. There are still, however, just enough Agnews to maintain the family tradition in Bond Street, a tradition which, with young Mr. Julian already ensconced for almost twenty years and still a relatively young man, shows no sign of being discontinued.

The family business is quite easily understood. Esprit de corps, loyalty, a sense of tradition, an expertise consciously and unconsciously transmitted through genes and environment, all these as well, I suppose, as greed, help to keep family firms in families; but there are also those curious families in which one, perhaps two generations suddenly flower in the same field. There is no formal enterprise which decrees that Menuhins should be musicians: no family orchestra for which they are put down at birth. Nor do the Edriches or Graveneys have family cricket teams, or the Clays a boat. The expectations that such a coincidence prompts are not always realised and when that happens there may be curious compensations. The Frys, for example, were almost as prodigious a cricketing family as the Graveneys and Edriches. C. B. Fry, the greatest Corinthian ever, the man who was offered the Albanian throne, played for England; his son captained Hampshire, and his grandson, C.A. or "Charlie", won an Oxford blue. Charlie's brother, Stephen, found the expectation overwhelming, was useless at ball games but compensated by becoming a boy wonder photographer with a full page in *Life* Magazine while still a Repton school boy.

Often these families have problems explaining the phenomenon, not least because they themselves do not find it as astonishing as the rest of the world. They take it as a matter of course. In 1982, twin brothers, Hugh and Robert Clay, won rowing blues at Oxford. Their elder brother, Henry, rowed in the Cambridge boat from 1974 to 1976 and their father, John, was in the Oxford boat in 1949 and 1950. Asked to explain this unprecedented family achievement John Clay, who is also chairman of Hambro's Bank, says that in his day, "The better oars chose Cambridge where I very much doubt I would have got a blue." Having thus shrugged off his own attainment he says, "Certainly all three of our children have benefited by good coaching. [They were all at Eton.] The impetus to rowing came from an absence of ball sense and perhaps a highly competitive turn of mind particularly between the twins." Clay senior is obviously not entirely happy with a verdict which almost suggests that any competitive Etonian brothers who can't play cricket will win rowing blues, but he nevertheless insists that it is "as near as we are likely to get at analysing the reasons".

Successful families rarely, it seems, acknowledge any assistance or debts. Such networks are regarded as quite bad form.

People are coy about family favouritism. When, for example, James Callaghan made his son-in-law, Peter Jay, ambassador to the United States in 1977* there was a spate of accusations about nepotism. The Prime Minister agonised publicly and it was maintained that the appointment was all due to the bouncy new Foreign Secretary, David Owen, a great admirer of clever Mr. Jay. How much simpler and even more honest and attractive if Mr. Callaghan had simply said "Obviously we would prefer to employ a Callaghan."

* His appointment evoked a note of congratulation from a fellow member of almost the only prep school network of note. "Another OD Triumph!" wrote Lady Antonia Fraser. She, like him, is an "Old Dragon" – a former pupil of the Dragon School, Oxford, where she won some notoriety as a rugger player. Old Dragons exhibit an unusual loyalty to the old school and to each other.

Elsewhere in parliament there are still family scions. Nicholas Ridley's ancestors have been Tory MPs for over 200 years. Southend has been represented by a member of the Guinness family since 1918. It is said that when the present member, Paul Channon, was elected MP for Southend West in 1959 (he was twenty-four at the time) the family brewery had to remove their local advertisements which were advising "Have another Guinness!" It is said just as unkindly that in 1970 old Sir Barnet (now Lord) Janner delayed his resignation from his Leicester constituency until after his election posters had been printed. With thousands of "Vote Janner" posters in their hands the local party simply had to adopt his son Greville.

Such scurrilous stories do less than justice to Paul Channon MP and Greville Janner MP and yet the family connections which would have been a matter of pride and honour if they had followed their fathers into a family regiment are regarded by most of us as slightly tainted. There is a whiff of the rotten borough about their franchise which will not quite disappear. They were selected and elected in the normal fashion and have been elected by the people ever since. It is not even a peculiarly British form of family networking. In the 1982 mid-term elections in the United States Adlai Stevenson II, son of the former Democrat leader, just failed to secure the governorship of the family state of Illinois. In California the recent governor, Jerry Brown, was the son of a former governor. In India Mrs. Gandhi is obviously committed to the idea of the family dynasty. And, as we've seen, there is always Rumania.

And yet . . .

Among the politicians' traditional enemies in Fleet Street there are a surprising number of family networks. Most, however, have been scrupulous about avoiding each other professionally even though they are close privately. William Deedes, the editor of the *Daily Telegraph*, was first employed by the *Morning Post* in 1931 in a direct trade between his uncle Lionel and the managing editor, Guy Pollock. "Pollock lived in a house on my uncle's estate at Chawton," says Deedes. "Pollock got a gun in his shoot then asked if Uncle Lionel would like a job for one of his two sons. He thought them most unsuitable but mentioned me. So I got the job." Since the *Post*'s merger with the *Telegraph* in 1937 Deedes has never worked for any other paper. His son Jeremy has always worked for the *Evening Standard* or *Daily Express*. The relationship is close but not professional.

Sir John Junor is another. Although editor of the *Sunday Express* he does not employ his own son Roderick who once worked with Bill Deedes on the *Telegraph*'s Peterborough column, and is now one of his special feature writers. Junor's daughter Penny *has* worked for the *Express* group (on the Londoner's Diary on the *Standard* where she was a colleague of Jeremy Deedes), but is now a freelance author who has had a regular column in *Private Eye* (the editor of which, Richard Ingrams, a keen networker, contrives to be on cordial personal terms with the Junors and the Deedes though not actually related).

An even more extraordinary example of a semi-negative family network were the Cudlipps, three brothers, all of whom became editors of Fleet Street papers though there was no previous family connection with journalism. The best known was Hugh, now Lord, Cudlipp, one time editor of the *Daily Mirror*. "No," he says, "there was no network. My two brothers and I became Fleet Street editors by different routes and with no personal influence (or pull) on behalf of each other. We all worked for different proprietors. Our old man, a commercial traveller in South Wales selling groceries to impecunious miners, had certainly no pull with Lord Beaverbrook or Lord Camrose. Though Camrose came from Wales, none of us ever worked for him. I left his brother's emporium (Lord Kemsley's) to join the Mirror Group because he wouldn't pay me ten bob over the minimum." Lord Cudlipp's nephew, Michael, also went into journalism but also avoided working with other Cudlipps. He was, successively, news editor at the *Sunday Times* and a deputy editor at *The Times*.

"The inky trade" and "arts and letters" do have sibling networks which function as networks and are acknowledged as such. The Greenes are a case in point. The key members are the brothers, Graham, the novelist, and Hugh, the former director general of the BBC. Hugh, or Sir Hugh Carleton Greene to give him his proper title, is chairman of the Bodley Head who are Graham's publishers. They are obviously a close and mutually supportive couple. On one famous occasion the *New Statesman* ran a competition in which the entrants were invited to submit the most plausible parody of prose from a Graham Greene novel. The winner (under a pseudonym) was Hugh, the runner-up Graham. Hugh's son, Graham C. Greene, is also a publisher but his firm, Jonathan Cape, do not, as yet, publish members of the family.

I only realised how well the Greenes operated as a family network when I went to Canada in 1977 as an associate editor of

Weekend Magazine, a weekly syndicated colour supplement which went out with the *Toronto Globe and Mail* and twenty or so other papers. It had a large budget and aspirations to match. Before leaving England I had agreed with Bodley Head that I would try to arrange an interview/profile with Graham for publication in *Weekend* and, we both hoped, subsequent syndication around the world. It would coincide with the publication of his novel, *The Human Factor*.

In Toronto I convinced the editor of the magazine that an article about Graham was exactly the sort of piece to persuade everyone that we were a journalistic force in the world, and accordingly filed a formal request to Euan Cameron, the publicity director at Bodley Head. Cameron replied that he would personally back my application but that my best course of action was to approach Graham's sister, Elisabeth, who looked after his affairs in London. Elisabeth, it transpired, was the wife of Rodney Dennys, Somerset Herald at the College of Arms. This was the first coincidence because several years before when I was working at the *Daily Express* I had gone to the College of Arms to research an article on some genealogical subject and been briefed by the Duty Herald who was Rodney. We had kept in touch since.

When Elisabeth replied to my letter there was a letter from Rodney in the envelope as well, remarking on the extraordinary coincidence and adding another. Their daughter Louise, an aspiring publisher, was living in Toronto with her friend Rick Young. I must get in touch with them. The inevitable outcome of this was that *Weekend Magazine* contracted Louise and Rick to fly to Antibes and spend a day or two interviewing Uncle Graham. To complete the networking it was agreed that the photographs should be taken by the Dennyses' other daughter Amanda.

It worked beautifully. Uncle Graham's nieces enjoyed a paid holiday in Antibes. *Weekend Magazine* got an exclusive story which was syndicated around the world. The author himself thought it the best article written about him. It was a fine piece of family networking relying in equal measure on a well composed family group in which everybody had different but mutually useful skills and positions; on a happy coincidence of timing and geography; and, most important of all, taking advantage of these with speed and no false modesty. Louise Dennys, incidentally, is now a partner in a Toronto publishing house and has become her uncle Graham's publisher. As a result his 1982 novel, *Monsieur Quixote*, was published in Toronto several months before appearing in London and New York.

It is never easy to evaluate the true strength of any network from outside. I was lucky to observe that particularly well oiled Greene machine in operation, otherwise I might never even have guessed what had been going on (the piece appeared, after all, under the by-line "Louise Dennys and Rick Young". There was no mention of a family connection). To an outsider, any coincidence of shared background, experience and, most of all, kinship, will be assumed to represent a network, but sometimes when you examine it you find that, despite these apparent links and ties, the individuals concerned simply don't get along, or even have a cordial loathing of each other. (More than likely if they have been at one of our great English public schools together.) There are also plenty of cases like the Cudlipps where, despite the network's existence with strategically placed siblings who liked each other enough to be of assistance, it was never actually called into play.

Lady Antonia Fraser makes this point in connection with the much vaunted family network of which she is a leading member. No less than five of the immediate family are famous and successful authors, mainly of historical and biographical works. Her father, Lord Longford, is among a wide variety of other things, the biographer of Éamon de Valera; her mother, Elizabeth Longford, has written about Wellington and Queen Victoria; her brother Thomas about the Boer War and she herself about Mary Queen of Scots and Cromwell. She is also the creator of a detective called Jemima Shore, who has become the star of a Thames TV series, and she shares her fictional talent with another sister, Rachel Billington. She has also extended this literary mafia by marrying the playwright Harold Pinter.

This impressive hand of Pakenham writers is generally known and widely remarked. Catholic families are inclined to be large, an obvious aid in network creation, and so there are cohorts of cousins. It is not particularly common knowledge that among these are, on the one hand, Harriet Harman, MP for Peckham and formerly the energetic left wing legal adviser to the National Council for Civil Liberties, and on the other, Ferdinand Mount, the well known right inclined political commentator and friend of Mrs. Thatcher. Lady Antonia and her historian brother, Thomas, are convinced that a future generation of historians and commentators will have a field day with this unlikely relationship. From it they will conclude that the Pakenham net encompassed both the

145

militant left and the radical right, reached into every crevice of the national political life, and knew no bounds. The conclusions would be interesting and entertaining but, according to Lady Antonia, essentially bogus. She concedes that if she and Thomas were future historians examining the 1980s they would do exactly this, and yet, living now and being on the inside of the alleged network, they know there is nothing in it. Lady Antonia says that although she knows Ferdinand Mount, she has never, as far as she knows, ever met Harriet Harman and belongs to the same political party as neither.

As far as her immediate family is concerned, they do operate as a network though, she says, the network is stronger vertically than horizontally. She feels a greater sense of matriarchy than of sibling loyalty. On one occasion when she and her mother were in direct competition for a place at the top of the best seller list, Lady Antonia asked her which gave her the greatest pleasure: seeing her own name there or her daughter's. "How can you ask?" replied Lady Longford, "you know that your success will always give me more pleasure than any of my own." "Because she is extraordinarily truthful I know she was telling the truth," Lady Antonia says, adding that as a mother herself she feels much the same about the potential achievements of her aspirant author daughter, Flora.

The network does not always operate in conventional or orthodox patterns. One of Lord Longford's hats is a publishing one, but the publishers of which he is chairman, Sidgwick and Jackson, has never cornered the market in Pakenham authors. Three of the family, Lady Longford, Lady Antonia and Thomas, are Weidenfeld and Nicolson authors but this is not because Lady Longford recommended her children. It was, in fact, Lady Antonia who first worked for Lord Weidenfeld – as an editor when she was freshly down from Oxford. She introduced her mother with a book called *Points for Parents*.

Thomas Pakenham was originally a Hodder and Stoughton author but moved to Weidenfeld when Robin Denniston, his editor, became deputy chairman there in 1973. Rachel used to be with Heinemann but is now with Hamish Hamilton. Although Lady Longford's introduction to publishing came through Lady Antonia, it was mother who introduced daughter to her agent, Graham Watson, the now retired head of Curtis Brown Ltd.

All this is agreeably cosy but when it comes to getting reviewed the Pakenhams feel that the appearance of network, rather than the reality, can operate against them. 1979 was an annus mirabilis, even by their standards. That was the year of Thomas Pakenham's Boer War, Lady Antonia's life of Charles II and Lady Longford's Wilfred Scawen Blunt. Lady Antonia remembers that Anthony Curtis, the literary editor of the *Financial Times* (whose brother John is a senior Weidenfeld editor), gave her mother's and brother's books to Lord (C. P.) Snow for review. Snow was then the *Financial Times'* senior reviewer and in both cases responded with enthusiastic notices. This effectively dished Lady Antonia's chances of the same treatment. A third Snow rave for a Pakenham, Curtis told her, albeit jocularly, would be too much.

She and her mother have read each other's manuscripts and made notes and corrections. They write very much the same kind of book and deal in many of the same subjects. For this reason they are often approached by the same editor, publisher or other potential employer and asked to write the same article, which opens the way to many a family leg-pull. If Lady Antonia feels like teasing her mother she will sometimes deliberately try to pass on work that she knows her mother would loathe. Thus a potential employer will call and ask: "I wonder if you possibly write us a couple of thousand words on Belgian ladies of the bedchamber?"

To which Lady Antonia will respond, gushing: "I'd love to but I'm afraid I'm just too busy. But I know that's one thing in the world my mother would absolutely love to write about, and I happen to know she's free at the moment. Let me give you her number. She's at home now."

The potential employer is later somewhat surprised and discomfited to be turned down by an extremely busy Lady Longford who very much dislikes the idea of writing about Belgian ladies of the bedchamber – even when he says plaintively, "But your daughter seemed to think there was nothing you'd like better."

Very soon afterwards mischievous daughter will get a call of remonstrance from mother.

All this networking seems to Lady Antonia to be just amusing or, if serious, perfectly legitimate. She has, however, always been irritated at allegations that she has traded on the family name. It is a difficult accusation to counter though in a sense it is easier for her to do so than a writer like Martin Amis, who may or may not have inherited his father's talent, but is assuredly stuck with his surname. A writer's success is very dependent on critical, and for that matter publishers', reactions. Particularly at the beginning of a career, readers are bound to make comparisons. Prejudice is inevitably aroused. Critics will ask if young Martin would have

147

received so much publicity if he had been called Smith. Or such a large advance. Or, dare one suggest it, have been published at all. The prejudice cuts both ways. Some will assume he's a genius because he's an Amis.

Lady Antonia, of course, has always written under the name Fraser, the surname of her first husband, the Conservative MP. She would also like it to be remembered that by the time her mother published her award winning *Victoria RI* she, Lady Antonia, was a thirty-one-year-old mother of five, a matriarch in her own right and, while appreciative of her mother's achievements, perfectly capable of directing her own career in her own way. When Weidenfeld published *Mary Queen of Scots* there was some pressure for her to capitalise on her mother's earlier success, certainly alluding to the family relationship in the blurb and perhaps even writing under her maiden name (which as Pakenham and not Longford still would not have made the relationship clear to everyone). She refused to do anything of the kind and thus reserved the right, when accused of cashing in on the family, of saying that if the critic knew that she was the Longfords' daughter it wasn't her fault. She certainly hadn't gone on about it. Now that one of her own daughters is embarking on a writing career she in turn is reacting just as Lady Antonia did. Despite pressure she intends writing under her married name. So watch out for a new writer named Flora Powell-Jones. And remember that whatever she or the others may say she is the latest of the Pakenhams, and enjoys the advantages of belonging to that formidable family network. But there are drawbacks, too, as mother has discovered.

As well as family, family bequeathes friends. In a formal sense the Church, ever pragmatic and with an inbuilt sense of the value of network, provides parents with the obligation to name special friends with the title of *god*parents, a pious euphemism which should blind no one to their equally important secular obligations. Godparents are theoretically supposed to oversee the religious upbringing of their godchildren until confirmation. In practice they are expected to remember birthdays and Christmas with generous presents.

Given the decline in Anglican religious observance, it is reasonable to suppose that although some parents do appoint non-religious godparents as putative guardians, the overall number of godparents is on the decline. The aristocracy, on the other hand, has tended to subscribe to the form if not the substance of organised religion and they still appoint godparents. And unlike the middle and lower classes they have never felt much obligation to duplicate the existing family network by appointing sibling godparents. Instead they have gone for friends and preferably for friends who are good for more than a pipe of port on the child's twenty-first birthday.

Take, for example, the godparents selected (in 1980) for the son of the Marquess and Marchioness of Bristol. The marquess, it should be said, is an ardent monarchist, which explains why there is a faint whiff of mothballs about his nominees, most of whom come from the world's throneless royal families. The godparents of the infant Frederick Hervey were: King Ahmed Fouad of Egypt; King Rechad al-Mandi, King of the Tunisians; Count Carl Joseph Henckel von Donnersmarck; Prince Tomislav of Yugoslavia; Prince Nikita Romanoff of Russia; Lord Nicholas Hervey; Queen Fadila of Egypt; Princess Marie Adelaide, Princess of Luxembourg; the Countess of Dundonald; and finally two unexpected commoners – Mrs. Peter Black and Mrs. Ben Rosenfeld. Not a network that everyone would wish but a network nonetheless, an obvious attempt to ensure the continued monarchism of the Herveys.

Even by the standards of monarchist aristocrats, that is an extravagant team of godparents but the difference of approach that it represents is real enough. In most families, certainly in those outside the upper and upper-middle classes, godparents are used as a modest attempt to bolster existing family obligation: one uncle and one aunt who are rather more committed than their siblings to maintaining a continuing interest in and responsibility for their nephew or niece. For the upper orders it is quite different. The most celebrated recent royal baby did not have quite the quantity bestowed on young Frederick Hervey – half to be precise – but there are certainly no siblings among them. Prince William's godparents are Princess Alexandra, the Duchess of Westminster, Lady Susan Hussey (for more than twenty years a lady of the bedchamber), Lord Romsey (grandson of Lord Mountbatten), ex-King Constantine of Greece and the South African born writer and explorer, Sir Laurens van der Post. Sir Laurens who will be ninety-six when the young prince attains his majority is possibly a little old to be much active use as a godfather, unlikely to be taking the boy on long hikes through the Kalahari. He is the token wild card of which Prince Charles is rather fond.

The others, however, are orthodox and predictable. They are

149

royal or near royal friends of the Prince of Wales already. By
making them his child's godparents he affirms their status as core
members of his own network, while trying to make sure that they
become in time among the founder members of Prince William's –
Lord Romsey and the Duchess of Westminster belong to the same
age group as the Prince and Princess of Wales and there is every
possibility that their children will become in time Prince William's
playmates, school friends, girl friends, shooting companions and
so on. Maybe even wife. That network would probably come into
being anyway, but the choosing of godparents makes it more
likely. Whether the young prince deviates from the pattern of
friendship thus prescribed will obviously depend on individual
character. Previous Princes of Wales have rebelled quite dramatically against their parents' notions of what would be suitable or
appropriate. But the pressure is there – as it is to a greater or lesser
extent on all children.

The family networks of Britain are not usually targets of criticism in the same way as the public school/Oxbridge networks of the
OBN, but they are often even more significant. What makes a
Pakenham a writer? School? University? Or being a Pakenham?
What makes a Pakenham a *successful* writer? That has something
to do with being a Pakenham, too. Agnews do not run Agnew's
because they were at Eton or Trinity, Cambridge, like Sir Geoffrey
(though he is also one of that impressive network – the former
Eton schoolmasters). They *run* Agnew's because they *are* Agnews.
It was not Rugby and Christ Church which directed the present
Bishop of Bath and Wells towards the Church. It was being a
Bickersteth.

8

Other Chaps' Networks

"If you want to be a proper newspaperman," I said, "You
got to be well known in the right circles. You got to be
persona grata in the mortuary, see."

Dylan Thomas, *Return Journey*

Most of the networks we think we are familiar with are networks
of privilege: the two OBNs and their constituent parts. Even while
we acknowledge the universality of family networks it is not
families like that of Sergeant Janes that spring to mind, it is the
Mountbatten-Windsors, the Cecils, the Pakenhams and their ilk.
Yet for every one of these visible OBN families there must be
thousands of others like the Janes who are unknown outside their
own small world. Every large family operates some form of
network. Networking is not simply the prerogative of the OBN,
there are other chaps' networks (OCNs) too. For once the
sociologists agree. A quarter of a century ago two of them, Michael
Young and Peter Willmott, looked at the ways in which families
worked. They did not look at the Massingberd 500 but at poor
families in the East End of London.

They concluded: "Every relative is thus a link with yet another
family, each family of marriage being knitted to each family of
origin and each family of origin to each family of marriage by a
member they have in common. The common member may be a
mother who is also daughter and sister, a father who is also son and
brother, a sister who is also wife and mother, or a brother who is
also husband and father. The interlocking pattern is repeated in
different forms throughout society in the way that is familiar. We
refer to all the relatives whom a person knows to exist, in all the
families to which he is linked in this way, as his 'kinship network'."

In other words it is not only the Massingberd 500 or even the
extended families of the OBN who operate family networks. And
if everyone has family networks then, presumably everyone can
have other sorts of network too. The principles of by-passing

151

bureaucracy; of scratching the other man's back if he scratches yours; of giving preferential treatment to those you know and like; these are not, surely, the sole prerogative of the OBN?

Almost the most conclusive answer to this question came from a member of my Old Sherborne network named Michael Selby. I first met him at a dinner party (that peculiarly OBN network tool) given by a mutual friend and we discovered that we had two things in common: squash and school (he had once shared a study with David Cornwell/alias John le Carré). Selby was in the Prison Service and, when I met him was governor of Brixton. Before that, he had been governor of Chelmsford which takes many of its inmates from the East End of London, where he had once run a boys' club. He had not been in the job long before he started to recognise old boys of the club. Not only did this give him an advantage in dealing with his now convicted charges, but he found that the boys' parents almost immediately started coming to him with their problems and worries, as they had when he was managing the club. Later, after he moved to Brixton, he found that every so often a new arrival in the exercise yard (Brixton is a remand prison for those who are charged and not allowed bail) would come up and introduce themselves with a, "Hello Guv. I was in Chelmsford." Once, walking in Balham market, he was accosted by an ex-con who recognised him from Chelmsford days. In a few moments a group of Old Chelmsfordians had gathered round and were reminiscing about the old days. "Just," says Selby, "like an old boys' reunion." This is not an entirely original thought, of course. Even in the thirties men like Kenneth and George Western pointed out the resemblance between the public schools and the prisons – albeit facetiously: "Don't forget Marlborough,* remember St. Pauls./And Dulwich and Hamlet and Stowe/And Wormwood and Dartmoor and Pentonville too/And Dr. Barnardo's."†

The context was startlingly unlike the public school, Oxbridge, Guards world of the OBN but the pattern was familiar. You belonged to the boys' club, made some friends, graduated to Chelmsford together, made some more friends, passed out and back in again through Brixton. Nor did the parallels cease there. The prison itself would be run on public school lines. The governor

* Some of Marlborough's buildings were planned by the architect who went on to design Wormwood Scrubs – according to an amusing but, alas, inaccurate piece of Marlborough folk-lore.
† See Appendix VII.

was headmaster and he commanded through two channels. The first was the formal, acknowledged structure of prison officers, corresponding to the schoolmasters; the other was the informal network structure operated by the inmates. At Chelmsford, Selby's informal network boss (head prefect if we continue the analogy) was a man named Ronnie Bender who had been a member of the Kray gang. Selby had a hold over Bender because he was the only person who could talk him out of the severe depressions to which he was prone. ("Never any problem communicating with the governor," confirmed Bender when I met him later.) On one occasion Selby learned through his official chain of command that there was a race riot brewing. His chief officer warned him there was nothing that could be done about it and advised him not to go down to the cells because it was too dangerous. Selby sent for Bender and asked him to fix things under the old pals act. There was no riot.

Latterly Bender's network influence diminished. He was in Chelmsford from 1975–8 but Selby's successor was less sympathetic to Bender's special position in the inmate network and Bender started to come unstuck. By the time I met him in the Weald wing at Maidstone Gaol he had just finished an extended countrywide tour of Her Majesty's prisons designed in part to disengage him from the network and to prevent him becoming the sort of unofficial regimental sergeant major figure he had been at Maidstone. He told me he was all against cliques and factions. "That's not what prisoners want. I'd break it down. Use my influence. I like to live in a happy prison. If I use my influence it's for everyone."

The official prison line is, of course, that all prisoners are treated absolutely equally and that privileged jobs like being butcher or diet cook go to those who earn them by good behaviour. In practice, they are frequently awarded to the key figures in the inmate network. Position in that hierarchy is determined partly on the impact a man makes in prison and partly on the reputation that precedes him. Strength of personality and leadership quality, however you define them, apply just as much in prison as they do in the Guards or the Church of England. And physical prowess matters in much the same way as it does at school. Bender had just made the final of the prison badminton and he worked out regularly with weights. That counted. He was one of the prison's strong men. And being a member of the Kray gang gave him obvious clout. At that time – the spring of '82 – he was, according to both

153

himself and the authorities, keeping a scrupulously low profile, despite poor history.

Everyone concedes that prisons contain a network of networks even though it is difficult for an outsider or, sometimes, a prison officer, to determine precisely how it works. Tobacco (two ounces for a fiver) is the inmate currency, though there is a drug currency too (probably swallowed in tin foil by visitors and passed in the prison loo but the authorities are, obviously, reluctant to find out for certain). There is usually one, maybe more, bookie in a gaol though Bender told me Maidstone didn't have one. (The governor said later he was pulling my leg.) And somehow there is a bush telegraph which operates among the criminal world inside and out and between the different prisons. Just what it is, and how it functions remains a mystery. "Mr. Selby could pick up the vibrations," said Bender. "You smell these things," said Selby, explaining how he sensed impending trouble.

When I visited Maidstone, George Davis, a well known London cause célèbre, had arrived the night before. Within an hour everyone had known. The prison was abuzz with the story, yet no one was supposed to know, and it is supposed to be impossible to communicate between one prison wing and another. As Julian Mitchell's OBN scandal had spread in *Another Country*, so the story had spread fast and mysteriously, as if by osmosis. As I heard this evidence of underground network communication, I cast my mind back a few days before to another example. Maidstone's was obviously a classic of OCN communication; the other just as classically OBN. I had been standing in the gallery of the stock exchange with the deputy chairman. As we gazed down on the floor teeming with hundreds of dark suits scurrying hither and yon, my companion said: "I could go down there and stand in one corner and start a rumour. And I guarantee everyone on the floor would know it within quarter of an hour."

You could hardly have two more different environments than the stock exchange and Maidstone Gaol and yet the ability to transmit gossip or rumour in this way is common to both. Other networks manage it too. Gypsy weddings, for instance, attract Romany congregations from far and wide, often from foreign countries; but nobody writes formal invitations, nobody telephones. The message is conveyed by the Romany bush telegraph – impenetrable from outside and yet a matter of easy unquestioning acceptance to those within the network. Such communication is a characteristic of the organic network in which mutual understanding is so ingrained that it becomes an almost animal empathy, rather like that which exists between couples who have been happily married for a very long time. It is equally common in the small networks of the OBNs as it is among other chaps' networks on the reverse side of the coin.

The recidivist criminal network is also characterised by an obvious and sharply defined sense of "contra mundum", just like OBN networks. The difference is that the élite OBN networks based on, say, Eton and Christ Church look down on the rest of the world with a sense of ingrained superiority, whereas the criminal fraternity is more inclined to take the worm's eye view. Both views are just as network inducing. There are, broadly speaking, networks of the oppressors and of the oppressed; those who bind together to keep the rest of the world in its place and those who do so in order to find a place in the rest of the world. Twenty years ago, Erving Goffman, the sociologist, described this latter category as the "stigmatised".

Some of the stigmatised, according to Goffman, suffered from peculiarities which "apparently discourage any group formation whatsoever". He cited speech defectives in this category and then proceeded to list a whole variety of stigmatised groups in ascending order of network sophistication (though he did not use that phrase). Ex mental health patients were unlikely to network. "The divorced, the aged, the obese, the physically handicapped, the ileostomied and colostomied" formed what he unkindly called "huddle-together self-help clubs". Alcoholics Anonymous he described as "almost a way of life for their members" while ex-convicts such as Selby's Old Chelmsfordians from a single prison were "mutual-claims networks". There were also "national networks of acquainted individuals (or acquainted once-removed) to which some criminals and some homosexuals seem to belong". He went on to mention parts of cities where "prostitutes, drug addicts, homosexuals, alcoholics and other shamed groups" had a territorial base, and concluded with urban communities, "ethnic, racial, or religious", which unlike the others were much like conventional residential communities and had the family as their "basic unit of organisation".

Since Goffman first produced that analysis many of his "stigmatised" groups have exploited their network potential to such an extent that we would no longer think of them as stigmatised, much less as "shamed". The divorced are now Singles; the obese are now Weight Watchers; above all; homosexuals are now "out of the

155

closet" and have grabbed an old word, changed its meaning and appropriated it for themselves: gay.

Almost any attribute or disability which puts you into a minority has network potential, even if it seems like a total liability. For years homosexuality had its underground networks, particularly in the theatre and among a well defined aesthetic-aristocratic group, the descendants of Oscar Wilde and Lord Alfred Douglas.

Peter Wildeblood, who went to prison in the fifties for homosexual offences, wrote then that, "One of the charges often levelled against homosexuals is that they tend to form a compact and exclusive group. They can hardly be expected to do anything else, since they are legally excluded from the rest of the community." In fact, although there were then compact, exclusive groups of homosexuals, most of them, fearful of criminal proceedings were "isolated, not only from the rest of the community, but from each other. The fear under which they live creates no freemasonry among them".

It may not have done then but it does now. The gay network has become a powerful and effective lobby group. With the threat of prison removed many gays emerged from the closet, to become readily identifiable and widely acknowledged. Gays wanting to meet other gays had only to read the personal column of papers like *Gay News* for information about gay bars or clubs from Aberdeen to Penzance, advice on where to stay in gay holiday resorts like Key West in Florida or Provincetown on Cape Cod or where to attend gay religious services. Homosexuality has become the pass to membership of a network, whereas it used to be a *barrier* to most network memberships.

Even now that homosexuality is legal it is not universally accepted. Coming out of the closet can still have professional consequences as the Queen's personal bodyguard, Commander Trestrail, discovered when he was forced to resign after it was revealed – in July 1982 – that he had had an affair with a male prostitute. It was the allegations of homosexuality which really precipitated Jeremy Thorpe's demise as a politician, although he was not found guilty of any offence. Many homosexuals are still afraid to admit the fact: A *Gay News* poll in 1981 found that only forty-three per cent of homosexuals were "out" at work and only forty-four per cent confided their homosexuality to their parents. The figures were much higher when it came to close but "straight" friends although for those over forty-five it was still only fifty-five per cent. Generally speaking, the younger you are the easier it is to be open about your homosexuality, but even so only fifty-four per cent of the under twenty-ones were "out" at work. For older gays, the tradition of secrecy evidently persists. Only sixteen per cent of male homosexuals over forty-five had told their parents and twenty-eight per cent told people at work. When you examine a particular area of life you can see how plausible those figures are. In parliament, for example, gay activists claim quite large numbers of homosexual MPs – usually around twenty or thirty. They know who they are and find that some are often sympathetic towards their cause, though others are not. But not one has publicly acknowledged his continuing homosexuality to his constituents. Their degree of acknowledgment varies but I was surprised that several quite well known MPs were alleged by gay activists to be actively homosexual and willing to take up, for instance, cases where homosexuals had been discriminated against; but I had never previously heard any mention of their being gay and the state of play is still such that I could not mention them in print for fear of a libel writ, even though homosexuality is legal, and even though they are prepared to admit their homosexuality in (semi) private. For many homosexuality still involves the enforced membership of a semi-secret society. But if they choose to use it there is a gay network available.

Julian Meldrum, who runs the Gay Monitoring and Archive Project and is therefore a sort of honorary librarian to the gay movement, has said that "social isolation and insecurity, a failure of the social support normally available through family, work mates, churches and official agencies" are common and persistent in the gay community. To counteract this, he added, "Gay organisations, and in particular London Gay Switchboard and *Gay News*, have brought gay social facilities into the open and provided many points of contact for isolated gay people, institutionalising options that have always existed [e.g. by writing to authors of books, writing to men convicted of sexual offences, writing to actors who took lesbian or gay male roles in films or stage plays, or writing to the Homosexual Law Reform society]."

Gay News reckoned some two and a half million homosexuals in Britain (male and female), rather a huge and unwieldy network. However, the taboos which still attach to homosexuality mean that they have to act as a network or as a large umbrella network for a host of smaller ones. Information on how to find other homosexuals was for long very difficult to come by, except for particularly strong and well established groups with the money

157

and connection to maintain contacts with a reasonable chance of avoiding prosecution. From time to time there were prosecutions of well known or aristocratic homosexuals, but for the most part, as anyone reading the diaries of Cecil Beaton (bi-sexual), Evelyn Waugh (heterosexual) or the autobiography of Tom Driberg (definitively homosexual) will know, the upper class gay network has operated effectively and happily throughout the twentieth century. It is by no means confined to Britain, and a London homosexual with the right introductions has always been able to infiltrate the equivalent society in New York or Paris or, most notoriously, Tangier.

It was quite different for the middle and lower class homosexual and especially – God help him – for the homosexual living in the countryside. It is true that there were homosexual minorities in various organisations – the forces for instance where T. E. Lawrence sought refuge – but rural England has always been more conservative in its public attitudes, especially towards sex. Without a recognised network, even semi-secret ones like those operated by the upper classes and the aesthetes, many homosexuals were forced either to suppress their sexuality altogether or to seek out contacts in public lavatories where they fell an easy prey to the police.

Despite the building of a gay network open to everyone there is still, it seems, a surprisingly large number of "cottagers" as the gay community calls those who make their contacts in public lavatories. As late as the end of 1981, *Gay News* issued a warning about police activities in Streatham: "We have been asked to warn readers who might find themselves in the Streatham area of London that the police appear to be using an *agent provocateur* to trap cottagers. Be particularly careful of Gleneagles and Streatham High roads. The alleged agent is about 6ft 2ins tall, West Indian, slim, about 19–22, and generally dressed reggae style. Police surveillance appears to have been stepped up in Croydon at the corner of Morland and Addiscombe roads, and in South Norwood (Portland Road), Norbury (London Road) and Brixton, opposite the town hall."

It is difficult to be sure which is the more depressing – the fact that homosexuals still feel compelled to hang around public lavatories to find partners or the fact that the police, apparently, employ men to discover them doing so. I would have thought that journals such as *Gay News*, with their detailed information on legitimate homosexual haunts as well as their quite explicit personal columns made it unnecessary. For example: "Friendly blond Londoner, pleasant looks, nice well developed physique, reliable, seeks permanent relationship, London"; or "Essex 32, schoolmaster type friend wanted". Difficult to see why the need for cottages or cottagers persists unless it is a positive preference; and advertisements like those have existed for years now, as far back as the sixties, in the pages of *Films and Filming* there were personal ads, many of an obviously homosexual nature. Thus, as early as October 1964: "Two Gay Bachelors early twenties wish correspondence, meet males 18–30," or, "Happy Holiday in Algarve, Portugal for unconventional bed and breakfast in Englishman's private home".

Most homosexuals remain relatively unflamboyant about their proclivities. Of that estimated two and a half million British homosexuals only some 2,000 are activists who campaign for gay rights, run gay organisations or are in any real sense professional gays. The rest are more or less reticent, some to the point where their homosexuality is completely repressed. But they all now have access to a real network.

In the early days they carefully avoided the music hall stereotypes of the limp wrist and flamboyant effeminate dress, eschewed mannerisms and affectations which might be thought camp, and generally did their best to avoid attention by blending as inconspicuously as possible with straight heterosexuals. In doing so they avoided the attentions of possibly censorious "straights" but also of their undeveloped contacts within the unformed gay network. Now enough homosexuals have come out, at least sufficiently to be recognised by their fellows, and the network has had life breathed into it. Its potential was always there just as it is in other "stigmatic" networks on a personal, national or even international level. In a free society it is surprisingly easy to turn the tables on the majority and make a viable network from an apparent handicap.

Also among Goffman's list of the stigmatised were ethnic or racial groups. Not all members of these racial groups are paid up members of their networks. Some indeed almost go out of their way – or appear to – to repudiate their origins, often, I think, because of their class connotations. It is, for example, perfectly acceptable, even quite smart, to be a Scot and affect at least a slight Scottish accent. In public life, David Steel, the Liberal party leader, plays this card to great effect. Being Welsh, however, and certainly speaking with a Welsh lilt is not so grand. It is noticeable that two of the Conservative party's most prominent Welshmen,

Michael Heseltine and Sir Geoffrey Howe, both look and sound like identi-kit Home Counties Englishmen, whereas in the Labour party someone like George Thomas talks like a character from *Under Milk Wood*, thus reinforcing his already sound working class support. I heard murmurings from the London Welsh network (otherwise known as the "Tafia") on the subject of Sir Geoffrey's repudiation of true Welshness and put the matter to him. "I would not have you nurturing any doubts about my Welshness," he replied. "Port Talbot was my home until my marriage in 1953, and I continued to practise at the Bar on the Welsh and Chester circuit until I was appointed Solicitor-General." Nevertheless, he is not a paid up member of the Tafia in the same way as Mr. Speaker Thomas, or Cliff Morgan or Sir Huw Weldon or Wynford Vaughan-Thomas or Harry Secombe or Clive Jenkins or a sizeable proportion of the best doctors in London, all of whom could be described, with no *serious* disrespect intended, as professional Welshmen.

This is true throughout the ethnic networks. There are those who glory in not being English and there are those who want nothing more than to be taken for an English gentleman. The Hungarian born humorist, George Mikes, has a vested interest in maintaining at least an element of foreignness, if only because his book *How to be an Alien*, published by another Hungarian, André Deutsch, in 1946, still sells 25,000 a year in paperback (having so far sold 450,000 in hard cover and 200,000 in the Penguin edition). However, we would scarcely know that his fellow Eastern European, Captain Robert Maxwell, hailed from Czechoslovakia if people like *Private Eye* didn't keep telling us.

Mikes himself maintains that Hungarians in Britain, estimated at around 20,000, are inclined to deny their network – a common practice among really sophisticated networkers, but not to be too readily believed. "They all say: 'Oh I hardly know any Hungarians,'" says Mikes. "But when you ask them, 'Who is your doctor?' he turns out to be Hungarian. 'Who is your solicitor?' 'Well as it happens, he's Hungarian, too.' 'And who is your accountant?' Yes, *another* Hungarian." Alexander Korda used to have a notice in his Hollywood office saying, "To be Hungarian is not enough." Mikes, meeting him once, remonstrated with him in a fraternal manner and protested, "But it *was* enough." Korda smiled and said, "Yes, I'm afraid it was."

I first encountered Mikes in the early seventies when he was the editor-in-chief presumptive of an embryonic humorous paper

backed by a humorously inclined millionaire. Alas, the millionaire
went suddenly and unexpectedly broke, and the magazine never
appeared. He was, of course, Hungarian.

The Australians are often supposed to operate a brilliantly
successful cultural mafia and certainly their influence in the London communications world would be thought "disproportionate"
if it could be proved that they were exercising some unfair network
advantage over the Poms. Australian Rupert Murdoch owns *The
Times* and the *Sunday Times*; Australians Clive James and Ger-
maine Greer have become gurus for our times; Bruce Page ex-
editor of the *New Statesman* and the Insight column of the *Sunday
Times*, hails from Melbourne; the poet Peter Porter comes from
Brisbane; the painter, Sir Sidney Nolan, a member of the Athe-
naeum, is a state educated Melbourne boy; the singer Dame Joan
Sutherland is from Sydney, as is Carmen Callil co-founder of
Virago Publishing. Dame Edna Everage, alias cultural attaché Sir
Les Paterson alias Barry Humphreys, is the most visible London
Australian of all.

Being Australian has hardly helped them. They are evidence of
the cultural sterility of their home country, now according to some
commentators a thing of the past. This meant that for years any
Australian with artistic pretentions had to come to London to find
a market for his wares. They are also products of the colonial
inferiority complex which traditionally decreed that if an Australian (or a Canadian or New Zealander) had not made it in London,
then he had not made it. The Canadian writer, Mordecai Richler,
who spent many years in London until returning to Montreal as
an acknowledged success (having become one in London)
coined a phrase to sum up this phenomenon. It is "world famous
in Canada".

The dramatically increased cultural self-confidence of the old
Commonwealth seems likely to mean that their best artists and
communicators will now stay at home instead of trying to take over
London. The Australians, in particular, have done very well at it,
but Dame Edna would argue that it has nothing to do with network
and everything to do with charm, beauty, talent and so on.
Brisbane-born Charles Osborne, literature director of the Arts
Council, says the crucial difference between the Australians and
the Hungarians is that, "Australians tend not to help one another
'get on' in a foreign country like the UK – they're far too envious
of one another."

Ethnic networks such as this operate at every level from the overt and official to the secret and unacknowledged, from the friendly and harmless to the downright sinister. At the most obvious end is the sort of activity conducted by various embassies. They all give parties, they all have lists. Some are quite exclusive, others not at all. At the Canadian High Commission, for instance, they use their large and well situated premises in Trafalgar Square for a whole range of Canadian events, to many of which any Canadian who happens to be living in London or just passing through is perfectly welcome. They held a large party, attended by Margaret Trudeau and others, for the royal wedding. When there is a Canadian election – not an event which receives very extensive coverage in the British media – they take the Canadian Broadcasting Corporation's coverage on a large screen, and hold open house for Canadian expatriates.

On a more restricted level, the High Commission arranges smaller gatherings if, say, a Canadian author such as Margaret Atwood, or Mordecai Richler or Brian Moore (an Ulsterman who lives in California – but still as a Canadian citizen) is in town; and, on a marginally more sinister note, they will, when occasion demands, lobby. All foreign embassies do this and it is one of those moments when, officially or unofficially, the national friends and sympathisers are tapped. Every country has its Anglo-Something friendship society; its group of sympathetic MPs and peers; of "makers and shakers" who for some reason or other have a connection with the country and can be activated in time of need.

This happened with the Canadians in 1980 and 1981 when they ran into trouble over the "patriation" of their constitution. The Canadians needed to create a powerful lobby group to act on their behalf. They concentrated their attentions on those members of both Houses of Parliament who had a Canadian connection. Thus, Lord Strathcona and Mount Royal, who had been educated at McGill University in Montreal and whose predecessor the first baron had once been governor of the Hudson's Bay Company and chief promoter of the Canadian Pacific Railway; and Jonathan Aitken MP, a great-nephew of Lord Beaverbrook and a nephew of Margaret Aitken who had been one of the closest friends of the Canadian High Commissioner, Mrs. Wadds.

Such lobbying is only the grand, political side of ethnic networking. More often it is a product of simple nostalgia and homesickness, a longing for home, which has led, for instance, to a proliferation of English pubs all over the world, especially in North America. They serve as a focus for the expatriate English – at least the expatriate English of a certain type. In Richmond, Virginia, I have found myself in earnest conversation with English exiles, drinking English beer, in ersatz English pubs (one called the Penny Lane, a Liverpudlian bar run by a former Liverpool footballer; the other Matt's British Pub, which is Evertonian in sympathy: the Penny Lane posts the English league football results on a black-board). In Toronto a whole chain of "Dukes" pubs (Duke of Richmond, of Clarence, of York) have made rich men out of their English-born proprietors and become meeting places for those who hanker after mother's cooking and home brews. When the England rugby XV visited Canada in 1982, tickets for the game could only be bought in advance at a cut rate through the Dukes pubs and a chain of fish and chip shops.

Most ethnic networks thrive on such evocations of life back home. The London Polish, for instance, began their London life – those who came during or just before the second world war – in South Kensington. Before his death in 1943 their Prime Minister in exile, General Sikorski, lived in Kensington hotels, first the Rembrandt and then the Rubens, and his people lived around him. Many still do, and the Polish Hearth Club, the main social centre for London's Poles, is still in the Museum district as is the main Polish restaurant, the Daquise. But after the war most of the Poles moved out to West London, to Ealing and Chiswick and Acton. The reason for this, evidently, was that the detached and semi-detached villas with their neat gardens and blossomed cherry trees reminded them of smart suburban Warsaw.

Of all these exile networks the Welsh is the most peculiar mixture of infiltration on the one hand and apartness on the other. They first came to London in the depression. Many of them started small dairies, rarely in the main streets but usually just off them. You could get sandwiches and snacks there too. These little shops have mainly gone now and the families who made money from them returned to Wales as rich people with large houses, rudely known as Plâs Llaeth (the Milk Palace) to prove it. Others began chemists' shops, more of which remain than the dairies. Yet others opened draperies and their names live on: D. H. Evans, Dickens and Jones, John Lewis.

In the early days, the centre of Welsh life in London was the chapel, just like home. There were said to be thirty-nine Welsh churches in London, though the number has dwindled and so has the enthusiasm. Once you had to queue to get into the Welsh church in Castle Street where Lloyd George worshipped (there

163

was an overflow in the vestry with a loudspeaker), and the congregations dressed soberly and respectably in their Sunday best or Dillad Parch as it's known in their own language. It was not so much that they were fervently religious, more that they needed to be together in that hostile, English world. They liked to sing together because singing together was something they could do better than anyone else and it gave them a sense of superiority as well as harmony. "If you can get together a dozen Welshmen," one London Welshman told me with pride, "you've got a choir."

The new generation of English Welshmen is a much smarter one. The new Welsh gravitate towards the great London hospitals and the stage, sometimes combining the two in the same family: Linford Rees, Professor Emeritus of Psychiatry at St. Bartholomew's Hospital and Honorary Bard of the Welsh Gorsedd is the father of Angharad Rees, the actress. They are called to the Bar: Lord Elwyn-Jones, the former Lord Chancellor, is reputed to "support everything" to do with the London Welsh; Lord Edmund-Davies, new president of the London Welsh Association, equally at home in Welsh and English, is a frequent speaker at London Welsh social gatherings. And, of course, like Sir Geraint Evans, they are world class singers: the chorus of one of the great London opera companies has sometimes been described, not wholly inaccurately, as the Sadlers Welsh.

The Albert Hall is the site of the greatest of the year's expatriate Welsh celebrations. It takes place on the evening of the Saturday nearest to St. David's Day which, in an ideal world, is the day, also of the England versus Wales rugby match at Twickenham. "To cry and laugh together," said Mattie Prichard, widow of Caradog sometime winner of National Eisteddfod bardic crowns and a bardic chair, and sub-editor, improbably, at the *Daily Telegraph*. "And dress up. They wear their Dillad Parch and it's a big night out. Not cheap. Not tatty. If it was they wouldn't go. They like dressing up, and if it was too cheap they'd smell a rat." There is also an annual dinner at the Savoy but the old Eisteddfod at the Central Hall Westminster has gone.

The core of official Welsh activity in London is the London Welsh Association in Gray's Inn Road, which used to be dry but now has a licensed bar, much to the dismay of the pubs in that part of town. (That apparently contradictory mix of puritanism and Methodism on the one hand and an indulgence in beer and maudlin song on the other is fundamentally Welsh.) Mrs. Prichard teaches advanced Welsh there once a week, finding that many of her pupils are older men who, in advancing years, conceive a sudden and passionate desire to assume real Welshness by learning the language of their fathers. The language, for so long forbidden in school by English authorities, is one of the most adhesive Welsh cements. For the last twenty years there has been a small Welsh school (the Ysgol Gymraeg) in Willesden Green where the children of expatriates can go to be immersed in their native language and culture from the earliest age.

Other, more or less formal, institutions are the London Welsh Rugby Club at Richmond, a notably more cohesive and passionate body than the London Scottish just down the road, who share their club and ground with Richmond Football Club, whereas the Welsh have a new club house and a large grandstand of their own. (The London Irish have a comparable rugby club except that it is in an inconvenient part of town, miles further out at Sunbury, and the pitch is peculiarly susceptible to flooding. It is, frankly, a bit Irish compared with the well orchestrated enthusiasm of the Welsh.)

There are also, one need hardly say, two London Welsh male voice choirs, both of which are based on the London Welsh Association. The London Welsh sing in bright red dinner jackets; the Gwalia sing in black; and they are said to be the greatest of friends in the bar, but the bitterest of enemies on the concert platform. And, like the English abroad, they have their pubs. There used to be the Hand and Racquet in Leicester Square and the Load of Hay in Praed Street, but pride of place among the Welsh pubs of London goes to the Cock Tavern in Great Portland Street. Every two years, when the Welsh national team plays rugby at Twickenham, the trains disgorge great crowds of supporters at Paddington Station and they make their way by common but largely unspoken accord to the Cock for long hours of traditionally Welsh song and tears, laughter and beer. There are leeks and daffodils and Clare, the landlady, pins a daffodil on the men's lapels, wearing a bright red cloak and one of the original hats from that great day in Fishguard when the French fleet was frightened away by a monstrous regiment of Welshwomen paraded on the cliff tops and looking for all the world like the Brigade of Guards.

The Welsh operate so effectively as a network because they are at one and the same time a part of British society, prominent and powerful and integrated, particularly in medicine and the law, on the stage and in parliament, and yet at the same time – for the most part – so conscious of their Welshness, continuing to feel a pride in it but also a sense of exclusion and of being patronised by the

English oppressors which is a powerful legacy of the past. "Contra mundum" in fact. It is a difficult balancing act to maintain but essential to really effective networking. Too total an assimilation may mean that you cut yourself off from your network, something that obviously happens with some Jewish or Huguenot or other old established immigrant families. It would be preposterous, surely, to think of Bishop Montefiore of Birmingham as a member of a Jewish mafia – he is too well absorbed, too obviously a member of the Anglican hierarchy.

Too extreme an alienation from power and authority in any area means that while you may network very effectively in a limited way it remains limited. Count Adam Zamoyski told me, for instance, that should he want a Polish plumber or a Polish carpenter he can always find one in the pages of a publication named *Polski London*. He has a constant stream of Polish charwomen provided, mainly by his aunts, through a mysterious network even he doesn't fully comprehend. But when it comes to networking in the upper echelons, the Poles, like the Sikhs or the Jamaicans, don't really rate. Zamoyski claims with a touch of bitterness that being Polish in England was a positive handicap until Solidarity and the Pope. The British had a bad conscience about the Poles and regarded them as a nuisance, felt in some distorted way that they had been responsible for the war, that they drank and womanised. For someone of his generation – he is in his thirties – being a Jew was much more popular, which is why for years, he thinks, most Polish Jews have been emphasising their Jewishness at the expense of their Polishness. Now there has been a shift in popular British conceptions, and, he argues, a Polish Jew would be better advised, if he is playing the networks, to try his Polish cards.

Networks are necessarily a function of a minority, so many English people never understand the strength of racial ties at first hand. It is salutary for an Englishman used to living at home in a permanent majority to experience the sense of being among a community of foreigners to whom he is an outsider. However friendly the natives that sense of exclusion, even in a well disposed "old" Commonwealth country like Canada is disconcerting. One does feel *foreign* in a foreign country and there is an abiding and mutual temptation, on hearing an English accent, to strike up conversation, to enquire where it comes from, to compare notes on impressions and experiences and, ultimately, to network. At home in England, obviously, one would not feel any bond with a stranger simply because he was English. The idea is manifestly ridiculous.

Yet abroad, even if one is only on a package tour to Rimini or a flight to Bangkok, one is suddenly divorced from all the usual networks of family and work and recreation. The roots that underpin them are all in England. But the need for the roots and the networks remain and once the Channel is crossed the strongest social cement we have is our Englishness, no matter how cosmopolitan and multi-lingual we may fancy ourselves.

The experience is useful in understanding why the tribal ethnic networks of Britain are strong. They are all, obviously, different, deriving their characteristics from their country of origin, the circumstances of their being here, the colour of their skin and even such apparent superficials as the food they eat, the clothes they wear and the games they play. Some of them are past masters at the network game; others scarcely understand it; but the potential is there for all.

Women did not feature on Goffman's little list of the stigmatised though some feminists would doubtless contest the omission.

There are women in parliament, on the floor of the stock exchange, in the boardroom and in court. There are distinguished female professors at the great universities and jet-setting international lady bankers as well as famous actresses and television speakerenes, Fleet Street hackettes, and publishers. "Publishers are publishers regardless of sex," explained one London editor, patiently. In some areas the women are little more than a token presence and in others they are either formally barred from doing men's work (in the Armed Services they are quite equal except that they never actually shoot people) or informally relegated to a role considered appropriate to the female sex. Every paper in Fleet Street, for instance, has a great many women journalists but there are no women editors and most women are employed on "soft" featurish stories which are assumed by their male bosses to not have a particularly feminine appeal.

Generally speaking, women have won formal acceptance and established a beach-head in professional and commercial life, but they remain a minority there and many of them think that they are being prevented from significantly enlarging the beach-head because that formal acceptance has not yet been turned into anything better. Women have not yet penetrated the OBN which, they feel, underpins and cements life at work. To do so some have started their rival new girl networks.

Even when a woman seems to be absolutely accepted as "one of the boys" or "part of the team" she may suddenly find that it is all an illusion and a pretence. One of the tightest and jolliest little networks in journalism – in any case, a tight, jolly profession, much given to small teams of people who, for a time at least, get on extraordinarily well together – was at the *Spectator* in the late fifties. It functioned as a mutually stimulating team network. It was, argues Katharine Whitehorn, who was one of the team and its only woman, a good magazine and recognised as such. That helped create a happy feeling of élitism among the staff but there was other cement too. "We were all in the same political condition," she says. "We were disillusioned socialists classified then as radicals (though it doesn't look very radical now). And we were all at that intoxicating moment when suddenly you realise you've got enough money and you can start choosing jobs for yourself rather than be thankful for whatever's offered."

The magazine was owned by Sir Ian Gilmour, later the leader of the wet Thatcherite cabinet ministers and known at the time as the Popular Proprietor (note the capital letters). The editor was Brian Inglis, and the leading team members were Whitehorn herself, Bernard Levin, Robert Muller, Karl Miller, Cyril Ray and Alan Brien (through whose good offices Whitehorn, recently sacked by *Woman's Own*, was employed at the *Spectator*).

The *Spectator*, being a weekly magazine, developed its own system of weekly rituals. One of these was that on Wednesday Whitehorn went to the local deli' and bought wine and pâté to be consumed on the premises. The original theory behind this was that on Wednesdays everyone was too busy to have a proper lunch, but gradually this office picnic became an event rather than a convenience – and, incidentally, a useful network builder. Guests were invited, some quite grand – "Roy Jenkins when he was thin; Lord Mancroft before he got pompous" – and Whitehorn was at the hub of it all.

Eventually the *Spectator* network began to disperse and move to other publications. Staff departures were naturally marked by suitable wakes. When Bernard Levin left there was to be such a party, arranged by Iain Hamilton, Inglis' successor as editor, who was not part of the original *Spectator* network. Whitehorn accordingly dolled herself up and came along to the office where she joined in the pre-prandial drinking. Nothing had been said to her about the form the party would take but she assumed they would be going on to lunch together. However as one o'clock approached the new editor looked at his watch, announced that it was time to move on to lunch, and said goodbye to Whitehorn.

Lunch, it transpired, was to be taken at the Garrick Club; and the Garrick Club did not allow women in for lunch (it didn't allow Bernard Levin in when he was later proposed for membership, but that is another story). Whitehorn was, naturally, flabbergasted, hurt, insulted and only partially mollified by Levin taking her off and pouring her full of champagne, thus making him very late for his own farewell lunch. In another context a formidable woman journalist, Evelyn Irons of the *Sunday Times*, had been described to the American Defence Department who were trying to prevent her covering one of their little wars, as "not a woman in the accepted sense". That was how Whitehorn regarded herself within the *Spectator*. She had indeed seemed to become "one of the boys" and yet, suddenly, she discovered that there were times when the old world, old style, old boy network, could work to exclude her from her friends in what she considered a virtually indissoluble little network.

If that happened to Katharine Whitehorn of all people, at the *Spectator* of all places, imagine what it must be like in Baton Rouge, Louisiana, or Phoenix, Arizona, for an American businesswoman trying to become accepted either within a large corporation, or, even more difficult, as an independent operator. Women in both places have recently come up against what one describes as "the frontier mentality" which is an even more red-necked version of our own Alf Garnett style male chauvinism. In both places women have chosen what has come to be a standard, well organised response. They have formed a network.

Even there it is possible to earn a living as a woman, just as it is in England, but that does not necessarily mean that it is easy. It certainly does not mean that women by infiltrating the boardroom also infiltrate what Americans call the locker room – a grander version of our own men's changing room, and scene, according to American business mythology, of many a shared confidence and under-the-shower-curtain deal. Most of the informal networks and the long established gentlemen's clubs are barred to women in the States and so too are such large unexclusive boosters as the Rotarians and the Jaycees.* Women, hardly surprisingly, feel stigmatised in a man's world.

* The Jaycees, like Rotary, do have a women's auxiliary and there is a move afoot to admit women to full membership. Indeed Baton Rouge recently held a debate at which the motion was, "Should women be allowed to join the Jaycees?"

In the past, successful women have often been loners, partly because their sex has excluded them from so many of the conventional networks. Once they have achieved their ambition and made it to the top many such women appear actively hostile to other women and to the idea of helping them on. Feminists call this the Queen Bee syndrome. Queen Bees are either afraid of competition from other women or they feel strongly that they have done it themselves and on their own, and any other woman who seeks similar success should have to make her own way too. Many successful women seem positively antipathetic to the idea of appointing other women to their boards, cabinets or teams and also to make a point of emphasising their lack of conventional feminity. It is said of Mrs. Thatcher, as it was of Mrs. Meir, that she is the only man in her cabinet. Something similar must have been said of Mrs. Gandhi. And it is interesting that these three most famous of the post-war world's women leaders should all have been almost defiantly unconciliatory and abrasive in their approach. All three were Prime Ministers when their countries went to war: they look to me like Queen Bees to a man.

At a less exalted level, however, competitive women have regarded what they perceive as the old boy network with a jaundiced eye. They cannot, apparently, join it, and they cannot beat it by taking it on on their own. The solution they decided lay in countering it with networks of their own. Hence a whole network of new girl networks (the NGN in fact) all over North America.

"Just meeting each other," said Mary Scott Welch, whose book *Networking* is both a history of the women's network movement in the States and a practical guide for would-be women networkers, "and realising that they shared feelings and experiences as women trying to make it in a male-dominated world – that was enough to keep any network group going in the early stages of its development".

The aims of such networks are unashamedly self-serving. No mention of morality, or ethics, let alone the Motherhood of God or the Sistership of Women. The Baton Rouge, Louisiana network, prospectus lists three separate purposes:

1. Continuing education of members. One or two professional seminars are held each year with national speakers brought in to discuss topics selected by the members.
2. Assist and support one another in whatever means possible. This ranges from financial assistance, to supporting those

who own businesses, to simply assisting one another with business problems.

   3. Promote members to serve on local boards, such as Chamber of Commerce, United Way, hospitals.

These goals are pursued at two regular meetings a month. The first is a coffee and doughnut breakfast in an office building owned by a member (membership of this particular network is confined to high flyers and is by invitation only). The second is at a private club where a local bank holds a membership. These are more formal affairs with guests and visiting speakers. Every Wednesday there is a quite informal lunch in a local restaurant – just an understanding that the girls, or any girls who happen to be free, will be lunching there, so why not drop by if you're not doing anything else? There is a monthly bulletin which must not exceed a page in length and all minutes and formal reports are kept to a minimum.

Networks like this are instant attempts to remedy the sexual imbalance, but, of course, part of the success of the old *boy* networks, even of rather dowdy ones, is that they contain a high proportion of really useful people. In the business world this means bank managers and insurance company executives, small businessmen, lawyers, accountants and so on. These people are usually – still – men. There must be a tendency for the women's networks to contain women with all the aspirations and drive in the world, but with not enough power and influence to make them mutually useful. Connections are vital for success, but only if they are the right ones.

Nevertheless the new girls' networks are an established part of life in North America today; the business wing of women's lib. They are still very definitely other chaps' networks in the sense that they are for those outside the OBN. But that could change. Throughout North America the women's networks are now powerful and pervasive. Already the idea has crossed the Atlantic and the odds are that before long Britain too will be over-run by them.

In Britain, "Network" was started by Irene Harris who earns her living by organising fund raising events, most notably the annual Woman of the Year lunch at the Savoy Hotel. She says that she formed the impression at such gatherings that, "A great number of influential women would like to have the opportunity to talk to each other on a more frequent basis concerning their careers."

Her aim, as expressed in her introductory address typed out on paper with a logo of rather limp female hands shaking each other, is very much the same as the aim of the network in Baton Rouge and elsewhere in the States – "To enable you to develop your contacts with others outside your own professional environment."

"Network," she continues, "will provide the opportunity for prominent women from all areas of working life to discuss matters of common interest such as managerial responsibilities, economic problems, international relations, combining family life with career, and of course, 'business gossip'." Unlike most of her American counterparts, she was able to offer such incentives as a "Network" rate for various hotels, wine merchants and health hydros as well as an impressive array of guest speakers, ranging from Daisy Hyams, then managing director of Tesco, to Lord Goodman who was her guest for dinner. (Oddly enough, Hyams was reported in the press a month before her speech as saying that, "I think there are prejudices against women in business, but if you start having an old girls' network you could make even greater prejudices.") Discussion subjects included The Working Woman's Guilt, Success and Divorce and Women and Civil Defence.

Network is not unlike American networks in its aspirations, and its literature is almost brutally explicit. Most of the questions in the form aspiring members are asked to fill in are designed to evaluate success, but one is, "How do you encourage career development of other women in your own organisation?" It is plain enough that anyone not interested in encouraging other women's "career development" would not be welcome in Network. Yet when I actually met Irene Harris I sensed a much less clear sense of purpose and also less cohesion. The common bond – women against the world – should have been strong; looked strong on paper; and yet at the end of our talk I found myself thinking that the Network was a rather flimsy, insubstantial idea.

Not, to be fair, that the women's Network network has anywhere defined its aims so that all the individual networks can agree on them. In the summer of 1982 the Canadian Networks held their first national conference in Vancouver. The movement is popular and successful in Canada – there are forty Networks in Toronto alone and 1,400 members of the Vancouver Network. The networkers agreed that it would make sense for them to have a national steering committee, but in the end they had to postpone its formation for a year. The ladies were quite unable to establish sufficient common points for the steering committee to do its steering by.

Like many other chaps' networks the new girls' networks are unashamedly singleminded in their approach. Like many of the stigmatic networks they represent the banding together of a minority group which believes it is getting a raw deal from the majority and is asserting itself. Strength through unity. No humbug. No pretension. Just a straightforward desire among NGN members to better oneself and one's fellow women. One commentator referred to these female networks as "creating a new kind of buddy system that works for them, and even though locker-room camaraderie may be replaced by a rather grim determination, work it still does". It is still early days for making that claim with any certainty. Grim determination is a valuable asset but successful networking needs loyalty and affection as well. It also seems to me that a network that actually calls itself a *Network* in its campaign literature is displaying its method and purpose too clearly. On the other hand, it is hardly surprising if the stigmatised members of the OCNs sometimes seem shrill compared with the bland self-assurance of those who belong to the OBN. The stigmatised are on the wrong side of the fence.

If you divide Britain's networkers into the successful high achieving old boy networks of the OBN and the less successful stigmatised other chap's networks, you sometimes stumble up against a curious hybrid form which might best be described as the sergeant majors' network (the SMN). It is a small but significant network group sandwiched between the OBN and OCN. For instance, as we have seen, the Windsor–Mountbatten–Spencer network is surrounded by a whole mesh of lesser family networks like the Penns and the Adeanes; the sergeant majors of the court. They are, literally, the power behind the throne. They make the arrangements, define the protocol, run the office. In the same way, Sergeant Janes' family complements the families of the Devon and Dorset officers' mess.

The sergeants' mess has its pride, its traditions, its links; its own networks. Indeed those who belong to such networks tend to believe, with some justification, that it is they who run the whole show. Where would Her Majesty be without her private secretary; without the comptroller of the royal household, and the rest of her other-rank network? Where would the commanding officer be without his regimental sergeant major?

In the Army, the NCOs' network echoes that of the officers. One of Wellington's commanders (General Sir Thomas Picton) said of his officers, "Damn it, Sir, they know nothing. We are saved by our non-commissioned officers who are the best in the world." The judgment was endorsed by at least one contemporary ensign and versified later by Kipling who wrote: "The 'eathen in his blindness must end where 'e began/but the backbone of the Army is the non-commissioned man." Field Marshal Lord Carver once said much the same to me though the point he was making was not to compare British NCOs with British officers, but rather with their foreign counterparts. Foreign armies don't have sergeants' messes in quite the same way as the British, and the phrase "Carry on sergeant major" is untranslatable.

Sergeant majors are not peculiar to the Services. The sergeant-major type is arguably at its most impressive in that other great British tribal network, the legal profession. In its evidence to the 1979 Royal Commission on Legal Services, the Senate of the Bar Council remarked, "There are still a few members of the Bar who would not take a day off without their clerk's approval . . . and who can almost be regarded more as their clerk's man than their own."

The exclusivity of the four Inns of Court to which all practising barristers belong is obvious. It is OBN territory. There are only just over 4,000 barristers; they are highly qualified; their training is lengthy; they are the only people in England who may plead in court; and they may not be approached directly by members of the public but only through solicitors. What is not always appreciated is that this approach is not made directly by the solicitor to the barrister but through their respective clerks, the barristers' clerks and legal executives, to give them their full title. These are the sergeant majors of the Inns of Court. It was claimed in evidence to the 1979 Royal Commission, "He [the clerk] combines the functions of office administrator and accountant, business manager, agent, adviser and friend." This last is a somewhat optimistic idea because, in my experience, for every barrister who lauds his clerk as "adviser" and "friend", there are another two who will vilify him as an extortionate adversary.

The two networks live together like Crown and courtiers. A barrister relies for his jobs on his network. Solicitors approach him either because they have worked with him before or because of his reputation. At the outset of his self-employed career the barrister has, obviously, no solicitors with whom he has worked in the past, and no reputation as a practising lawyer. The senate of the Inns of Court and the Bar publishes a small booklet for those "contemplating a career at the Bar" and this makes no bones about the clerks' influence and importance.

> The clerk is an important part of the mechanism of chambers, especially in the early years of a young barrister's career, before he has become known to solicitors and been able to build up a practice [i.e. a network] of his own. It is part of the clerk's job to acquaint himself with his principal's special aptitudes; and, when occasion arises, to recommend suitable young members to solicitors. It is in this way that a personal practice is born. Its growth and the character it assumes will largely depend on the attributes of the person concerned, the reputation of his chambers, and the guiding hand of his clerk. It is he who deals with solicitors, negotiates fees and arranges his principals' timetables.

These network creators are literally capable of making or breaking a barrister's career. Evidence to the royal commission conceded that some clerks withheld work from a barrister in their chambers "because of personal antipathy or some prejudice relating to class, race or sex". Yet, until recently, no qualification at all was necessary for a man to become a clerk, and even now the admission standards are scarcely onerous. A clerk must have an English 'O' level. That is the sole academic requirement.

There are about 230 clerks, one for each set of chambers. These chambers, north and south of Fleet Street, have the comforting air of the Oxford and Cambridge staircases on which so many of their occupants once lived and perhaps first met each other. The names of members are inscribed at ground level, painted in black italics on a white board. Some of the larger sets might have as many as thirty or more barristers, others as few as half a dozen. Some specialise in obscure aspects of tax or property, some are generalists. Some have a reputation for espousing unpopular causes. Some are smart and fashionable, others dowdy and workmanlike. Some make a habit of defending known criminals. Some have a reputation for dealing with black clients only. The reverse also applies. But they all have clerks.

The typical set of chambers, if such a thing can be said to exist, has a senior clerk, a junior clerk, and a boy. No chambers would have more than one senior clerk though a larger one might have two juniors and perhaps three boys. These three grades represent the entire career structure. The boys, school leavers now armed with their single 'O' level, make tea and run errands, chiefly carrying briefs tied in pink ribbon from chambers to courts or solicitors' offices. They are paid very little and they are treated in a manner which some find distastefully Dickensian. The distinction between officer-class barristers and other-rank clerks is scrupulously observed. Many modern school leavers do not care for it and the Bar is finding it difficult to attract likely lads. This is short sighted of school leavers because those who do choose it find that after the early years of drudgery and penury the later rewards, both financial and influential, are extraordinary.

Originally a senior barrister's clerk was paid two and a half per cent of his employers' fees. Then it was doubled to five per cent, or, as it was quaintly known, "the shillings in the guineas". Before the war, ten per cent had become commonplace, which meant that clerks were not only getting more than junior barristers, they were actually getting more than the mean average if they worked in a set of chambers which contained more than ten barristers. When, after the war, the numbers in chambers rose sharply, some clerks were earning more than three times the average barrister, a situation which even most clerks acknowledged was getting out of hand. Today ten per cent is virtually unknown, and there is a plan to pay clerks a fixed salary plus a much reduced percentage, but even so, a successful senior clerk can earn more than £35,000 a year – a tempting prospect for a school leaver with virtually no qualifications.

In the past much recruiting was done through family connection. Cyril Bachelor, a former chairman of the Barristers' Clerks Association, joined Sir Leslie Scott's chambers between the wars on the recommendation of his uncle. Scott, later a Lord Justice, led a crack set of chambers with a lucrative line in Indian princes. Bachelor's uncle had become a clerk through the good offices of his father who had worked as coachman to Lord Halsbury, three times Lord Chancellor and the man who gave his name to Halsbury's Laws of England. In time, Bachelor succeeded his uncle as senior clerk in the chambers led by Sir Melford Stevenson. In turn, he persuaded his son to follow in his footsteps, although his son later opted out.

Such impressive ancestors as Lord Halsbury's coachman are not easily come by, but the nature of the job and the relatively small numbers involved mean that most people come in because of some personal connection. It is not a job you would be likely to hear about were it not for some form of connection like this, and only a personal connection would be likely to be able to persuade a potential clerk that the job, so initially unappealing, could yield such rewards in later life. Once in, advancement continues to be based on contact and luck rather than easily defined procedures. The crucial promotion is to a junior clerkship, and that depends on impressing the senior clerk in one's own chambers as well as catching the eyes of the clerks in those other chambers where a vacancy may fall. The Inns of Court, like most closed communities, are introspective and gossipy. If chambers are looking for a junior clerk, other clerks will be aware of it and they will know enough about their own juniors to decide whether or not to press their claims. And a good clerk will know exactly how much importance to attach to the recommendations of his fellows. Such jobs are not openly advertised nor are they open to formal competition. Instead they are allocated after very much the same kind of informal soundings and conversations and bush telegraph work which characterises all appointments at the Bar right up to that of Lord Chief Justice.

"A senior clerk," says one of their number, "will notice someone who looks bright and when he does he will go to his clerk and say 'I want to poach your fellow'." Such mobility is accepted in the early stages of a clerk's career. The first move – from mere boy to junior clerk is usually made at about twenty, the second at twenty-five. But by the time one has reached the position of second-in-command it is time to sit still and wait for the top job to fall into one's lap. It invariably does.

Something of the nature of the position and of the clerks' feelings about it can be deduced from the fact that during the war many of those who went away to fight left their wives to mind the shop. This apparently worked satisfactorily and was accepted by all concerned – perhaps most importantly by the barristers themselves. A body of men popularly considered one of the most aggressively misogynist in Britain had been confronted with a choice between breaking with the conventions of sex or the network. They decided to keep the network intact.

177

9

Boosters and the Clubbable Instinct

> At each place was the Boosters' Club booklet, listing the members. Though the object of the club was good fellowship, yet they never lost sight of the importance of doing a little more business. After each name was the member's occupation. There were scores of advertisements in the booklet, and on one page the admonition: "There's no rule that you have to trade with your fellow Boosters, but get wise, boy – what's the use of letting all this money get outside of our happy fambly?"
>
> Sinclair Lewis, *Babbitt*

One of the fundamental problems with a network is the balance between fun and self-interest. The OBN is always likely to prove too strong for the NGN because men genuinely enjoy the exclusive company of other men, whereas women, on the whole, don't much enjoy the exclusive company of other women. The really effective networks tend, paradoxically, to be the ones that do not set out to be effective at all. The regiment and the family do not come into being primarily as mutual self-help organisations and yet over the years that is what they have become.

Networking, like sex, is one of the few activities at which the gifted and enthusiastic amateur has a built-in advantage over the purely professional.

It is often the lack of naked self-interest which makes a network truly effective. The strength of a blood tie or of patriotic or ethnic networks lies partly in the fact that the relationship is inborn. There is nothing contrived about it and therefore nothing suspicious. Self-interest is bad social cement because it *is* selfish. The bond only survives as long as it is of use to oneself; once the use goes the fair weather friendship founders. Other members of such networks realise this so that the effectiveness of their network membership is correspondingly diminished.

Sinclair Lewis, who satirised the ersatz self-promoting network in his novel *Babbitt*, identified four reasons for men such as George F. Babbitt, his self-important, self-righteous middle American estate agent, belonging to such associations as "the Rotarians, the Kiwanis, or the Boosters; to the Oddfellows, Moose, Masons, Red Men, Woodmen, Owls, Eagles, Maccabees, Knights of Pythias, Knights of Columbus, and other secret orders characterised by a high degree of heartiness, sound morals, and reverence for the Constitution."

Three of Lewis' alleged reasons were harmless if silly. The first was because "it was the thing to do"; the third because it enabled ordinary Americans to assume "such unctuous honorifics as High Worthy Recording Scribe and Grand Hoogow to add to the commonplace distinctions of Colonel, Judge and Professor"; the fourth was because it meant that the hen-pecked American male had a legitimate excuse for being away from home whenever there were meetings or other business to attend to. The second reason was the one which caused offence: "It was," wrote Lewis, "good for business, since lodge-brothers frequently became customers."

Although Lewis' target included any number of recently created middle American networks he was mainly concerned to have fun with the Rotarians, the archetypal "booster" which had been started in Chicago in 1905, seventeen years before Lewis' novel appeared. Its founder, Paul Harris, was a lawyer who belonged to no traditional network and therefore set about creating one. The idea had a brilliant simplicity. Harris recognised that although lawyers had much in common with other lawyers, accountants with accountants, candlestick makers with other candlestick makers, they were all in competition with each other. The lawyers might well operate a protective cabal which fixed fees, and have a vested interest in creating as much work as possible for lawyers, but in a competitive society each lawyer was out to get clients, and if getting a client for oneself meant taking a client away from one's fellow lawyer, then so be it. The community of interest between the lawyer and the candlestick maker might not be obviously apparent, but lawyers needed candlesticks and candlestick makers needed the law. How neat it would be if the lawyer, the candlestick maker and the accountant formed a tacit agreement that they would work with each other and not with any other lawyers, candlestick makers or accountants.

Harris' original Rotary (so called because members met in rotation at each other's offices after business hours – though there are other theories to explain the name) was restricted to one man

179

from each trade or profession. It was, at least at first, shamelessly boostering. The modern British Rotary offers a Sample Address to Prospective Members, a sort of model for local Rotary Club chairmen, and even this is forced to admit that, "In the early stages it was an obligation upon the members of the Club that they should do business with each other. If there were a butcher, a baker, a candlestick maker, anybody requiring meat, bread or candlesticks would be expected to turn to his fellow member rather than to anybody else."

Almost from the beginning, this self-interest was mingled with protestations about the moral basis of the Rotary movement. The 1915 Annual Convention of Rotary Clubs which met in San Francisco laid down a Rotary Code of Ethics for Business Men of all Lines but although this was full of talk about the elevation of standards and the necessity of service it was full of giveaways. "He profits most who serves best" concludes maxim two of the code, while number seven proclaims the need to, "Understand that one of the greatest assets of a professional or of a business man is his friends, and that any advantage gained by reason of friendship is eminently ethical and proper."

Over the years, such protestations about morality and ethics have been greeted by a persistent whistling and catcalling from the stalls. Sinclair Lewis himself remarked that a Rotarian type after-dinner speech would invariably ramble on about "a thing called Ethics, whose nature was confusing but if you had it you were a High Class Realtor and if you hadn't you were a shyster, a piker, and a fly-by-night." George Bernard Shaw said he tried talking about ethics to Rotarians and, "I never saw men more astonished in the whole course of my life. I tried first in Liverpool and then I tried in Edinburgh. It is quite true that these men came together and that they lunched, and told one another funny stories, but I really could not see that any of them had any idea in their heads that the Rotarians had any other object or purpose." G. K. Chesterton, as a Catholic rather than an atheist, took an even sterner view of the Rotarians because, he argued, their friendship for each other lacked surprise, mystery or God. "It is," he said, "a form of comradeship that is gross, common, vainglorious, blatant, sentimental and, in a word, caddish . . . there is something vulgar about such companionship. It lacks spiritual dignity."

If such criticism seems slightly over the top you can at least see what they were getting at. The early Rotarians had said that one of their aims was "to promote the scientising of acquaintance as an opportunity for service and an aid to success". If you believed in the spirituality of friendship, like Chesterton, or in less God given forms of altruism (let alone proper English), you were likely to take against Rotarianism. Rotarians themselves have taken account of such hostility. The word "scientising" has now been dropped and the idea of "success" eliminated. In the early days Rotary members drew a name from a hat after every lunch. It was the duty of every member to spend the ensuing week putting as much business as possible in the way of the name from the hat. That no longer happens. In fact the contemporary official view is almost prissy. "That aspect of the Movement," says the official "sample address", "has largely disappeared now and no Rotarian is expected *necessarily* [my italics] to trade with another Rotarian except in so far that members of a Club find it pleasant to do business with fellow-members just for the sake of the friendly relationship which exists between them.

"But I stress that there is no sort of obligation, and that no questions on this subject would ever be asked in these days."

This last may well be true, but it begs the questions. No self-respecting networker lays it on the line in quite such an obvious fashion. It is just that there are certain assumptions, and they are contained in that phrase about members of a club finding it pleasant to do business with fellow members. In practice there is a tendency for local Rotarians to deal with other Rotarians. It is inevitable and its inevitability is one of the reasons for joining.

There are more than 1,400 Rotary clubs in Britain* with a total of more than 60,000 members. Potentially that means more than 1,400 bank managers always sporting their little badge and looking out for it in customers' lapels; 1,400 vicars on Christian name terms with the superintendent of police; 1,400 car salesmen who know exactly where to go for a cut price carpet. In its essentially OCN way, it is a formidable network.

In other countries it enjoys a much higher profile. The chairmen of large public companies in France, Germany and Italy are practising Rotarians. In Britain it is a Poujadist network, just as it was in Chicago in the early years of the century. Its members are independent businessmen, professionals, managers of local branches of banks and insurance companies – the sort of men who

* Worldwide membership of Rotary is almost a million and there are 19,484 clubs in 157 countries. Any British Rotarian who is away from home is entitled to lunch in any of these other clubs. All he has to do is produce his membership card.

tend not to belong to other networks and, because they are bosses, tend to be isolated at work. Each club is supposed to have only one representative of each trade or profession and this naturally makes for a much tighter and more exclusive network. Since the beginning of the movement, however, ways have been found to get round this rule. Even Rotary's official spokesman admitted there were two bank managers in his branch – one perhaps as a bank manager, the other as a financial adviser, he wasn't sure. George Bernard Shaw reported that when he lectured the Rotarians on ethics he found the clubs stuffed with men from the same profession or trade. "In the printing business, for instance, you had the machine represented, and the printing represented, and the paper represented and I do not know what else; at any rate, it is perfectly easy to get as many men who are virtually printers into the clubs as you like. That does not matter; the more the merrier."

It may be merrier but it dilutes the network. One representative from each trade and profession means, in theory, that it is easy for Rotary folk to stay together and for Rotary folk to all be friends. More than one means a choice. Choice means a loser.

The Shavian–Lewis view of Rotary is that it is a self-interest network masquerading as an altruistic and charitable enterprise, the whole decked out in high-flown mumbo jumbo. To be fair, modern Rotarianism has largely shed the mumbo jumbo and raises huge sums for charity. It is, nevertheless, a classic network: creating social links between men who can be of mutual professional help because of them.

Freemasonry, often bracketed with Rotary, is a booster club of incomparably more overblown mumbo jumbo, though with genuine and ancient historical roots. It is also, unlike Rotary, a secret society, although, for all its rather melodramatic subterfuges, it is so open a secret that the freemasons publish their announcements on the Court pages of *The Times* and the *Daily Telegraph* and hold their grandest rituals in the Albert Hall. Like Rotary, it is neither a political nor religious organisation in a sectarian sense, though its enemies contend that its elaborate ritual and ornate language, coupled with that quasi-secrecy, have made it a religious sect of its own. It is traditionally regarded as anti-Catholic, though it might be fairer to argue that it is the Catholics that are anti-masonic. Some Greek, Italian and French groups in the eighteenth century became agnostic, and as a result Pope Clement published a bull in 1738 forbidding Catholic membership.

In Britain and Ireland it took almost a hundred years for this to be enforced, and well into the eighteenth century there were predominantly Roman Catholic lodges even in Ulster.

Like Rotary in Britain, its numbers are declining. (Rotary is, however, increasing in popularity in Japan and the Pacific – yet another example of the Orient adopting an aspect of industrialised society and, in time, refining it.) Masonic reticence means that I cannot produce statistical evidence to support my view that masons are not what they were. I know that when I talked to a distinguished elderly bencher at one of the Inns of Court he acknowledged the existence of a local legal lodge but was unable to think of a single member under fifty. And I understand that Prince Charles, unlike both his predecessors as Prince of Wales and his own father and grandfather, is not a mason. This is not objective proof; but they are interesting straws in the wind.

The Grand Lodge of England was founded in 1717 but the first evidence of transition from "operative" to "speculative" masonry came in Scotland in the seventeenth century. Before that, masonry, which claims to be descended from the rule book of the masons who built King Solomon's temple in Jerusalem, was a guild or trade union of stonemasons. Its secrecy had the understandable object of preventing any outsider gatecrashing the profession. As the Rev. Robert Foxcroft, who made a television programme about the masons for the BBC, puts it, "It was a practical way of maintaining a closed shop." The seventeenth century Scottish operatives gradually admitted more and more speculatives to their organisation. Usually they were local gentry or distinguished passers-by, and initially they lent respectability and tone to the plebeian masons. Eventually the speculatives outnumbered the operatives until the society became what it is today – an organisation of men from every walk of life. Freemasonry still has a strong hold in parts of the construction industry but you certainly don't have to be a builder to belong.

They have been described, in another phrase from Foxcroft as the Mafia of the Mediocre. There is some truth in this. One lapsed mason I talked to had been told that he would be expected to join when he assumed the headmastership of a public school. (It was not an order but it was an understanding.) He was appalled by what he found, describing it as a lot of local grocers and undertakers dressing up and addressing each other by grand titles. A real OCN in its most disparaging sense. He attended two or three meetings of the lodge and then quietly dropped out.

This element of Rotary, of boosterism, subscribed to by town worthies and tradespeople, has an element of truth in it, but masons, who appear extremely snobbish, are proud of their royal and aristocratic connections. In the case of the royal family this dates back to 1874, when the Marquess of Ripon resigned as Grand Master and became a Roman Catholic. He was succeeded by the Prince of Wales, who was duly installed at the Albert Hall. Subsequent members of the royal family came in through a Royal Naval lodge (Number 2612) but Prince Charles is supposed to have broken this tradition, like the great Duke of Wellington, who was bullied into masonry by his family as a young man but refused to have anything to do with it in later life.

Masons claim a curious ragbag of the world's great men as their own. These include American presidents (Washington, both Roosevelts, Truman, Johnson and Gerald Ford), the third Aga Khan, Winston Churchill, Lord Halsbury, Stamford Raffles and Cecil Rhodes; numerous generals and admirals including Alexander, Haig, Jellicoe, Kitchener and Nelson; the explorers Amundsen and Scott; sundry spacemen including John Glenn and Virgil Grissom; Sir Joseph Banks, the eighteenth century naturalist, Montgolfier, Boswell, Casanova, Gibbon Goethe, Sheridan, Swift, Trollope, Voltaire, Bach, Haydn, Mozart, Sousa, W. C. Fields, Clark Gable, Houdini, Harry Lauder, Buffalo Bill, and the man who invented the guillotine. Most lodges do not admit women, though Dr. M. H. R. O'Connell, a leading Irish mason, writes that in 1712 the Honourable Elizabeth Aldworth was initiated in Irish lodge No. 44. I know one woman who claims (and I have no reason to doubt her) that she is a member of a Scottish lodge.

There are over a million masons in Britain and the organisation is said to be worth more than £25 million. It is much given to good works; raised £½ million for the Royal College of Surgeons; runs a benevolent association which looks after masonic widows; subsidises masons' sons at public schools; and poses no visible threats to the fabric of society.

Elsewhere this is not the case. The maverick European lodges are, unlike British ones, often highly politicised and anti-clerical. The English lodges are still full of Anglican clergy. (Lord Fisher of Lambeth used to be the masons' Grand Chaplain before the war.) In 1871, however, the Grand Orient Lodge of Italy stopped requiring members to swear on the Bible at their initiation ceremonies – something that would be quite unthinkable in Britain. In

Propaganda Two

May 1981 the "Propaganda Two" lodge in Italy under the Grand Mastership of a Tuscan industrialist named Licio Gelli, an old friend of the Argentinian ruler Juan Peron, brought about the downfall of Arnaldo Forlani's Christian Democrat government. The lodge was so secret that only Gelli knew the names of the members but when the list was discovered at his home it contained two ministers, three under-secretaries, 175 senior military officers, bankers, and nineteen judges. It was alleged that this secret sect "combined business and politics with the intention of destroying the country's constitutional order".

It is perhaps significant that in 1864, a decade before the Prince of Wales became English Grand Master, the Italian Grand Master was Garibaldi. Now the English Grand Master is the Duke of Kent while the Grand Master of Italian lodge P2 was, until recently, the sinister Signor Gelli. As long as the royal family remain in charge it seems unlikely, to say the least, that English masonry will subvert the realm; there is nothing about English freemasonry to excite suspicion, nothing to make it more sinister than its half brother Rotary, except for its secrecy.

But the secrecy does excite suspicion. It suggests that the freemasons have something to hide which, in Italy, and perhaps elsewhere, they obviously have.

In crudely boosterish network terms, secrecy helps. "There is a widespread suspicion," says Foxcroft, "that it provides a cloak for unscrupulous business dealings, that there is a network of free-masons who use the secret passwords and recognition signals to gain an unfair advantage." Like other networkers masons like to do business with other masons and masonry creates opportunities for men to meet people who may, in a purely commercial and business sense, be useful to them. In this it is, like Rotary, a classic booster organisation creating an immediately favourable re- sponse, if not on the telephone then certainly on the handshake – or possibly through some signal of greater secrecy. But it is hardly exclusive. Its huge membership is limited only by age and sex, a willingness to take part in its peculiar rituals while professing a belief in the Fatherhood of God and the Brotherhood of Man. Non-masons do not know, publicly, which of their acquaintances, associates or friends, are masons. Because of this they suspect that there is some form of conspiracy among masons, a conspiracy from which they are excluded. In a sense they are right. Masons have a bond with each other and, just like Rotarians, they will use that bond to help each other in a way which, to non-masons, will often

185

seem unfair. But the bond for all its ritual and secrecy is really no more than the bond of the boosters and the bond is weak.

Weak bonds have their uses. Rotarians and masons, unlike brothers or compatriots, are unlikely to die for each other even though they may put a little work each other's way, but then putting a little work each other's way has a day to day usefulness which greater sacrifices don't. In professional life the closest network ties may be useless if one's nearest and dearest do not work in jobs which impinge on your own.

Part of my scepticism is based on my feeling that they are clubs for those who are unable to get themselves elected to any *proper* club. The Groucho Marx sentiments are mine exactly: "Please accept my resignation. I don't want to belong to any club that will accept me as a member." In the OBN a club is as much of a status symbol as one's school or college. You are pleased, in your *Who's Who* entry, to put "White's" or (if you are Alan Pryce-Jones) "The Artillery (Galveston, Texas)" or (if you are Sir John Jardine-Paterson, "the Royal Calcutta Turf (Calcutta)". OBN members are not pleased to put "Rotary, (Grantham)". But as far as Grantham is concerned it is the Rotary Club that counts and no one has ever heard of White's, much less the Royal Calcutta Turf. Every network to its place.

In British society as a whole the most significant of the formal network assisting clubs are those usually associated in a general and imprecise way with the OBN. This means – more or less – the essentially Victorian gentlemen's clubs situated – more or less – around Pall Mall and St. James'. Over the last few years these places have fallen on progressively hard times. Some, like the Bath, have vanished altogether, sold out by the committee amid a welter of recrimination from the members; others like the Guards and the Cavalry are now amalgamated; yet others, of which the Army and Navy is the most obvious example, have adapted to the times by giving more room to women and cutting their cloth to suit the, relatively, reduced circumstances of their members. "The Rag", as the Army and Navy is known, is much less like the officers' mess and much more like the NAAFI than it used to be (though its members are, of course, still recognisably officers, gentlemen and members of the OBN).

Yet the conventionally successful Englishman still seems to belong to at least one London club. It still seems to be something you do when you join the Establishment OBN and are invited to have your name in *Who's Who*. As we entered the 1980s all but three of the country's twenty-three top civil servants belonged to a club and so did practically all Mrs. Thatcher's cabinet – even if it was only the Tory party's canteen, the Carlton. Generals naturally belong, as do judges. Even the unconventional Lord Denning is a member of the Athenaeum as, still, is the Archbishop of Canterbury – unlike the recently retired Archbishop of York, Stuart Blanch, and his friend the Bishop of Bath and Wells, both of whom belong to the much cheaper and much less fashionable Royal Commonwealth Society. At one time the Athenaeum was full of bishops, but bishops are increasingly the poor relations of the Establishment and simply can't afford it. "All diocesan bishops used to belong to the Athenaeum," said one of their number, "but inflation and the failure of Church stipends to keep up with inflation I think has changed all that a great deal and now most bishops stay with relatives or sleep uncomfortably in son's and daughter's flats when up in London." "I have neither the money nor the inclination to join," said another. But the Athenaeum still has seven of the Civil Service's permanent secretaries, as against the United Oxford and Cambridge's five and the Reform's two. It has no cabinet ministers, which will come as a surprise to Chris Mullin, editor of *Tribune*, who makes it the centre of the Tory party network in his thriller, *A Very British Coup*.

In North America I was told by one analyst, Peter Newman, the former editor of *Macleans Magazine* and author of *The Canadian Establishment*, that the rising stars of the smart élite still feel it advisable to belong to the old world clubs but, unlike their fathers, they no longer feel that it is necessary to actually go to them. In Britain, as in North America, most clubs are like morgues in the evening since it is no longer the done thing for a man to spend his evening in all male company. And at lunch they have to compete with an increasing number of restaurants which with few exceptions lay on not only better food at comparable prices but also provide the ambience and gregariousness of a good club without insisting on membership. Why lunch at the Carlton or the Reform when you can go to Langan's Brasserie?

By dark many of the London clubs are either half empty or little more than hotels. Members don't go there to meet other members and manipulate the networks over good cheap claret and nursery food; they use them, for the most part, as a place to entertain their friends or, God forbid, their clients. Others which are perceived by some outsiders as OBN havens have no exclusive qualities other than a long waiting list and a subscription. The MCC, for instance, has 18,000 members who achieve membership simply by finding one member to sponsor them and another to second them. Neither is difficult for anyone passionate about cricket (though there is a waiting list of 8,000). And being passionate about cricket is the only reason for joining. Membership entitles you to entry to Lord's for every day of cricket played there but confers no real social prestige or network membership. It's the cricketing equivalent of renting a box at Covent Garden. But cheaper.

To have any network value over and above being some sort of status symbol (however unconvincing) and a convenient place to lunch, a club needs to be full of useful people who talk to one another. Many clubs appear to contain only rather dim mutual strangers who studiously ignore one another. The Lansdowne may be useful for swimming and the RAC a good place to play squash but it is difficult to imagine anyone bumping into anyone there and learning something to their mutual advantage. (Uncharitable about the RAC since there *is* a chance of meeting Nigel Dempster on or around the squash courts, though even the incorrigible Dempster doesn't start serious networking till later in the day.)

The Service clubs obviously have a network value in the sense that if a relatively junior officer happens to be in London for the day it does him absolutely no harm to bump into a senior officer, who has wandered across the park from the Ministry of Defence, and join him for a gin and tonic or lunch. Otherwise the most clubbable clubs are Pratt's, the Beefsteak, the Savile, the Turf, Boodle's, the Garrick and White's. Of these, the two last operate the most successfully. Both contained members of Mrs. Thatcher's first cabinet and, though neither is first and foremost a political club, the cabinet members give a good clue to the tone of each place. The White's men were Lords Carrington and Soames and Sir Ian Gilmour. The Garrick members were Norman St. John-Stevas and Mark Carlisle QC. (The Attorney-General, Sir Michael Havers, is also a Garrick man.)

White's, it follows, is grand in the old manner – Aneurin Bevan was once assaulted on the steps, though it was asking for trouble to go there after referring to the Tory party as "vermin". It is full of old money and for a certain sort of Englishman it is the only club worth contemplating. The waiting list is long and the blackball is used frequently. Unlike most clubs which are essentially places where members take other people, White's is a club where members go on their own in the hope of seeing their friends. The difference is crucial. It is in the nature of the club that anything as vulgar as business dealing does not take place there, but one man – not a member – told me a business story involving White's which gives some idea of its members' influence. This man and his partner, who *is* a member (though he won't be much longer if the members at White's guess his identity) were embarking on a fortnight's business trip to Texas. They had never been there before and had no contacts at all. After a day at White's chatting up the members they had enough Texan millionaires in their address book to give them three meetings a day throughout their trip.

The Garrick has no such class or money pretensions. Indeed, most of its members would be regarded by most of White's members as common and poor. Membership is comprised of lawyers, actors, journalists, writers and publishers. It is quite usual for members to turn up on their own, have a drink at the bar and then go downstairs to lunch at the long table in the front dining room or make up a small group to lunch with friends at another table. The "shop" talked is of a well informed if sometimes speculative nature but its most interesting network function is as a market place for books and book ideas. Some books never go outside the Garrick until they are actually published and it has certainly been known for a very famous Garrick author to use his Garrick agent to – in effect – auction his unwritten manuscript among the various Garrick publishers.

Of all London's clubs only one combines sociability with undeniable power. Charles Dickens, in *Our Mutual Friend*, made Mr. Twemlow venture the opinion that the House of Commons was "the best club in London". Today the verdict is questionable. The accommodation is overcrowded, the food poor and the décor dog-eared. But more than any other parliament in the world Westminster strikes the outsider as being, in an inimitably British way, more of a club than a legislature. Whenever I go there I find it hard to remember that members have been elected by the people and not by the other members.

One reason for the House of Commons' extreme clubbability is that it keeps strange hours and does not require its members to be in the chamber the entire time. It also serves, indeed seems to actively encourage, strong drink (unlike other parliaments which like other navies are often "dry"). Because a member may be required to vote at any moment he can never go too far away. The wealthier MPs have flats or houses fitted with "division bells" close enough to the House to make it possible to hotfoot it from home to chamber in time to vote. But most members, even those with

189

adjacent dwelling places, spend a lot of time hanging around bars. There are a great many of these about the House, all with their particular character and all tailor-made for a particular sort of networking. The Smoking Room next to the members' dining room, scene of practically all the old parliament chestnuts about the repartee of Sir Winston Churchill, has most of the leathery characteristics of a St. James' club and is therefore favoured by Tories and the sort of Labour MP who has either joined the SDP or is about to. The Kremlin Bar is the parliamentary equivalent of the local working men's club, except that it invariably has women there as well as slightly randy Labour men drinking Newcastle Brown. A different sort of networking goes on in Annie's Bar where MPs traditionally leak bits and pieces to their favourite lobby correspondents. And the Pugin Room is not used for internal networking, though it could be the scene of some intrigue involving non-professional politicians. "It is," said one well brought up Tory MP, "where one takes one's nicer constituents for sherry."

The larger less wieldy associations occur on both sides of the House. The Labour left has its Tribune Group, the right its Manifesto Group; while the Conservatives have the left-inclined (relatively) Bow Group and the rightist Monday Club. The smaller more convivial groups tend to be Tory. One of the most interesting is the "One Nation" Group which was founded by Sir Angus Maude and Lord (then plain Cuthbert) Alport in 1950. Its original members were the leaders of that peculiarly talented group of Conservative MPs who first entered the House that year and which included Edward Heath, Iain Macleod and Enoch Powell. It still meets for dinner every Wednesday and it still includes the principal Conservative "wets" or moderates, although members have to resign if they become ministers. They do rejoin on ceasing to be ministers so that Sir Ian Gilmour and Norman St. John-Stevas both returned to the ranks of One Nation after leaving Mrs. Thatcher's team.

One Nation's inspiration like its name comes from Disraeli and it is the antithesis of Thatcherism. Lord Alport wrote, in 1981: "The fact that today the term 'One Nation' is regarded by the contemporary Conservative establishment as evidence of dissidence, 'wetness', or whatever other epithet the Prime Minister may concoct for us, is a sad reminder of the extent to which the present leadership of our party has fallen below the high ideals of a generation ago."

Alport said that when it began One Nation "sought to elevate and modernise the social policies of the Tory party. We sought to wean the Conservative party, post 1945, away from the image of the party of 'hard-faced business men who had done well out of the first and second world wars'. We sought to capture and hold the middle ground of politics."

Some such form of common ideological commitment is almost always the pretext for these associations. The 92 Club is One Nation's tough right wing counterpart headed by the former Royal Marine, Major Pat Wall, author of *Student Power* and *The Soviet Maritime Threat*, leading member of the Conservative Southern Africa Group. Other more or less Tory left or left-centre groups include Nick's Diner, named after Nicholas Scott the member for Kensington and Chelsea ("mainly men who were trendy and popular in the early seventies," said one critic waspishly, "and are starting to look a bit fly-blown"), and the Guy Fawkes, which also dines though its members are of a newer vintage.

But the smartest, socially and intellectually, are the Blue Chips who dine every other Thursday at the home in Catherine Place of Tristan Garel-Jones, the MP for Watford. The Chips campaigned en masse at the Croydon East by-election in 1981 (to no great effect, the seat was won by William Pitt – no relation – for the Liberal/SDP alliance) and is broadly on the same ideological net as the One Nation group; but it is not so much its shared political view that marks it out as its highly developed sense of network. Individual Chips seem to get on with each other at least as well socially as politically. Nearly all were at public schools (four at Eton) and rather over half at Oxford. Nearly all of them entered the House of Commons after the 1979 election (though Lord O'Hagan, the fourth baron, sits in the Lords and the European parliament where he represents Devon) and they are very much of an age, nearly all belonging to the generation born in the early to mid-forties. They tend to have sharp and independent wives. One wife is Sarah Hogg, well known for her TV impersonations of Mrs. Thatcher and now a Channel Four newscaster; another is Caroline Waldegrave, who runs Prue Leith's successful cookery school. Not all of them are blue blooded by any means, but there is a strong sense of dynasty – political as well as aristocratic. Viscount Cranborne is a Cecil, representing the family constituency of Dorset South, and heir to one of the great political titles: Marquess of Salisbury. Douglas Hogg is Lord Hailsham's son and his wife, apart from being a successful journalist, is also the daughter of another old Tory warhorse, Lord Boyd-Carpenter. Richard Needham, the MP for Chippenham, is actually the sixth Earl of Kilmorey but he does not use the title. Michael Ancram is the son and heir of the Marquess of Lothian; and William Waldegrave, the son of Earl Waldegrave. And he is clever too: a Fellow of All Souls, no less. The Chips weekend with each other, which is agreeable since several have very splendid houses, and they even sometimes go on holiday together. From time to time they serve as godparents to each others' children – there is a strong Roman Catholic caucus, including Ancram (who is married to the daughter of England's leading Catholic layman, the Duke of Norfolk), Chris Patten, the member for Bath, and John Patten, the member for Oxford. The Pattens are close friends but not, surprisingly, related. In short, it is a remarkably cosy little organisation and it would be surprising if they fail to dominate a Tory government before the century is out.

In network terms I think the more interesting clubs are those, like the Chips – without the apparatus of permanent premises and servants – where the main purpose of the meeting is to generate a flow of interesting, and preferably useful, information. These can be very small. Some of the most effective informal little clubs of this century were based on railway carriages. For whole working lifetimes little groups of men would join commuter trains at stations like Dorking or Sevenoaks or Twyford, travel together in the same compartment, alight together, then go their separate ways, only to return together on the same train and in the same compartment that evening. Some of the time they would read *The Times* or the *Daily Telegraph* in silence but some of the time they would talk. The talk might have been of cricket or politics but sometimes it would have been the sort of professional gossip which provides an efficient networker with exactly the sort of inside knowledge to give him the unfair advantage in life that he is looking for. Douglas Muggeridge of the BBC (Malcolm's nephew – the Muggeridges are a quite large, interesting family network) told me that for years his father travelled up to the city from Sussex in the same compartment as his stockbroker. On the way up in the morning he would brief his broker on the day's plans. On the way home at night they would conduct the post mortem. A first class compartment in the old days sat six – an ideal size for a small cabal – and ensured absolute privacy. Now the open plan train is destroying that sort of club premises and the only railway based networks are much looser associations: the action groups of commuters trying to pressure British Rail into providing a better service.

An element of conviviality distinguishes all these club networks. They are for the most part full of "clubbable men" – a definition originally coined by Boswell for Dr. Johnson. The most effective networking usually needs the pretence at least of informality and happenstance, rather like the convention (dying if not dead) that it is bad form to discuss business at lunch until after eating is over and the loyal toast (metaphorically speaking) been pronounced. A club which meets for the sole purpose of networking would – *pace* the new women's networks – be a pretty grim sort of club, a club which has eating and drinking as its primary and avowed purpose is never *just* that; it's not natural. But practically all small network type clubs centre on food and drink and are sometimes dictated to by them. One such consists of Lord (Victor) Rothschild, Woodrow Wyatt, David Somerset, Michael Tree and Michael Broadbent, head of Christie's wine department. It meets irregularly, eats and drinks well, and rejoices in the name the Drink Tank. (Rothschild was the first Director-General of the Central Policy Review Staff more widely known as the Think Tank.) A bottle of wine divided between five ensures one generous glass each. Each man produces a bottle. The same thought governed the now defunct Bordeaux Club which was limited to six members representing, more or less, Oxford, Cambridge and London, on the grounds that a bottle produced six glasses. Each member was expected to produce a very good bottle.

Sydney Smith, writing in the Cambridge Review of 26th February 1982, recalls Sir Stephen Gaselee, chief librarian of the Foreign Office in the 1920s, who left the Cambridge University library, "Several rare books and an extraordinary collection of menus of the very numerous meetings of groups sharing the ambition to explore the associations between fine food and outstanding wines." On 10th June 1927, says Smith, Gaselee lunched at the Restaurant Basque "with five others – the right number to have an adequate portion from each bottle: Haut-Brion 1914; (Gruaud) Larose 1899; Mouton-Rothschild 1893; Lafite 1870; and Yquem 1858. Two other of the participants I had later the pleasure of tasting, indeed drinking, wines with – Sir Thomas Barlow and his elder brother Sir Alan. The Lafite 1870, to judge from my later experiences with this vintage, would by then have thrown off the *gaucheries* of unduly prolonged youth."

Oxbridge and the wine trade are particularly prone to such clubs, the best of which are quite consciously designed to give insiders a chance to mix in convivial circumstances with well disposed and – perhaps – potentially helpful outsiders. Thus the Saintsbury Club* formed in 1931 by Maurice Healy backed by André Simon, Sir John Squire and A. J. A. Symons. Harry Yoxall, a member for thirty years, writes that the original intention was that "half should come from the more literate members of the wine trade and half from the more vinously educated men of letters", though he concedes that the qualifications have become shaded over the years. The fifty members meet twice a year at the Vintners' Hall and reckon that though the food is not as good as their French counterpart, the Club des Cent, the wine is better. Meetings are held on St. George's Day and Saintsbury's birthday. Wine trade apart, literary members have included Hilaire Belloc, Henry Cecil, Vyvyan Holland, James Laver, Compton Mackenzie and Stephen Potter, while among what Yoxall says "may loosely be called personalities" he recalls Chips Channon, the Duke of Alba, C. B. Cochran, the Duke of Devonshire, Prince Vsevolde of Russia and Lord Woolton. The modern members seem a less colourful collection.

Oxford and Cambridge are positively riddled with such organisations, with Cambridge enjoying a reputation for higher living and a liking for interminable "feasts", while Oxford probably has the edge for political intrigue. The most self-conscious attempt to maintain an intimate, gastronomically bolstered link between senior dons at both universities and their more distinguished alumni is "Ad Eundem" founded in 1864 by W. C. Sidgwick and H. Sidgwick. The first dinner was held at Oxford, the second at Cambridge and the third at Greenwich, and dinners have rotated between the university cities and London ever since. Originally there were eight Oxford and eight Cambridge members but since 24th May 1879 there have always been fourteen from each place. Of those fourteen, seven are "in residence" and seven not so that in practice there are always fourteen dons and fourteen non-academics. Dinners are sumptuous and heads of colleges vie with each other in attempting to prove the superiority of their cellars and kitchens. Membership is considered an honour although not by everyone, and an early edition of the club notes remarks laconically that, "We have not recorded the names of the few who, having been elected, declined to join the Club." A fairly typical

---

* Professor George Saintsbury, 1845–1933, author of *Notes on a Cellarbook*, the father of modern winemanship. See Appendix X for a full list of those attending the 101st dinner.

member is the newly ennobled philosopher, Anthony Quinton, president of Trinity College, Oxford, and a self-confessed devotee of what he calls "sedentary pursuits". The dons tend to be similarly dedicated to sedentary (and convivial) pursuits – men such as the archaeologist Glyn Daniel and John Sparrow, the former warden of All Souls. The graduates are inclined to be clubbable high achievers of the Robin Day, Peter Parker class.

Of course, Ad Eundem is not a pressure group or a lobby or trade union any more than the Saintsbury or the Drink Tank. Members of such organisations are given to protesting that they "really are just dining clubs", but, of course, anyone who knows anything about networking cannot believe that *any* dining club is ever *just* a dining club. Food and drink are essential but so too is conversation and conversation among members of such exclusive little groups is bound to lead to the exchange of more or less privileged information, the creation of mutually shared confidences and to links and prejudices which provide the means, at least potentially, of doing what networks are all about, which is by-passing the usual channels.

Some such clubs do it more consciously than others; some excite more resentment among outsiders. In the world of the public school headmasters, for instance, there are two dining clubs: the Twenty-Seven and the Gang. Not all headmasters belong and those that do tend, though not always, to be headmasters of the most prestigious Great Schools. Headmasters of lesser schools, naturally, are often resentful because as Dr. John Rae, the headmaster of Westminster, has pointed out: they "in a characteristically English way created an inner, charmed circle and made those who were excluded suspect that it was here that the effective decisions were taken". In the case of the headmasters the Headmasters' Conference is the formal, public debating chamber, but it is the exclusive, clubby gatherings, well evoked in the name the "Gang" which produce the confidential chats and exchanges. Headmasters, by dint of their office, are in a solitary position. It is difficult to confide in anyone about the problems which exercise them most, particularly about the shortcomings of their staff. If a headmaster wishes to complain about "how dreadful directors of music are" (evidently a common complaint) he is unlikely to raise the matter with his own director of music, with whom he is presumably dissatisfied and is hardly going to bring it up in public debate at the annual meeting of the Headmasters' Conference unless he wants resignations, recriminations and a fuss. But it is precisely the sort of remark he can make to his companions at a dinner of the Gang.

The same applies to most people at the apex of a pyramid of power. For those in government geographical proximity means that if, say, the head of the Civil Service wants a quiet word with the permanent secretary to the Treasury he can always find a quiet corner (there are plenty) of the Athenaeum or the United Oxford and Cambridge. But it is not so easy for headmasters, who are scattered about the country.

The headmasters, unlike the dons, restrict their membership to practising headmasters. Their meetings are not concerned with the sort of cross fertilisation that inspires Ad Eundem; but some of the headmasters of the Anglican public schools do belong to one of the more intriguing of these groups, a body known as "Nobody's Friends" which dines three times a year at Lambeth Palace. Nobody's Friends or just plain Nobody's excites very much the same sort of resentments as the Gang and the Twenty-Seven. "I've always felt the title was the very worst form of English inverted snobbery," complained one bishop, adding that, "I've never thought of them as an especially significant group of people." Others regard them as being very influential and their dinners as being the most important networking occasions in the Anglican calendar. Yet others produce the old refrain: "Nobody's Friends really *is* a dining club."

The club was started in 1800 by William Stevens, a man "trained to a mercantile life" who could have been rich but preferred to give most of his money to charity. He "found leisure for literary pursuits, particularly for the study of theology and Church government: and he lived in habits of friendly intercourse with some of the most pious and learned men of his age".

One of Stevens' friends who had heard him going on about these friends "of sound principles in Church and State" said he would like to meet such people "in the face". Characteristically, one can't help feeling, Stevens was only too happy to do what Rotarians would later call "scientise his acquaintance". Equally characteristically, he always referred to himself as "Nobody", even publishing his collected writings under the title, *The Works of Nobody*. Hence the club's name which, it should be said, in fairness to the founder, was not actually thought up until after his death in 1807.

The first meeting was attended by Stevens himself, the founding members and, "Two noble lords and persons of the first station for talent and worth in the three learned professions, and others of a literary character who delighted in the conversation, admired the principles and honoured the prominent and active virtues of Mr. Stevens' character." From the first it decided "not to meet so often as to make attendance burdensome, nor so seldom that the Members could not keep their friendships in good repair".

The club has met three times a year since then, except during the war years this century, and the only real changes have been the time of meeting (it was half past five in 1822), the cost (five shillings in 1890) and the dress (evening dress was normally worn until 1939). In 1980 the club had sixty members, of whom half were clerical and half lay. Apart from these members there was a provision for up to thirty "extra-members" who are, "Privy Councillors, Bishops, Judges and other persons deemed to have qualified on the grounds of special service to Church and Queen." The Club motto is still "Pro Ecclesia et Regina". Extra members are balloted for as soon as possible after they have been nominated but ordinary members have to spend at least two years on the waiting list and four "negative votes", better known in less polite society as blackballs, are enough to keep a candidate out.

The notes compiled by Nobody's Friends' secretary in 1941 say that, "When a new Member is elected he is expected, in the words of one of the earliest rules, to make an *éloge* on himself at the first meeting he attends: in other words to justify his presence. If the justification is regarded as satisfactory by Members – and there has been no case in which it has not been so regarded – the health of the new Member is drunk and he becomes thereupon entitled to all the privileges, amenities and, I will venture to add, the pleasure and happiness of being one of Nobody's Friends."

All of which sounds very cosy and jolly, as indeed it is and as it is meant to. It is now run by Michael Kinchin Smith, lay assistant to the Archbishop of Canterbury, a grandson of a Governor of Hong Kong, married to a daughter of a Master of Magdalene, Cambridge, former president of the Oxford Union, Coldstream Guards officer and for almost thirty years a BBC administrator – a man, in other words, with his finger on the pulse of many networks, not the least of which is Nobody's Friends.

197

10

The Sergeant, the Peeress and the Meaning of "Friend"

> You could do a lot worse than become a fixture at a place
> where the eminent gather, although I wouldn't suggest
> actually eating there because it can be terribly expensive.
> But a glass of milk costs very little, and an order like that
> will get you remembered as mildly eccentric and therefore
> rich. Give the bartender outrageously generous gratuities
> (you can afford to on glasses of milk), and he will then allow
> you to call him Freddie and introduce you by name to his
> wealthy clientele. In that setting, on those terms, the
> automatic presumption that you are a "someone" will
> allow you to seize whatever opportunities fate puts before
> you.
>
> John Wareham, *Secrets of a Corporate*
> *Headhunter*

The world is full of bogus OBN members – men wearing the
striped ties of schools they never attended and colleges from which
they never graduated; people who affect exaggerated and essentially counterfeit accent and idiom; sometimes even really ambitious professional con-men who award themselves a title or at least
the honorific "Sir" in front of their name – or perhaps "Colonel"
or "Captain". It is still, I suspect, easier for an officer and gentleman to pass a dud cheque or induce a little old lady to part with her
inheritance than it is for an obvious "other rank".

Such deliberate dissimulation is not always necessary if one
wants to "crash" a network. The Establishment OBN is inhabited
by many men who are not Foundation OBN members but could
pass themselves off as foundationers. They are usually accepted
quite happily by those who really were at public school and
Oxbridge. You may have to subscribe to the conventions of the
network, and accept the club rules but provided you do so it is
possible, I think, to infiltrate all but the most starchily punctilious
networks – and the starchiest are not always the ones most worth
belonging to.

One of the most fascinating instances of this is the case of the man known in the smartest circles of wartime London as "the Sergeant". "Who is this Sergeant I hear so much about?" the King is supposed to have asked, somewhat huffily. He seemed to be everywhere. His friend, James Lees-Milne, encountering Lady Cunard by his hospital bed one day in 1943, wrote: "The whole of London congregates round the Sergeant's bed. Like Louis XIV he holds levées. Instead of meeting now in Heywood Hill's shop, the intelligentsia and society congregate in public ward no. 3 of St. George's Hospital." He was, as far as one could make out, an American Army sergeant, possibly something in intelligence, with nothing known about him except that he seemed to be everywhere with everyone. Dinner with the Duff Coopers; dinner with Harold Nicolson; lunch with the provost of Eton. Logan Pearsall Smith, another of the Sergeant's conquests, checked up on him through mutual friends and pronounced him "aristocratic (according to American social rules) rich and popular." Chips Channon, walking with Lees-Milne in Hyde Park, "Asked me whether Stuart (the Sergeant's real name was Stuart Preston) was really rich or really very poor. Everyone was asking, for Stuart is extremely mean with money if he is not poor. I honestly did not know. Was Stuart an imposter, he wondered. I said such an idea had not occurred to me. I thought an imposter was a person masquerading as someone who he wasn't."

This was a good answer for Channon. An American himself, he had married Lady Honor Guinness and, like many converts, sometimes seemed a more fervent Guinness than if he had been born one. It was also true. The Sergeant had not cheated his way into the embrace of London society. There was no deception involved. He had never pretended to be anyone else. There was never any need. People were more than happy to accept him for what he was.

He now lives in Paris – "still an Anglophile, but a less dazzled one" – and when asked how he came to be part of what looks, forty years on, like a dazzlingly exclusive and impenetrable network, he says, self-deprecatingly: "I can only say that in 1942 I was aged twenty-one, very much of an Anglophile and – I must admit – romantically snobbish. I don't regret it."

The old, of course, like the flattery of the young, especially when it is sincere. James Lees-Milne says, "Old ladies like Lady Desborough, Lady Islington adored him for he took immense trouble, going to visit them by train at Panshanger or Dyrham. They told him stories of Edwardian days and whispered confidences which they would not have done to a young man who was not a foreigner. And not only old ladies. Old men of letters like Maurice Baring and Logan Pearsall Smith were much taken with him. They exchanged little gifts of autographed books with flattering dedications, and other things."

There is nearly always an aristocratic mafia of elderly ladies around London; most of them charmingly susceptible to men like the Sergeant. But he had achieved social success beyond the sphere of the dowagers. James Lees-Milne explains what he thinks the reasons were: "He was a well-bred American of the upper crust. He was very personable, intelligent, well read, passionately interested in the arts and literature, particularly English. It is true he had an historic interest in old families and knew exactly who was who, who was related to whom etc., often to the surprise of the socially eminent. He was a sort of passionate pilgrim, Henry Jamesean."

Lees-Milne had met him before the war, in 1938, with Harold Nicolson "at whose feet he sat". Nicolson was a useful sponsor, the best possible introductory passport. The sergeant was a civilian then but Nicolson predicted that he would be back in uniform, and so it turned out. On 30th December 1942 he telephoned Lees-Milne to announce his return, in khaki. "In those days," continues Lees-Milne, "he was rather good looking with great charm, very outward looking and cheerful (which he no longer is). The London hostesses were delighted to find an American soldier who would be an asset at their wartime tables of spam and other austere fare that they could muster. Thereby they would be doing their bit to help greet our gallant allies from across the Atlantic. Stuart became a cult. He had – still has – a rather beguiling soft voice. He played up like mad. He was invited everywhere. Dukes and Duchesses, even crowned heads, were fascinated.

"Now the Sergeant never put a foot wrong. He was after all well brought up and knew what was what. He made no enemies except among those of his own generation who were jealous of his success (I mean among the English young) and resented this interloper. He was never bitchy; never criticised, never said unkind things about others."

Nowadays the idea of 'society' is preposterous. The sixties took care of that. Society, if there ever was such a thing, has become irreversibly Dempsterised, penetrable, it seems, virtually at will. It may help to be a hairdresser, or perhaps, though fashion changes so fast that it is impossible to know for sure, a photographer. The only certainty is that anyone who wishes may now join the world characterised as society in the various gossip columns. It is an infinitely crashable party as this little piece of alleged social climbing analysis in the *Tatler* by its former editor, Tina Brown (alias Mrs. Harold Evans), demonstrates with bizarre precision:

"Take Timothy Swallow," she suggests improbably, asking us to suppose that he is "the diminutive social meteor who works on the William Hickey column." According to Tina Brown, "In a single train journey from Doncaster eight years ago he shed his family, his home town and his Yorkshire accent. After a spell working in the china and glass department at Peter Jones his social breakthrough came when he met the punk figure, Jordan – herself a media creation – in a shop selling Cambridge Rapist masks in the King's Road. Swallow had indeed met his Amazon, for Jordan introduced him to Quentin Crisp who in turn introduced him to the talent spotting proprietor of a gay magazine. For a time he commuted from Doncaster to London every Friday, working in a crumpet factory during the week and covering Society for the gay magazine at weekends. Now he was only a bullshot away from the Fleet Street diaries and their passport into the social hub of London. He made it to the inside."

A latter-day Sergeant, networking his way into latter-day "society".

As far as society goes nowadays nobody seems to know what or where the inside is. In the old days there were more rigorous efforts to codify procedures and to establish who belonged to the social network at the apex of society. For those who cared about such things, there were girls who had "come out" and girls who had not. Those who had were called debutantes, or debs, and their *coming out* ensured that they would meet eligible young men known as debs' delights. Fond mothers hoped that their daughters would marry one of these and produce offspring who would one day become debs and debs' delights in their turn.

This social network existed for more than a hundred years and was quite distinct from the titled aristocracy. It consisted, quite simply, of those who had been presented at court and introduced to the monarch. This meant that they in turn were entitled to present someone else at court and introduce *them* to the monarch. The system has its echoes in every club for which new members have to be proposed by an existing member and also in the formal system of social introductions. English people, unlike Americans, remain shy of approaching strangers on their own account. They still feel that they need to be introduced through the good offices of a mutual friend. The introduction can be perfunctory, the ensuing contact monosyllabic, but it confers formal acquaintanceship, and thus network membership. It entitles you to approach on your own with outstretched hand and glassy smile. Thus, "You may not remember, but we met at the Jones' cocktail party." (Or the Cohen Barmitzva, Or the Kelly ceaolidh, or any other function you can come up with.) And so with the monarch. There were those who had been introduced, and those who had not.

The network was self-enlarging. A woman was presented and in turn presented others who in turn . . . and so on. A complete list of all "Levée and Drawing Room Notices since 1773 and Registers of all ladies presented since 1826" is filed at the Lord Chamberlain's office. Latterly it was the ladies that mattered. It became the custom for married women to present their unmarried daughters at court whereupon they became debutantes.* This in turn meant that they were entitled to "do" the season. The season consisted of a series of social events, including private parties given by girls' mothers. At the end it was hoped that the girl would have met and become engaged to one of the suitable debs' delights who were to be found at these various functions. Thus was society perpetuated.

The system was flawed. Some of those who had been presented at court had fallen on hard times and were obliged to turn their network membership to financial advantage. For years an advertisement appeared in the personal column of *The Times* saying, "Peeress will chaperone debutantes." This was non-committal enough but immediately afterwards there followed the words: "Every advantage." This meant that the impecunious peeress had herself been presented at court and would arrange the same for your daughter. You paid half on signing the contract and half on delivery.

By 1958 the Queen and especially, it is said, Prince Philip, had had enough. Presentation was becoming increasingly popular. More and more people wanted to be presented. One can only assume that mothers were more and more prolific and/or socially ambitious and that the impecunious peeresses had become more impecunious and hence more voracious. In any event, the Queen "felt reluctant to bring these [the Presentation parties] to an end because of the pleasure they appeared to give to a number of young

* See Appendix XI for full list of regulations governing presentation at court.

people and the increasing applications for them". However, there were so many applications that they either had to increase the number of parties or "seek some other solution". That solution was to give more garden parties. These somewhat impersonal affairs can accommodate several thousand people at a time. The Presentation parties, confined to the Ball Supper Room and the Ball Room, where the curtseys were made, were for about 500 at a time, of whom 200 were debs, 100 the married ladies doing the presenting and another 200 parents and sundry hangers-on. At the garden parties presentations are made by a staff member, and anyone can be presented. The atmosphere is quite relaxed; etiquette scarcely applies; and even journalists are invited. The decision was an obvious attempt to destroy the network.

Naturally enough this was fun for the masses but none at all to those who wanted their daughters to "come out" and join the society network. Amazingly enough, the withdrawal of the royal warrant and the end of the formal presentations did not kill off the idea of debutantes and the "season".

For almost twenty years the focal point of the debs' coming out became Queen Charlotte's Ball. To begin with, various minor royals came along and cut a ceremonial cake. Princess Alice of Gloucester, Princess Ann of Denmark and Princess Tomislav of Yugoslavia were among the cake-cutters but after a while it was felt that since royalty had done away with formal presentations it was wrong for any royals to give substance to the aspirations of the new substitute season. In 1976 Queen Charlotte's Ball stopped and another smart(ish) dance called the Rose Ball took its place. It is not the same.

Nevertheless the thing persists, for as Henrietta Calder-Smith, 1979's Deb of the Year, remarked perspicaciously: "It's a way for families who don't know anyone to introduce their daughters to people." Every year, still, about 150 girls in their late teens attend a round of parties and other functions at which there will be a regular supply of suitable young, and not so young, men. (The girls don't go for the younger men, and the girls' mothers are apprehensive about the older men, who are thought, as the saying goes, to be unsafe in the back of taxis.)

The Mr. Fix-it, or network king of what remains of this London Season, is the social editor of the *Tatler*, Peter Townend, though it must be said that when approached on the subject he is surprisingly coy. Others have found the same. One then young man who had reasonable credentials for service as a debs' delight tells me that soon after meeting Townend he found himself invited by some perfect strangers to a dinner dance at Hurlingham, a country club in south west London often used for such functions. Mother, father and daughter greeted him with outsize but rather bewildered grins; son looked knowing and told him to get a drink. The only person he knew in the entire gathering was Townend but when he accosted him and said, tentatively, "Can't think why I was invited; don't know a soul," Townend looked blank and said it was nothing whatever to do with him. My friend swears that he found out later that Townend had acted as official adviser on the guest list and was indeed responsible for getting his name included. He found the affair so gruesome that he escaped by the french windows after dinner and was never invited to another.

Townend told me that the sort of people who want their daughters to come out these days send the girls to private schools like Benenden and North Foreland Lodge and probably live in Hampshire, Gloucestershire or Sussex, with Hertfordshire coming up fast.

Sometimes the pressure to come out is put on by the girls whose friends from school are all doing the same; sometimes it is the parents who think it is the done thing, a way of winning social acceptance for themselves and their daughters. Those from outside the OBN who are uncertain of how to proceed are advised to contact Townend.

"What usually happens," says Townend, "is that Mrs. X will say to Mrs. Snooks that she was thinking of bringing out Annabel. Mrs. Snooks says, Yes she would like to bring out her daughter too. They probably know five or six people who are in the same position." They confer, these mothers, and a series of tea parties are arranged in town. The tea parties are held rather late nowadays and often turn into drinks because so many girls have jobs or are at secretarial colleges. Tea parties are attended by about twenty girls a time and they compare diaries. Each one will be giving some sort of party during the season and they have to make sure that the dates all fit in. Tea parties, incidentally, should be quite near central London. There was one in Kew recently which evidently caused some raised eyebrows. When I told Townend I lived in Richmond he said firmly that that would never do. Far too far out.

Private dances, at least in London, are almost unheard of now because of the expense. Twenty years ago you could dance at the Hyde Park Hotel every night of the week, networking for all you were worth, but when a recent party was held there few of the girls had ever previously set foot in the place. Halls of City livery companies come cheaper but they are not keen on the music and the mess. Most Mums therefore give a cocktail party, sometimes combining with as many as two other hostesses. Others give a dance in the country, which is fine if it is in Hertfordshire, but not if it is Devon or Yorkshire because they are too far for the Londoners. Cocktail parties are bad luck for the debs' delights because whereas in the old days they could freeload their way through an entire season they are now expected to take a girl out to dinner after the drinks.

Townend himself gives a cocktail party at the beginning of the season at which girls meet men. It is the beginning of the year's network. Throughout the season he advises, helps, encourages, plugs other people into his contacts and, very occasionally, tries to warn people off. Some people, still, simply aren't suitable. Precisely how he arrives at this conclusion is not absolutely clear. The clue lies in the fact that while it may be possible to buy a girl a smart education at Benenden which guarantees her a nice accent and good manners, it is sometimes too late to do the same for her parents.

Sometimes, says Townend, a group of half a dozen girls will meet at a tea party and become inseparable. "They'll go to *everything*," he says. Other girls start the season with a steady boyfriend who is invited to everything as well. That, emphatically, is not the point.

It is strange that the ritual should have survived without the piece of royal flummery which was its justification. Betty Kenward no longer lists the private parties in her Jennifer's Diary in *Harpers and Queen*; nor, since the Murdoch take over, does *The Times*. More and more alleged debs, like Michael Heseltine's daughter, protest that they are not debs really – and because that one absolute test of presentation at court has vanished there is really no way of saying one way or the other. "If a girl," said Jane Ellison, in a *Sunday Times* article about debs, "is not on Townend's list she is not a deb. It is as simple as that." Which, with all due respect to Mr. Townend, seems a bit of a come down from a curtsey to the Queen as the criterion.

But still it continues – living proof of the social pretensions of the wealthy; a summer long attempt to provide a daughter with a nice husband and nice friends – a personal network for life; above all, perhaps, an attempt to become part of that elusive chimera: society. Yet with the royal element removed, the most visible permanent elements in the society of the season are the events themselves and a handful of social journalists like Betty Kenward and Peter Townend. Otherwise the members of the caravan sprout with the spring and wither with autumn, somewhere near Oban, where various Highland flings finish the entertainment. Next year it will be another network of 150 girls and their parents, and then another, and another. They are like the graduates of a college except that they have no college, only a temporary allegiance to the fag end of an old idea.

The idea behind those half forgotten presentations was essentially familial. Mothers presented daughters who in turn presented their daughters. A combination of social climbing (by the new rich) and financial failure (by the old smart) diluted and finally destroyed it.

The new method of getting into this curious demi-monde of debs and debs' delights is simply to be accepted by Mr. Townend. You must also have money, but that (for the girls' families) was always true. Mr. Townend's acceptance is not, as far as I can see, terribly difficult to achieve.

In network-crashing, the infiltration of polite society or simply the making of friends and contacts, it is the first introduction that matters. It is the key to the whole network. The Sergeant penetrated wartime society in London largely on the strength of that first introduction to Harold Nicolson. Nicolson was seen to accept him. Therefore he was all right. In the old days of presentation at court someone had to perform the introduction, even if it was only the "impecunious peeress". Nowadays it is Mr. Townend. The introduction is essential. In polite British society, one still does not introduce oneself, and certainly not *cold*. It is necessary to be able to explain that you are a friend of a mutual friend, at the very least.

The majority of us do not share the social aspirations of the Sergeant or even those supplicants who beat a path to the door of Peter Townend. But there are occasions when all of us could usefully apply network principles. The method as revealed by these examples is available to us all, and even the most solitary of us has some sort of network available if only we would recognise it. We all have families and we have friends of some sort. Even if you don't class most of the people you know as friends you must know some people, even if they are quite casual acquaintances. Some of those people might be useful. It is who you know that matters, not how well you know them. We all have our own private personal networks – friends, acquaintances, fellow members of Rotary,

206

people we know at work, play golf with, meet on the train or live next door to.

Some have larger PPNs than others, though sociologists have, of course, tried to determine their exact average size. One man from UCLA in Berkeley, California, even produced a serious scholarly paper entitled "What do we mean by 'Friend'?" in which just over a thousand Californians were asked ten key questions such as, "How many people had helped with tasks around the house in the previous three months?" and, "How many people would you ask for a sizeable loan?" (The answer seemed to be that the average Californian had 18.5 friends, and the paper concluded that, "Researchers should be wary about using this vague term.")

The OBN is as peculiarly British as the public school system on which it is based, but the idea of network is universal. I realised this with somewhat depressing force when I went to Toronto to cut myself off from my source material and write a draft of this book. In Britain I found that one network led to another, that every time I spoke to a member of my own personal private network in order to discuss, say, his membership of some branch of the OBN, he would tell me about some other branch or about another chap's network or a booster. In Britain, it appeared, the whole of life was a network of networks and investigation of it could easily take until the end of time.

In Canada I not only discovered a similar network of networks, even down to a miniature imitation OBN based mainly on Upper Canada College and a handful of other public schools, I also found that Toronto was the headquarters of The International Network for Social Network Analysis. This institution, based on the Sociology Department of the University of Toronto was started in 1977 as a "clearing house" and, according to its "Co-ordinator", Barry Wellman, it has 300 members from all over the world, most of them social scientists, mathematicians and statisticians. It has a magazine called *Connections* and is affiliated to another called *Social Networks* (described dauntingly as "an International Journal of Structural Analysis").

Much of what these "network analysts" have to say is fairly impenetrable or downright depressing since their main purpose appears to be to reduce life to algebra. The jargon is full of "nodes" and "blockmodelling" and "matrices", such as, "The total number of organisations to which an individual belongs is the sum of the row corresponding to that individual." Professor Wellman and his colleagues seem to be more concerned with "the pattern of ties" and "the nature of links" than with the individuals involved in such relationships. Individuals, as far as I can make out, are merely nodes.

Wellman himself in a working paper on "Network Analysis from Method and Metaphor to Theory and Substance" deplores the emphasis on "the persuasiveness of verbal descriptions" and "descriptive techniques, verbal persuasiveness and esthetic (sic) appeal for acceptance". Instead he wants "more comprehensive structural formulations"; more mathematics; more "top-down structural analysis".

So far so bad; but what *is* appealing about the various academic studies by INSNA members and sympathisers is the catholicity of subject matter and an absence of critical cant. In Britain the idea of the "social network" is popularly associated almost exclusively with the idea of the OBN and its smaller components. It is also, almost always, A Bad Thing. Whenever there is a scandal in Britain the phrase "old boy network" is trotted out to explain it. It was the explanation for the Blunt, Philby, Burgess, Maclean debacle; it was the explanation for security lapses at Buckingham Palace which allowed an intruder to make his way into the Queen's bedroom. For many people it appears to be the single most important cause of Britain's decline and fall.

For Wellman and his fellow academics, however, networks are by no means restricted to the ruling classes let alone to the public schools. Certainly there have been academic studies of OBN type networks of power such as one called "Interlocking Corporate Directorships as a Social Network" by Koenig and Gogel but generally speaking the academics are at least as concerned with networks among ordinary people. These might be families in the East End of London, or the citizens of Hobart, who suddenly found their inter-city networks sundered when the river bridge linking them collapsed. Academic network analysts have considered the use of networks in "parenting", "job getting", "schizophrenia" and the "urban village". They have considered how Third World immigrants have kept their old networks intact in industrialised societies.

They do not seem to agree about much. Some are psychiatrists; some are sociologists; some are mathematicians; and they bend the concept of networks to their own ends just as they bend the language to exclude the layman (thus forming their own network from which non members of the International Network for Social Network Analysis are naturally excluded). They are however united in the belief that throughout the world and at every level of society there are a whole series of eccentrically composed informal organisations which exist independently of the formal. Everyone has his or her own network. Everybody belongs to other people's. There are networks like the OBN itself so huge and impersonal that they resemble multi-national companies and there are networks so tiny that they are scarcely more than "dyadic" ("one-to-one") relationships. And however you do it, whatever your standpoint or methodology, the network analysts are agreed that, in Wellman's words, "The most direct way to study a social system is to analyse the pattern of ties linking its members." It *is* instructive to discover that so many of Mrs. Thatcher's cabinet ministers have Cambridge/Bow Group links or that sergeant majors and barristers' clerks follow family traditions or that the inmates of Her Majesty's prisons have network ties which persist after they have been released. The network connections of Sir Geoffrey Howe or Sergeant Janes of the Devon and Dorsets or Ronnie Bender of Maidstone Gaol help us to understand the world about us.

For the individual, of course, it also does away with the idea that networks are, necessarily, for other more privileged people. Nicholas Tomalin, the journalist, who devoted one of his 1960s *Sunday Times* Atticus columns to his idea of what networks were about, wrote that to those outside a particular network it always looked like "a bigoted cabal of clannish intriguers dedicated to the promotion of self-interest and the exclusion of outsiders". This is as true of an obvious élite within an élite – the Tory Blue Chips perhaps – as it is of that little group who monopolise one corner of the saloon bar every evening and talk too loudly about their Jaguars. To those of us on the outside they are both equally resentable.

From the inside, however, it looks (to borrow another of Tomalin's phrases) like "an inevitable coming together of the most talented, charming and like-minded souls in any given field". It does not, really, matter very much whether you are on the inside of a genuine élite – a Fellow of the Royal Society perhaps – or if you are merely one of a small group of old friends which meets regularly on the terraces at, say, Stamford Bridge or Anfield to support the home football team. The view from within is much the same. You feel rather smug about it, you derive some feeling of reciprocal support from it and you sense that even if this network has, most of the time, a minor role in your life, it might, in special circumstances, be useful in some other way.

Just as North America seems to be the place where an academic acceptance of the ubiquitousness of network is most widespread, so Americans, at least since the foundation of Rotary and the writing of *Babbit*, have been the readiest to publicly accept the idea that networking is a tool available to all. The Booster as an artificially contrived network form is as much an American concept as the organic OBN is a British one. It is just one reason why the epidemic of women's networks began on the other side of the Atlantic and why it is still so much stronger there.

I even discovered an organisation called the "Open Network" in Denver which operates as a sort of profit making booster for every man. Like the INSNA its central belief is that networks are pervasive and ubiquitous and that networking is available to everyone no matter what their education, social background, marital status or anything else. INSNA is an organisation for the academic study arising out of that belief; the Open Network sets out to help people put those beliefs into practice. They have a short practical booklet telling you how to play the "networking game" and for thirty-five dollars they will tell you more. They will even talk on the phone for up to an hour, provided you pay the phone bill.

There are times, when the Open Network's language is as obscure as the sociologists' – though in an entirely different way. For instance, they say, quite reasonably, that the need to practise networking is most obvious when someone makes a radical change in their life – by moving home, changing jobs, going to university. The point they make is that in doing this you move out of your old network, which is an infinitely variable group of vicar, bank manager, golfing partners, people you meet in the pub and so on, to a new world where, probably, you don't have the first contact essential for building a network. "Suddenly," according to the Open Network, "whole new universes are glimpsed, and an exploration takes on the characteristics of intergalactic space travel. There are new languages to learn, new customs, and sometimes it seems as if even the laws of nature have gone askew. We think that the ability to change galaxies and to contact other universes is vital for the flourishing of the human explorers on this planet."

It is possible to be fairly ho-hummish about the way the ideas are expressed while at the same time sympathetic to the ideas themselves. The Open Network argues that the average adult American (for their purposes but any mature adult in a Westernised society would be the same) lives with a personal network – PPN in my jargon – which they estimate at about 250 people. Most people's PPN is probably much smaller and, of course, there is that startling suggestion that the average Californian has only 18.5 friends.

If you suddenly cut yourself off from this laboriously if unconsciously acquired PPN you have to build a new one. The Open Network offers five cardinal rules.

(1) Be useful.
(2) Don't be boring.
(3) Listen.
(4) Ask questions.
(5) Don't make assumptions.

Their most valuable advice is never entirely articulated, however, though it constantly lurks beneath the surface of their message. It is, essentially, that human contacts are more useful than written information. The Open Network makes a clear distinction between its network operation and a library or archive. In response to a query they say they would not, like the archive, offer "a shopping cart full of paper" but a postcard with two addresses on it. After that it is up to you, but after these initial introductions you will find yourself being passed along a network chain rather as I was when I began researching the network idea myself. As Nicholas Tomalin said in his *Sunday Times* article, the crucial beginning of a networking ploy is that you receive "a warm response on the telephone from other networkers. All other benefits flow from that." Tomalin knew, naturally, that a good newspaperman is the sum of his telephone numbers (mainly ex-directory), but the principle has a universal application. The first contact or introduction is crucial. Once – in the old days of *proper* debutantes – an introduction to the monarch served as a passport into the whole of society. Once it had been observed that the Sergeant was a friend of Harold Nicolson, he was guaranteed a free passage in Harold Nicolson's world. One contact always leads to another, provided you pursue it.

Networking can help with the crucial problems in life – most notably job getting, but it is often much more mundane. The lowest common network denominator is *blat*, the Muscovite word for circumventing the usual channels in order to get tickets for the Bolshoi or a joint of beef without having to stand in a queue from the early hours of the morning.

211

In Moscow, Michael Binyon, when *The Times* correspondent, revealed the existence of something called *blat*. "With 'blat'," he says, "most of life's daily obstacles can be overcome. It might just happen that your aunt works in the shop where the shoes are sold: she can not only put aside a good pair for you, but can also purloin an extra pair which you can donate to someone whose acquaintance you would like to cultivate: perhaps a doctor willing to take a bit more time over your case or a seamstress who can run you up a nice dress privately during her working hours.

"Or instead of standing for hours at the little window of the box office for the Taganka Theatre, Moscow's most celebrated and fashionably innovative playhouse, you can call up your friend in the administration and persuade her that those top party officials are not going to turn up at the last minute for tonight's performance and she can certainly risk getting rid of at least two of the precious seats that are always reserved 'just in case'.

"No money," concludes Binyon, "need change hands."

At its crudest, networking means cultivating people, currying favour with those who can do you favours in return, but the essence of really successful networking is that it must never be too blatant. There has to be a convincing pretence of enjoyment in the network relationship. Even if transactions are almost entirely commercial, the commercial element has to be played down if not wholly concealed. To take an example of British blat, the British have for centuries made a practice of giving out "boxes" on St. Stephen's Day, the day after Christmas. These were originally alms for the poor but gradually the "Boxing Day" tradition evolved into a ritual handing out of sweeteners to the regular tradesmen with whom people dealt – dustmen, milkmen, grocers and so on. As early as the last century the system began to go sour because – like the old-fashioned tip which has now become a mandatory service charge – the gift became an expectation and an obligation to such an extent that some tradesmen would turn up at the door before Christmas, hand outstretched. The Christmas box became like protection money. If you didn't pay the dustmen a suitable "box" they would give poor service during the following year. Dustmen still do this, but the system has fallen into such general disuse that it has, paradoxically, become possible for the network conscious housewife to revive it.

Most housewives who do not shop solely at an impersonal supermarket operate a form of network. They choose to patronise a particular butcher, baker, candlestick maker or what-have-you

212

because they believe that his goods are superior to his rivals and they expect – in return for their consistent patronage – to receive superior service as well.

The assiduous networking housewife will cultivate these relationships in all sorts of ways, one of which once more, is to give a gift at Christmas. A bottle of Scotch, prettily wrapped, is an insurance of only getting the best cuts from the butcher. So are smiling nicely, taking the trouble to pass the time of day, and generally chatting up, all of which are common sense and common courtesy but, curiously, not always practised. Arriving recently in Santa Fe, New Mexico, a completely strange foreign town, my wife and I were unable to find a decent butcher. Asking one of our few contacts we were told that our diagnosis was correct but that Nancy who worked in the meat department of the leading local supermarket was a surprisingly competent butcher. Our contacts said that they had gone to her for years. When they returned from travels abroad they always brought her little gifts and they always remembered her at Christmas. As a result they ate very superior meat.

This sounds cynical, and to be truthful networking does sound cynical, but the paradox is that it cannot be too cynically practised if it is to be successful. Guards officers, to take one of the best known examples, operate their network quite consciously and ruthlessly and yet it is founded on a very real sense of tribal camaraderie. That is why it works. By the same token you have to (quite) like your butcher and derive at least some pleasure from plying him or her with occasional gifts. A network which is founded entirely on self-interest is fragile and, ultimately, doomed. The art of networking is to do it naturally and with pleasure, giving as well as receiving, acknowledging that there *is* an equation but recognising that sometimes you will seem to be giving more than you get back.

Some situations lend themselves more to networking than others. The accountant or scientist who joins a company in early life and remains with it throughout his career will have less scope for networking than the entrepreneur, the agent, the merchant banker or the journalist. But even he will, willy-nilly, be involved in *some* form of office politics, have to indulge in some sort of personal relationship at work, no matter how perfunctory. Even a genius is well advised to cultivate allies, even if it only means buying a secretary a box of chocolates or colleagues a round of drinks. ISCO's *How to Apply for a Job*, advises school leavers how to behave during a job interview. It does not (at least not in print) suggest flaunting the old school neckwear but it does advise candidates that the interviewer (being human) "is likely to judge you by the general impression you make on him at least as much as by your record on paper. He wants to find out not only whether you can do the job, but whether you will fit in with colleagues in the organisation." That advice holds good even after landing the job. It not only means that you are likely to stay in it, it also means that if, perhaps through no fault of your own, you are thrown out of that job in mid-career, you have a supportive network which can be marshalled in finding a new one. The evidence of those professionals engaged in "Outplacement" and finding jobs for the newly redundant, suggests that, particularly in times of high unemployment, such networks are indispensable.

11

Outplacement and Hot Contacts

It is wonderful what a little determined charm will do, plus
American cigarettes.

Noël Coward, *Diaries*

In the late 1970s and early 1980s a really attractive executive job
advertised in the national press was attracting an average of
between 700 and 800 applicants, most of them with at least the
minimum stipulated qualifications. Many companies had even
stopped acknowledging the applicants, let alone interviewing
them.

When the jobs outnumber the suitable applicants the head
hunter reigns. Reverse that and you create a need for someone to
assist the potential employee in the same way that the head hunter
helps the potential employer. Hence something called "outplacement". Head hunters find people for jobs. Outplacement agents
find jobs for people. Or, because nowadays that is a tall order and
the outplacement people are nervous of promising what they can't
deliver, they "help people find jobs for themselves". Because that
is a demonstrably tall order they have to be ingenious, and in this
case their ingenuity means networking. Their most important tool
is the private personal network.

Like other outplacement men, Theodore Simpson, a partner in
the London firm of Sanders and Sidney, used to be a head hunter.
He was in "search" with Heidrick and Struggles (a Wodehousian
name, but actually real). Simpson is a committed network man
who talks nostalgically of the Brussels mafia which grew up during
his time in advertising there. He ran the European end of an
American agency whose main client was Alitalia. In his present
work he applies network principles singlemindedly, constantly
trying to inculcate them into the minds of men who often have no
idea what he is talking about.

Individuals do not hire the services of companies like this.
Outplacement agencies are only employed by companies and they

are employed as part of a redundancy package. When a company fires a man and feels more than usually guilty about it they will throw in the services of an outplacement agency on top of the redundancy payment, the right to keep the firm's car, the video and whatever else they choose to offer the departing employee. During the inevitably painful dismissal meeting the man doing the firing will say that in the next room there is someone who will help the victim find a new job. His services are free, a generous gesture from the company, but they are not negotiable for cash. The redundant executive can take it or leave it.

If the sacked employee chooses to take it, which is statistically more likely than not, the first meeting takes place in conditions of some shock. Horror stories abound. Men are in tears, men are in incoherent rage, men are, invariably, taken by surprise. At the rather exalted level at which outplacement operates no one, apparently, ever expects the sack. Outplacement agents do not normally set an absolute figure but they are unlikely to take on a man who has been earning under £15,000 a year.

Sanders and Sidney themselves offer no guarantees and no panaceas. In fact they claimed, when I spoke to them, that it normally takes about five months for someone on their books to find a new job and that between a half and two thirds of those under fifty actually end up in more highly paid ones than before. But that is a fluctuating average; and they do concede failures.

The one virtually sure way of not getting a job, Theodore Simpson tells his new client, is to sit at home answering advertisements. In a world in which only qualifications and merit counted that might work but, he insists, the world isn't like that. In return for their fee (a percentage of the client's annual salary paid in advance and not dependent on results) Sanders and Sidney give the man office space in their Mayfair premises and thus provide him with an immediate illusion of still being in employment.

If nothing else, this is good for the self-esteem, and without confidence there is no way our man is going to fight his way back into employment. His new office provides him with a share in a secretary, desk space and a phone, and his new mentors help him to put together what they call a "marketing package". He has some smart writing paper printed (carefully omitting any mention of anything as off-putting as an outplacement agency); he constructs as laudatory a curriculum vitae as he can manage and he is forced to think hard about the sort of job he wants to do – and *can* do. Deryck Sidney says that while the writing paper and general presentation are necessary, they are only embellishments.

He is not seeking to help men con their way into jobs. The CV, for instance, may be laudatory but it must be honest. "There is no point," says Sidney, "in helping a man get into a job which he cannot do."

This stage is conventional enough and is unlikely, on its own, to do much for our displaced executive's future. Stage two of the Sanders and Sidney scheme involves networks. It builds on what has already been done by something which their jargon calls "contact development" and which is really the instant activation of your dormant PPN. Simpson tells his client: "You must write down the names of men you know and who might just be useful. The guy next door, the wife's brother-in-law, any bloody person."* The average person, faced with this demand, is unable at first to think of more than half a dozen such people – less than a third of the average Californian PPN – but this social paralysis is more apparent than real. "Everyone has contacts," says Deryck Sidney. "The man may think he hasn't but he has." Nevertheless the names have to be dug out like splinters. Some, salesmen for instance, have no trouble reeling off a long list, but the man who has just been fired after twenty years in accounts "in a green eye shade on a tall stool" is a natural introvert with a life history of solitude. He does not know anyone and, what's more, he does not *want* to know anyone. Gregariousness does not come easily to him. In the rare case of a man who really does have virtually no usable contacts he is sent off to the library to look for likely strangers in the reference books and trade journals. These will be identified as "cold contacts". They are better than nothing but part of the network trick is to use your own friends, otherwise known, of course, as "hot contacts" to warm the cold ones up. If the list of hot contacts is sound and extensive the network is in place, ready to be activated. If there are nothing but cold contacts it is more difficult but the aims and aspirations are the same.

Rule one is that you do not ring the first contact on your list and begin by saying, "Hey, you'll never guess – those bastards threw me out." The initial approach has to be low key and positive. You

---

* In her novel *Bodily Harm*, Margaret Atwood remarks sadly: "He is a contact of hers, which is not the same as a friend. While she was in the hospital she decided that most of her friends were really just contacts." This may be a cause for emotional regret, but in the harsh practical terms of the contemporary job market it could scarcely matter less. Here contact counts as much as friendship.

tell your contact that you have come to an important crossroads. You are leaving your present employers and embarking on a new and exciting period in your life. What you need more than anything is some really authoritative and helpful advice. Since the one thing you have always respected about this particular contact is the quality of his opinions, you wonder whether you might possibly come in some time for twenty minutes or so and pick his brains. You tell him you'd like some suggestions to improve your CV and that you'd welcome the names of anyone he thinks might be worth contacting. And so on.

This spiel invariably works with hot contacts and sometimes with cold, provided you can get past their secretaries. Even top executives are susceptible to a little well judged flattery, though Deryck Sidney says, "We teach (and believe) that people (including top executives) want to help those who are clearly being positive and are trying to help themselves." Simpson seems less sure. "Nobody *wants* to see you," he says. "It's tough."

Once you have made the first interview the technique is to prise some names out of the contact. It then becomes possible to phone or write to them with the introductory "Joe Bloggs suggested I call you". Without that you're dead. With it, you have at least a fighting chance. The golden rule about not actually asking for a job remains. It doesn't do to be seen to be desperate. If there is a job there and you are the man for it, the fact will emerge without your asking. If there is no job, no amount of asking will create it.

The secret is to get into the contact's office, face him across his desk, accept that you are indeed a friend of Joe Bloggs and therefore a member of the network. Then, given luck, the contact will begin asking questions about your background. If he is impressed he may possibly say, "Come back on Thursday." This is code for there being the germ of a job involved and in Simpson's words, "Gradually, imperceptibly, a job begins to form. That's the time to move in: before it becomes a job and the head hunters are hired." Then it is advertised and becomes open to the horrors of public competition. By being there, with a personal recommendation from Bloggs, as the job is born, you are half way to getting it. It is known in the trade as "the hidden job market". According to Simpson, "There are jobs out there being born every minute."

Within two years of being taken on, practically all their clients will have found jobs not *simply* on merit – with so many well qualified candidates chasing so few jobs there is no way any employer can make an appointment based solely on merit. By creating an ever expanding network of contacts, however, even a man who has returned from years abroad can develop enough useful and relevant friendships and acquaintanceships to get ahead of the field.

Deryck Sidney is anxious that his enterprise and outplacement in general should not seem like a "high class con". "We consider," he says, "that we are doing a skilled and professional counselling job to help the man recognise what his objective should be. We then tell him how to go about obtaining this objective. This means using the contact development approach – but not cynically and with unctuous flattery and untrue credentials. He must be credible, creditable and honest and hard working."

Networking, in short, creates opportunities and chances and openings. Consolidating them requires other skills but when it comes to getting a job the use of network, or contact development, puts you ahead of the competition and means, in theory, that you should at least get the interview if not the job.

To see how it worked in practice, I asked Sanders and Sidney to recommend one or two of their clients. Using their own network principles I was given the names of three men who had recently succeeded in getting jobs after being on the Sanders and Sidney books. All agreed to see me. One, an American banker, stood me up and failed to acknowledge my subsequent letter. The other two insisted on total anonymity, partly because they did not want their new employers to know that they had been clients of an outplacement firm, and partly because – I think – they were not keen for their friends and other contacts to realise quite how singlemindedly they had been used in pursuit of employment.

Of my two remaining clients, one had defied the Sanders and Sidney principles by getting his job through an advertisement in a trade journal. He worked in a field which was small and specialised so that such advertisements were quite detailed in their requirements. Although the network had nothing to do with his application, he later discovered that he knew someone who had previously worked for the advertiser and this was certainly helpful in his evaluating the job, and possibly in helping the employer come to a decision as well. When he accepted the job there were two others for which he was in the running, and both came through the network.

This man also won a number of part time contracts for consultancy work and these tended to come through contacts who had heard, on the grapevine, that he was looking for work. Although he had plenty of useful experience he was short of formal qualifications and also felt that he lacked the right social background for some jobs for which he was perfectly suited. The licensed trade, especially the big distillers' companies for instance, spurned him because, he felt, he was obviously not "an officer and gentleman", real or home made. He did approach about twenty contacts as advised by Sanders and Sidney, but found many positively depressing. "They were all very sympathetic, but nothing actually materialised. Several of them did make me think that, at forty-seven, I was over the top. I don't blame them for that. In fact I tend to share that view. You need people who are spunky and who are prepared to take risks and by the time you get to my age you're not inclined to take risks." His problem, he admits, was self-confidence, and he was grateful to Sanders and Sidney for bolstering it.

As far as networks go, his experiences seemed to me inconclusive. He himself did not appear particularly enthusiastic about the *idea* of the network and yet he had tapped a number of contacts for work, especially for part time consultancies. Also the area in which he worked was sufficiently small and specialised for it to function as a network in much the same way as, say, the Headmasters' Conference or the Church of England. Jobs did not, on the whole, go to outsiders and, at his level, most people were aware of each other.

The other Sanders and Sidney client was different because his skills were more general. He was experienced and adroit in the arts of management and he did not particularly mind what his employer manufactured or produced. He had been a divisional director of a large but ailing company with an annual turnover of about £100 million. He had been with the company for twenty-eight years since finishing his national service, and on the whole his career had been uphill all the way.

Towards the end of 1980, however, he had started to have a rather unrewarding time. The firm's declining fortunes were no fault of his but he had been given the unenviable job of negotiating the closure and re-organisation of plants employing several hundred men. This task had been complicated by the fact that the man who had been his immediate superior had recently been moved on and replaced by someone with whom Mr. X, as I shall call him, did not enjoy quite the same rapport. The various structural reforms he had carried out were so effective that he had, almost without realising it, managed to delegate most of his duties to others. Another section of the firm was after the more profitable part of his empire; and as the result of a report by a team of business efficiency consultants the company was engaged in making cuts of twenty per cent all round. In retrospect, he really should have realised that his career was at risk, but a lifetime in the service of the same employer with an absorbing responsibility for a work force of 2,000 men meant that he felt quite secure.

One Friday morning in March 1981 his secretary told him that his new boss wanted to see him that afternoon at three. Mr. X had to leave early that afternoon so he asked to bring the appointment forward to just after two. He had no idea what it was about and scarcely gave it a thought. He assumed it was something routine, even trivial.

By three o'clock he was out of work.

Like the Monopoly player who is sent to gaol his sentence took effect with a shocking immediacy. He was told to leave the office at once, without even talking to his secretary, nor to the team of half a dozen subordinates with whom he had been working most closely. After some argument it was agreed that he could come in on Sunday morning to clear his desk. His redundancy terms were, ironically, the very ones that he himself had negotiated for the management during the recent factory closure. They included, of course, the services of Sanders and Sidney.

"All through my career," he says, "I had been asked to take over new jobs at a moment's notice, so although I could see my present job disappearing it never occurred to me that I'd disappear with it. I thought something would crop up. It always had done in the past."

In a sense it was the collapse of his own office network which helped to bring about his downfall. When he first joined the company he did so because he was recommended to the managing director by his father. The two men were friends. All the time that this original managing director remained in office Mr. X knew that, although nothing could save him from his own mistakes and failures, he did at least have a kindly guardian at the top of the heap, who would presumably have something to say about his protégé's summary dismissal after more than a quarter of a century's loyal service. And the departure of his friendly boss and the substitution of a hostile one obviously made that dismissal more likely.

That weekend he felt desperately depressed. He had no real financial worries because his redundancy payment was generous, his wife had a part time job and the children's private education had been paid for. But he did feel he had been consigned to the scrap heap and he sensed that in his late forties he was not at an easily re-employable age. This was particularly galling because until now he had reckoned on at least fifteen more years of good and profitable work. The prospect of Sanders and Sidney did not fill him with any particular optimism since he knew nothing about them.

When he finally went for a long interview with them he was told, "Don't talk to the neighbours; don't approach friends, don't panic." By then he had done all three as well as answered six job advertisements in the *Sunday Times*. His morale was in shreds. Going over his past career, which was actually very successful, he found himself remembering only the down moments, the slights, the criticisms, the failures. The first problem for Sanders and Sidney was therefore to restore his self-confidence.

This took about a fortnight during which he was made to list and elaborate all his achievements (the top fifteen in order of merit), his virtues, his abilities and qualifications. His wife wrote a report on him which she let him see, though one of the rules of the game was that it could be kept from him. This in itself was a useful morale booster since she said his main failing was "taking on too much – he never says 'no' ". Part of the therapy was working hard at the business of getting a job and coming to realise that it was a job in itself. He had dreaded idleness but now found that he was as busy as ever. His wife also entered into the spirit of the game and one morning gave him a fearful rollicking because he was fifteen minutes late starting "work". After two weeks he was almost buoyant and had worked so effectively that he had even persuaded his old boss to give him an enthusiastic reference.

He had not, however, answered any more advertisements. Sanders and Sidney told him there was no point unless he found one which fitted him so specifically and in such detail that he was the only conceivable candidate. This was unlikely. Job advertisements for men like Mr. X are impossibly vague, usually placed by head hunters who are guarding the true identity of their client and phrased much like this typical example selected at random from the *Sunday Times*:

Deputy Managing Director to succeed on his forthcoming retirement the present Managing Director of this successful building company, turnover £30 million, part of a larger group. Candidates must have a good track record in the profitable direction of general building contracting as well as the drive and flair to lead the development and diversification of the company over the next 10 years.

Not much there to get your teeth into, and certainly not if you intend to invoke the rules of networking and contact development, as Mr. X, under Sanders and Sidneys' tutelage, was about to do.

When it came to writing down the names of friends and acquaintances his first list ran to almost 200 entries. He based it on several different segments of his life. There were old school friends in surprising numbers because although he had worked in several different parts of the United Kingdom he had recently returned to the home of his youth and renewed friendships with men who had once been at the same day public school. Some of his contacts were business associates, both from his own company and from client or associated companies with whom he had done business; others were business competitors; and then there were social contacts – fellow members of the local sailing club – and members of the 41 Club, alumni of that Rotary clone, the Round Table.

"The objective was not to get offered a job," he says. "You are asking for help. When you write [he is not a telephoning man] you emphasise that you don't expect a job but that you know the guy is knowledgeable and you want to see if he has any bright ideas. Most people are flattered if you ask for their advice!"

Sensing that many people are sensitive about too obvious a mixing of business with pleasure even though they themselves may do it all the time, he was scrupulous about making his approaches to social contacts brisk and businesslike. One of those on his list, a director of his own company, was a fellow member of the local sailing club. In this case Mr. X "made it my business to bump into him" and outlined his predicament. His friend seemed apprehensive, even embarrassed by such an obviously opportunist use of social acquaintance to promote professional ends, but was obviously greatly relieved when Mr. X said, "Don't commit yourself now. I'll ring you at the office in a week and come and see you there." You could make the contact informally but the nuts and bolts had to be screwed into place in office time and space. That was the etiquette of using your PPN.

Mr. X's fifteen primary contacts were:

(1) The main board director of a large retail chain. Fellow member of the 41 Club.

(2) The personnel director of a cigarette company. An old school friend not seen more than twice in the previous five years. ("Always identify yourself," he says, "by prefacing the introduction with something like 'Do you remember that chat we had at London airport last December?' ")

(3) The managing director of a competitor who had previously been a senior manager at his former employer's.

(4) A senior manager with one of the big five banks, a former customer.

(5) A member of the local sailing club who ran his own business.

(6) A chief purchasing officer for a large company who had been a customer and had also once been made redundant himself.

(7) Another chief purchasing officer who had been a customer of Mr. X's.

(8) A chartered accountant in private practice in London, who was also a member of the 41 Club.

(9) A local doctor and JP who had been at school with him and had useful contacts in the neighbourhood.

(10) A school friend who was a successful executive with a food company.

(11) Another school friend, this one the secretary of a large public company.

(12) The old chairman of his previous employers, now retired and in his seventies.

(13) A former supplier of imported goods.

(14) A former customer in a large international organisation.

(15) The same.

Mr. X's network of fifteen therefore consisted of four old school friends, and one member of the sailing club and two of the 41 Club. Almost half, in other words, came from the social side of his PPN. The remaining eight were from the professional – two former colleagues, five customers and one supplier.

Sticking carefully to the plan of campaign outlined by Sanders and Sidney, he was scrupulously un-hectoring in his approach to these men. He did not ask them for work, but for constructive help. In particular he wanted a second outer network of secondary contacts. "I needed a name," he says, "and I needed permission to use the first guy's name in my approach. Or, better still, you try to make sure the first guy rings 'Buggins'. And you must make sure they do it. You have to leave it so that you can ring back and say, 'Did you ring so-and-so, and what did he say?'"

"You get a very variable response. Some people offered lots of sympathy and a huge lunch but that wasn't what I wanted. Others would give me half an hour and be very brisk about it, but I would come away with up to a dozen or so new contacts."

While he was working on this network building he also sent out a round robin, which included his impressively composed, curriculum vitae, to a list of management consultants compiled by Sanders and Sidney – another network of its own.

In the end, however, the job he actually landed came not from one of the people on his primary network nor from the round robin but from a network contact he had overlooked. After his dismissal his old job was in effect carved up between three successors. Eventually, after the initial acrimony had slightly subsided, he was allowed back into his old office to effect some sort of transition. In the course of this the man who was taking over one of the thirds happened to remark that he himself had recently been approached by a head hunter who had had a specific job in mind. Mr. X expressed interest and his successor asked if he would like him to telephone the head hunter to see if an interview could be arranged. He did and it was. By the time Mr. X called on the head hunter that particular job had gone and it wasn't entirely appropriate anyway. But the head hunter was impressed and said he would be able to place him "maybe not for six or twelve months, but we'll do it".

This was the introduction which eventually led to an appointment. After a series of meetings, some nail biting delays and several long intense interviews Mr. X began work as the managing director of a company employing about 120 men – small beer after the 2,000 he had been responsible for in his old job and in certain respects a move back to where he had been ten years before. But there were compensations. He had much more freedom of movement; his new boss left him alone and delegated far more than his old one. He was allowed to generate new business himself, look for new markets and at the same time enjoy direct contact with his work force. When I saw him about three months after he began his new work he seemed genuinely happy and fulfilled.

His success came through a network connection he had scarcely considered and which led on to a management consultant or head hunter. In all, his approaches to the head hunters on Sanders and Sidney's list, a lukewarm if not quite cold network, resulted in five interviews and eight specific leads. His own Personal Private

Network of hot contacts led on to an outer network of thirty-five secondary contacts, five of which were repeated several times. These were opportunities or openings known to more than one member of his primary network. In these instances there were specific jobs which seemed, to his friends, to suit Mr. X perfectly – so much so that they were prepared to recommend him personally. Another ten were specific recommendations to companies which seemed likely and relevant but where his contacts did not know whether there was a suitable vacancy. These, Mr. X concedes, were less likely to yield a job than the first five but they were still possible. A further ten introductions were to more head hunters with whom Mr. X's primary contact had a special relationship of his own. None of these actually led anywhere but he felt that these head hunters would take special trouble with him because of the personal introduction. The final ten were long shots – introductions to a variety of industries and organisations where Mr. X's experience was of only moderate relevance and where there was no sign of a job being available. But at the time he finally accepted his present post Mr. X was involved in serious negotiations for about five other jobs, any one of which, he believes, might quite easily have led to "a very worthwhile job".

A final droll twist to his job getting efforts was that once he had proved successful he sent out a form letter to all the head hunters with whom he had been in correspondence – even those who had responded with a xeroxed form letter of their own. Many of these previously offhand consultants responded with fulsome personal notes. They now saw him not as a boring supplicant but an exciting potential job giver.

The head hunters were, somewhat belatedly and cack-handedly, playing the network game. They owe their livelihood to an intelligence system which is sustained as much by odd leads like this one as by rigorous scrutiny of the financial pages. By writing to them as he did, Mr. X became a name not a number. The bond was extremely weak, but it existed. At least any subsequent phone call could begin with, "You may not remember, but we corresponded a little while ago . . ." Which might not produce a very favourable response, but would at least gain the head hunter a hearing.

Mr. X had never previously used his network because his career had run smoothly without it, but once the necessity arose he realised that he was at the hub of acquaintances which could swiftly and painlessly be turned to his advantage. Other men, particularly the self-employed, journalists, agents of all descriptions, all entrepreneurs, use their networks daily; in setting his network in motion so quickly Mr. X was creating from scratch the sort of apparatus whose careful nurturing is other people's life's work.

He was using his PPN.

12

The Butler, the Godfather and the Jacuzzi

Where you are tomorrow may well depend on whom you
meet tonight.
Sarah Weddington, Assistant to the President of
the United States addressing a meeting of the
Washington Women's Network, Washington, DC

Laura Corrigan was a lumberjack's daughter from Cleveland,
Ohio. In 1921 she arrived in London with the express intention of
breaking into English society. She was a total stranger. She knew
no one and no one knew her. In her native America she had tried to
become a society figure in both Cleveland and New York but,
despite spending vast amounts of her steel magnate husband's
money on lavish entertainments, it was a total failure; she was
unable to buy her way into American society.

Her only contact in London was another American, Cora,
Countess of Strafford, the widow of Mr. Colgate the toothpaste
millionaire. They had a lot in common. Over dinner with Cora it
transpired that Edward VII's friend Mrs. Keppel was off to Europe
and wanted to let her house in Grosvenor Street. The house would
make a magnificent base for an aspiring society hostess but there
were much greater advantages to the deal than opulent premises.
For an extra consideration, Mrs. Corrigan took over not only Mrs.
Keppel's house but her Visitors' Book and her butler, Rolfe.

During the first few weeks of her tenancy Mrs. Corrigan got
Rolfe to stand outside the house and wait for friends of Mrs.
Keppel's to pass by. When he saw them he would ask them in for a
drink to meet his new mistress. The ploy worked. Mrs. Keppel's
friends became Mrs. Corrigan's friends. Then the invaluable Rolfe
suggested that Mrs. Corrigan should hire the services of an impecunious aristocrat called Charlie Stirling. Stirling, rather like today's
Peter Townend of the *Tatler*, was a man who seemed to crop up at
absolutely all the best parties and to be on friendly terms with all
the best hostesses. Before long he had engineered an invitation for

Mrs. Corrigan from Lady Londonderry, the most fashionable hostess of the day.

When she died in 1947, Mrs. Corrigan's memorial service was organised by Chips Channon, the Duke of Buccleuch and Alan Lennox-Boyd (later Viscount Boyd). It was attended by duchesses, ambassadors, the Cavendishes, Londonderrys, Herberts, Thynnes and other aristocratic members of the social world. Even Princess Marina, then the Duchess of Kent, who had become a close friend, made an exception and attended a non-royal memorial service for the first time. "An amazing woman," recorded Chips Channon, "sexless, devoid of any outward physical attractions and never consciously amusing, yet she made an international position for herself in the very highest society which she wooed and cajoled."

Verdict:

A triumph of networking set on its way by the one crucial hot contact with the sympathetic toothpaste millionaire's widow; aided and abetted by a butler who was himself a resourceful networker and mentor in the style of the good regimental sergeant major or barrister's clerk; oiled by a plentiful supply of dollars; and given crucial impetus by a passionate interest in the people she was cultivating. It helped to be foreign. An English parvenu would have been detected because of accent and other unmistakable signals. But Mrs. Corrigan, like the Sergeant, was difficult to place.

"My name is Threepwood."

"Oh yes?!"

"Galahad Threepwood."

The name touched a chord in Sam's memory. It was one the late Berkeley Bagshott had often mentioned when in reminiscent vein. The conversation of his intimates of the old days was always inclined to turn to Gally as they probed the past.

"Oh really?" he said, beaming in his turn. "I've heard my father speak of you."

"So you *are* old Boko's son. I thought so."

"You were great friends, weren't you?"

"Bosom."

"That was why he had me christened Galahad, I suppose."

"Yes, it was a pretty thought. He told me he would have asked

229

me to be your godfather, only he didn't feel it would be safe. Starting you off under too much of a handicap."

"Well, it's awfully nice of you to look me up. How did you find my address?"

"It was given me by Sandy Callendar as I was leaving Blandings Castle this morning."

"Oh?" Sam gulped. "So you've met Sandy?"

"I've known her quite a long time. We first met in New York when she was working for Chet Tipton, a pal of mine. He, poor chap, handed in his dinner pail and she came to London, looking for a job. I ran into her just when my sister Hermione was wanting a secretary for my brother Clarence, so I recommended her and she was signed on. This morning as I was leaving she gave me this parcel to post. I saw your name, the S.G. struck me as significant and I decided to deliver it in person, just in case you were the fellow I thought you might be, if you see what I mean. I don't know what odds a bookie would have given against your turning out to be Boko's son, but it seemed a fair speculative venture, and the long shot came off."

Verdict:

P. G. Wodehouse had a sound grasp of the principles of networking especially as applied in certain reaches of clubland OBN. This extract from *Galahad at Blandings* neatly illustrates the natural networker's constant eye for the main chance and the luck and coincidence which that so often produces. The run of chance meeting in this episode may seem unlikely but if, like Threepwood, you *think network* such coincidences fall into place more often than not.

Godparents are real parents' first attempt to construct an extra-family network for their children and with luck they will not only be some sort of moral support in years to come, not only a source of book tokens and premium bonds, but also actively useful in an accepted network sense. There is – obviously – an element of risk or fluke in this. Parents cannot be sure how children will turn out and where their interests will lie. Nor can they be sure of god-parents. The close contemporary and friend of parents in their twenties and thirties may look a golden certainty for power and influence only to become a broken promise when the godchild needs him twenty or so years later. Or, more often, just irrelevant.

My own parents' choice of godparents was touched with just the necessary stroke of luck. One godfather, an uncle by marriage (we tend to keep one godparent in the family) was a naval officer who retired to work at an Outward Bound School and run a golf club. Dutiful and kind though he was, he was unable to offer any network help since at no time did my interests include the Navy, golf or the Outward Bound. My godmother, a lifelong friend of my mother since they served together in the ATS, has been just as dutiful. Her husband's career in the Colonial Service and a naturally gregarious disposition means that she has a network of friends scattered about the world so that no matter where one is going she is always good for an address or two. This has been enjoyable but relatively marginal.

The trump in my modest hand of godparents was a man my father met during the war (a great network breeding time since that shared experience produced precisely the mutual confidence and trust which are the base of the most effective networks). Commissioned as a true Dorset man into the county regiment, my father found a convivial fellow officer in an Old Harrovian with no readily discernible local connection, Peter Wilson. Their friendship was cemented during the Italian campaign when my father served with the Hampshires and spent short leave periods with Wilson who was then working on the Forces' newspaper, the *Union Jack*, with fellow *Daily Mirror* journalists, Hugh (later Lord) Cudlipp, Bill Connor ("Cassandra") and the novelist Hammond Innes.

When I was born in 1944 Wilson became my godfather.

It would be wrong to say that he was a model godfather. He was far less punctilious than the other two. Gifts, though lavish, were occasional; moral support not obviously evident. But the luck was that I decided, as a child, that I wanted to be a journalist. By then Wilson had become a famous, outspoken, globe trotting sportswriter (christened, in typical *Mirror*-ese, "The man they can't gag"). I asked him to contribute to a school magazine I was helping to edit. He did. After leaving school and before going up to university I asked if he could fix me up with some sort of holiday work at the *Mirror*. He could and he did. For a month as an eighteen year old I worked in the *Mirror* newsroom (to the indignation of my contemporaries and of journalists who had no such network connection). Thus my introduction to Fleet Street.

I don't believe I could have pulled that string if Peter Wilson had only been a friend of my father. It was the extra involvement of

231

being my godfather. He was not just part of my father's considerable network, he was part of mine too.

Since then, the National Union of Journalists, anxious to promote the interests of its own formally constituted mega-network
against small irregular networks like mine, has become more
vigilant and more powerful. I am less confident of helping my
godchildren into Fleet Street than Wilson was of helping me but if
the call comes I shall certainly try.

Verdict:

An extraordinary piece of networking luck since there was nothing
to suggest, in 1944, that I would be interested in a journalistic
career in 1962. But the successful networking is often about taking
chances in the first place and capitalising on them ruthlessly if they
come off. It takes a networker to select unorthodox godparents in
the first place and it takes a networker to make them work for him
as he comes of age. It also helps, as always in networking, if the
parties involved are at least moderately fond of each other.

By the time Harold Evans was appointed editor of *The Times* he
had had plenty of time to build up a loyal and dedicated network of
colleagues. He had arrived in Fleet Street as a sort of journalistic
Mrs. Corrigan, an unknown outsider from the *Northern Echo*,
Darlington, whose main Fleet Street contact was Hunter Davies,
his old colleague on the Durham University newspaper. Since
becoming editor of the *Sunday Times* in 1967 he had shrewdly
consolidated his position not just as a crusading, award winning
editor, but also as the centre of an effective professional PPN of his
own creation.

In 1981 Rupert Murdoch, the new proprietor of Times Newspapers, switched Evans from the Sunday to the Daily as successor
to the arch OBN figure of Sir William Rees-Mogg. It was no secret
inside or out that Evans was intent on wholesale reform and – most
significantly – breaking the existing old *Times* network and bringing in his own panzers to do the job. Veterans of his early years at
the *Sunday Times* recalled that his ineffectual efforts to get rid of
long serving old guards there had led to the nickname "the man
with the rubber hatchet" and, alas for Evans, the same happened
when he reached *The Times*. One or two of the long serving *Times*
men proved unexpectedly difficult to dislodge. Some left but
others stood firm. John Higgins, the arts editor whose fondness for

opera, preferably in some exotic foreign part, was a source of irritation to the Evans school of self-consciously gritty investigative newshounds, refused to budge. Charles Douglas-Home, despite a high level flirtation with the *Daily Telegraph*, hung on as deputy editor. The leading writers complained about the dreadful indignities inflicted on their deathless prose by the vulgar ignoramuses of the new regime. So, less stridently, did the OBN literary editor Philip Howard (Eton, Trinity Oxford, Black Watch). But they stayed.

There were genuine differences of style and understanding. "Where others saw eccentricity, authority and charm" wrote the *Tatler* (edited by Evans' wife Tina), "he saw public school cliques, pomposity and fancy verbiage." Howard once told him that "When you wrote for *The Times* you were prudent also to assume that many of your readers knew more about the subject than you did." Evans couldn't understand this. "He looked at me," says Howard, "as if I was daft."

Instead of trying to win over the old guard, Evans tried to persuade as many as possible to go while importing his own network with indecent haste. Anthony Holden, a former *Sunday Times* "Atticus" who had been best man at his wedding (in the garden of *Washington Post* editor Ben Bradlee), became features editor; *Sunday Times* designer Edwin Taylor came over to produce the charts and diagrams of which he was so fond. Another old *Sunday Times* man, Oscar Turnill, was recruited from *The Times Literary Supplement* to add strength to the visual side of things. Peter Watson who had briefly chosen the "Review Fronts" at the *Sunday Times* was brought in to edit the *Times* Diary and Brian Macarthur, Evans' former chief assistant at the *Sunday Times* (though he had once worked at *The Times*), became the *Times* news editor.

Evans made no secret, inside or outside New Printing House Square, of his impatience with old *Times* ways and old *Times* men. Throughout his editorship there was a war of the two networks – Evans' PPN and the old *Times* men. Then, in the spring of '82, quite suddenly, very reluctantly and amid mutual rancour, Evans left with a golden handshake. Most of his PPN also folded their tents and *The Thunderer* reverted to the rump of the remaining old *Times* men under the editorship of Lord Home's (alias Sir Alec Douglas-Home) nephew Charles.

Verdict:
A classic case of over-networking. Evans had two possible network

options. One was to get rid of the whole of the existing *Times* network which had been left over from the previous regime. Had he managed this he could have installed his own PPN with impunity, but the hatchet once more proved rubber and he was unable to oust all the incumbents. That being so, his other option was to woo the existing network, win them over to his side and (perhaps) slowly infiltrate his own men. Instead he charged in with his own interloping PPN, antagonised the existing network and was defeated by it within the year. Philip Howard says that Evans "failed mainly because he did not understand what *The Times* was about and the sort of readers it has". But no boss succeeds with a divided staff and Evans' cardinal sin was to set network against network. Not only did he fail to understand *The Times* and its readers; he failed to understand its journalists.

Just as Harold Evans was losing his network battle at *The Times*, another editor was building a team for a brand new paper where there was no entrenched old guard waiting to beat off invaders from another network. This was Bernard Shrimsley, former editor of Rupert Murdoch's *Sun* and *News of the World*, and the paper was the *Mail on Sunday*. When Lord Rothermere asked him to start it, he was the only member of the staff and there was no question of anyone being foisted on him. It would have been possible to draft in staff from the sister *Daily Mail* but that paper's editor, David, now Sir David, English, was reluctant to give up any of his writers or executives and the only *Daily Mail* network member to be poached by Shrimsley was Christopher Fildes, the city editor.

For Shrimsley it was an obvious opportunity to draft in his journalistic PPN en masse and yet of his forty-four initial appointments only five were people he already knew: an astonishing denial of network principles, especially in the incestuous world of Fleet Street.

This reluctance to play the network game is perhaps partially explained by his single most important hiring. As his deputy editor he chose his younger brother Tony.

On the face of it this would appear to be as flagrant an example of over-zealous networking as anything attempted by Harold Evans at *The Times* but, sibling relationship aside, Tony appeared well qualified for the job. He had previously worked for Lord Rothermere as political editor at the *Mail* and when the *Mail on Sunday* was first conceived he was editing Sir James Goldsmith's weekly news magazine *Now!* This obviously made him unavailable as associate editor under Bernard but before any alternative decision was made *Now!* folded and its employees were out on the street.

Scrupulously trying to avoid any accusations of family favouritism Bernard addressed his telegram of condolence to his brother and the staff to "The Editor-in-Chief *Now! Magazine*" rather than actually mentioning the Shrimsley name. He said he would be interested to talk to any displaced journalist who was prepared to try his luck on another speculative venture, but he said nothing specifically to Tony, even though the thought was very much in his mind. Instead he waited for his proprietor, Lord Rothermere, and sure enough he did not have to wait long.

"What about Tony?" ventured his Lordship during one of their regular conversations about the new paper. Bernard said he had no doubt that Tony was the best man for the job but that because he was family he hadn't liked to suggest and people might talk and perhaps . . .

Rothermere told him, politely, not to be silly. If Tony was the best man for the job he should hire him. And hired he was.

Elsewhere, Bernard hired from all over Fleet Street. In this sense it was, very loosely, a network operation because – apart from *Now!*, from which he recruited the production department en masse – he scarcely went outside London.* Shrimsley's first ten appointments were from *Now!*, the *Evening News*, the *Daily Mail*, the *Tatler*, *Cosmopolitan*, the New York Bureau of Rupert Murdoch's News Group, the *Sunday Times*, the *Observer* and the *Evening Standard*. He only knew two of these personally and was, brother apart, quite consciously against a policy of "just taking on half a dozen of your old chums". He hoped that instead of importing loyalty and esprit de corps in the form of a ready made network (the Evans' philosophy) he would be more likely to weld a close knit team if he started from scratch with a group of strangers who had no old prejudices about each other.

---

* It is notoriously difficult to make the transition from the provinces to Fleet Street, not necessarily because of lack of ability or qualifications but because provincial journalists are not on the Fleet Street network. A case in point is Tom Stoppard (*Western Daily Press* 1954–8, *Bristol Evening World* 1958–60) who failed to land a job as an entertainments reporter on the *Daily Express* and had to make do with play writing instead. "Something of a relief," he says, "I wasn't at all sure that it was a job I wanted."

It is a matter of history that he failed. Ten weeks after the launch in the spring of 1982 Bernard resigned, to be followed soon after by brother Tony. He was succeeded temporarily by Sir David English who later installed Stewart Steven, a long time member of *his* PPN who had worked with him since his days as an associate editor of the *Daily Express* in the late sixties. The ultimate paradox was that as soon as the Shrimsleys were out of the way English brought in the existing *Daily Mail* network which he and Bernard had earlier agreed to keep well away from the *Sunday* operation. He even included Ann Leslie, one of the few *Daily Mail* writers Bernard *had* wanted to use. English had turned down Shrimsley's request. Not only did English import his PPN from the *Daily*, he even gloried in it and made it part of his publicity campaign. "More star writers from our sister paper, the *Daily Mail*, join the *Mail on Sunday*'s own team," crowed the page-one puff in Sunday July 18th's issue. "Now it really is the *Mail on Sunday*."
Verdict:
As with Evans' failure at *The Times*, there were non-network reasons for this disastrous passage in Shrimsley's career, but the network considerations are fundamental. Evans sought to impose his own network on an existing one which he could not break; Shrimsley had – literally – a blank piece of paper. Unlike Evans he was able – almost obliged – to bring in as cohesive, loyal and properly understood PPN as he possibly could. This, with the exception of brother Tony, he signally failed to do; and it was this, more than anything else, which was the cause of his undoing.

In December 1980 a letter from the Prime Minister's husband to one of his wife's ministers was reprinted on the front page of *The Times*. It was a rare public example of the essentially discreet and personal art of networking.

Mr. Thatcher's letter was addressed to the Minister of State for Wales, Mr. Edwards, or rather, since this was a networker's appeal, "Dear Nick". He began, on the principle that flattery will get you most places, by telling the minister what a busy fellow he was and how sorry he was to have to bother him. Then, very properly, he declared his interest: he was a consultant to a company which wanted to build sixty-three houses and a motel on a site just below Harlech Castle. The local County Council had turned the application down and Mr. Thatcher's firm had appealed. At the time of writing, eleven months later, the appeal hearing had still not been set up and Mr. Thatcher complained that, because of this, "Hundreds of thousands of pounds have been locked into an unproductive asset." With that he signed off: "Kind regards, Denis."

The letter, written on 10 Downing Street paper, had the desired effect because "Nick" scribbled on a note at the bottom "The explanation had better be good and quick, ie this week," a command presumably directed at some unfortunate civil servant in the Welsh Office. The effect was, however, rather spoiled when the letter turned up on the front page of *The Times*.

Verdict:

An adequate, if clumsy piece of networking of the "pulling rank" variety, absolutely ruined by putting it in writing and sending it to a public office where it would inevitably be seen by the mischievous and the ill disposed. If Mr. Thatcher had been a really class networker he would have taken the minister to lunch.

Six examples of networks in action. Three successes and three failures. The successes owe much to intuition, a sort of haphazard hunch – playing characteristic of the most effective networking. As a rule, top networks are by-products rather than ends in themselves. The best, Eton, say, or the Guards, are not networks first and foremost; they exist primarily for education and for fighting. But the fact that their networking is secondary makes them more, not less, effective. Too obviously singleminded an approach tends to be counter-productive and the less a network *looks* like a network the more effective it is likely to be.

This is more clearly understood by those born into the networking pink than by those beneath the networking salt. If you divide networkers into haves and have-nots you find that the "have" networkers exploit their connections with an apparent ease and nonchalance which *almost* disguises their determination while the "have-nots" networking creaks with conscious effort. Threepwood and Mrs. Corrigan's butler were both consummate networkers and yet you would hardly, even when on the receiving end, realise what they were up to. Denis Thatcher and Harold Evans were similarly enthusiastic but much less sophisticated, and the fact that they were so obvious in what they were doing made their networking that much less likely to succeed.

The great networking families, schools and Oxbridge colleges, together with a host of smaller OBN oriented networks, all instil principles of discretion and effortlessness, not to say guile. For their members, networking is so much second nature that they scarcely realise that they are networking at all. Such networkers acquire networking technique and apparatus early in life and the only real lesson they need is to keep both well oiled and in good repair.

For the have-nots it is more complicated. Despite most popular prejudices networks are not the sole preserve of a hereditary plutocracy. We all have our PPNs; there are powerful *stigmatised* and *other chaps' networks* as well as *sergeants' mess networks*; it is possible sometimes to create networks from scratch; and many existing networks can be penetrated by anyone capable of combining a gregarious and plausible manner, a genuine interest in people (no substitute will quite do), with an eye for the main chance. Mrs. Corrigan is a case in point. Likewise her fellow American, the Sergeant. Even supposedly minor schools – not even public ones – can occasionally take on network qualities which would be the envy of all but the most leading of Waugh's Leading schools. A few years ago I interviewed the archaeologist, Dr. Glyn Daniel, a life Fellow of St. John's College, Cambridge, writer, broadcaster, friend of the royal family, the prototype establishment don. Dr. Daniel let slip the fact that no less than three of his sixth form contemporaries were now knights of the realm. And where, pray, was this? Eton? Winchester? Harrow? Why no. It was the Barry County School in Wales.

Even the least likely schools may have network qualities waiting to be exploited. Likewise families. No PPN worth its salt can afford to be without a wife and one or two relations, and the easiest way to crash any network is to marry into it. As Sir Geoffrey Agnew said, when surveying his exclusively family board of directors, one of them is there simply because he had "the good sense" to marry an Agnew. Not everyone perhaps can – or indeed wants – to make a dynastic marriage, but the option is always there. You may not be able to marry a royal, or even one of the Massingberd 500; but in every community there are network families whose ranks, if you're so inclined, may be worth joining. If you can marry money, you can also marry network.

Of course this sounds cynical and it is one of the undeniable problems of network that its principles do sound cynical when baldly stated. None of the anecdotes of successful networking recounted above – Mrs. Corrigan, Threepwood and my godfather Peter Wilson – reveal meanness of spirit or a singleminded selfish cynicism; but the terse statement of the network philosophy under-lying them can look less than altruistic. Because of this, "network" is often a pejorative word. We take refuge in aphorisms about not mixing business with pleasure, we suck our teeth at the idea of "exploiting" those whom we know socially, and in doing so we lose sight of the fact that one of the defining features of friendship is that it involves helping each other. It is mutual – a two way process – but it is a fact of life, and by no means a disreputable one.

For the networking have-not who reaches adult life with little or no network apparatus, scarcely the beginnings of a fledgling PPN, the first rule must be to *think network*. Just as the outplacement experts at Sanders and Sydney tell their clients to write down *everyone* who *might* be of help in getting them a job, so the aspiring networker should regard anyone he meets as potentially useful. Just how he is going to be useful, just what you may (ultimately) want them to do for you is neither here nor there. Nicholas Tomalin in his 1964 Atticus column on networks wrote that network membership guaranteed no more than an initially favour-able response on the telephone. "All other benefits flow from that." But precisely what those benefits may be varies according to individual and to circumstance. Just as the best networking has an almost organic quality, and grows almost without the participants being aware of it out of some other form of association, so it should never be too clearly focused. It never occurred to me when I started to correspond with my fellow crime writer, Dorothy Hughes, that one day I would be writing this book as a guest in her New Mexican house; but from the beginning I think (but can't be certain) that I sensed some (mutual) benefit might come of our networking.

Paradoxically, the typical Englishman is bad networking ma-terial even though he may be a hard-core OBN member. If he comes from networking stock and is brought up in networking institutions he reaches adulthood with a sound skeletal PPN, but even he (and much more the non-OBN man) is bad at grafting on to what he has. He is even worse at building from nothing. He will not talk to strangers in railway carriages and bus queues, much less expect to turn such chance acquaintanceships into anything more enduring; he will not ask business associates home to dinner; he will act the wallflower at parties of all kinds rather than go through

239

the possible (but highly unlikely) humiliation of introducing himself to an unknown fellow guest and being rebuffed. In the United
States I once belonged to a racquet-ball club (roughly equivalent to
a squash club) where the manager (and proprietor) greeted me by
my Christian name after I'd been in no more than twice and
introduced me to anyone else who happened to be in the foyer. In
my English squash club there are members with whom I have
shared a changing room for years, yet still we have exchanged
nothing more than a curt nod. We don't even know each other's
names. In the States, sitting in the communal jacuzzi, people are
apt to rise up out of the foam and shake hands very formally with a
brief announcement of their name and occupation. An invitation,
if you like, to network.

This natural British reticence often makes networking difficult
for beginners. It is necessary to break down one's own reserves and
that of one's potential fellow networkers. My experience (admit-
tedly highly personal) and my suspicion (unprovable but based on
said experience and years of observation) is that the other man's
reserve is usually no more than balsa wood. People – especially
English people – are almost pathetically apprehensive about being
rebuffed but if you *do* make the first overture the rebuff hardly ever
comes. And if it does, so what?

This lack of self-confidence is one reason for many people's
bogus disapproval of networking. "Oh, he only got the job because
he plays golf with the boss", "Oh well, he's a friend of so-and-
so's," often disguises one's own inability to make and use connections rather than any genuine moral objection to the practice. It is
an admission of one's own failure to network.

This is not to say that networking is an absolute good. If the
promotion and protection of friends becomes the be-all and end-all
it is obviously not. That way lies the cover-up of crime and
incompetence, and the promotion of the second-rate likeable at
the expense of the first-rate dislikeable.

"Surely," I suggested to Malcolm Muggeridge, "you hired
people you *liked* when you were editor of *Punch*." It seemed so
obvious. *Punch* with its celebrated "Table" and its genial air of
chummy mutual congratulation is just as much a club as a magazine – like *Private Eye*. The editor, surely, can hire any mate he
likes. No reason at all to take on someone you don't much care for,
who might rock the boat, and Old Mug, of all people, strikes one as
the sort who would prefer to have kindred spirits around the place.
He did not, of course, answer the question entirely straightfor-

wardly. Instead he said, smiling, "I took on Claud Cockburn because I thought he was a good writer."

Irresistible talent is relatively rare. More often in competition of any kind, whether it is for an archbishopric or the very best possible service at the local butcher, other considerations come into play: network. All other beings being equal – and that phrase is crucial – the bishops, the Prime Minister and the Crown (who in effect choose archbishops between them) would rather have an archbishop they *like*, who they get on with, and can actually regard with affection. At the other end of the scale, the man in the striped apron is not going to reach under the counter for a particularly choice cut of sirloin for any old Tom, Dick or Harry. He is going to do it for someone he likes, for someone who has the good manners to be a regular and appreciative customer, and who would, if called upon, return the favour in whatever way was asked. That, in the end, is what networking is about. It is about the preferment of friends. That is why it is a pervasive fact of life, not something to be condemned or applauded but simply something to be recognised. It is the principle that in every area of life people have personal preferences. They like some people more than others and they enjoy helping them. They will deal with others, of course, politely perhaps, but without the real sense of enthusiasm reserved for fellow members of their various networks – the people who together comprise their PPN.

"One must be fond," wrote E. M. Forster, "of people and trust them if one is not to make a mess of one's life and it is therefore essential that they should not let one down."

Which is not only a succinct and perceptive statement of the principle of friendship, but also of the principle of networking.

Epilogue

It was Blunt who began my curiosity about networks. That curiously nonchalant acceptance of the OBN in his languid interview in the *Times* boardroom:

"Then you joined MI5. How did you join? Did you apply, or was it arranged for you, or how?"

"Well, like all those . . . that kind of recruitment, it was done simply. Someone who was in MI5 recommended me. I was recommended."

"The old boy network?"

"Yes."

Later Andrew Boyle, the author who had done so much to unmask Blunt, suggested that the "first casualty" of that great spy scandal was "the traditional public school convention of mutual trust between colleagues who shared the same privileged social backgrounds". Curious that so perceptive a writer should think those network ties so easily unknotted. Curious too that he, like others, should imply that they are the prerogative only of the privately educated. Class does create network bonds but not indiscriminately. At the top it is called the OBN; at the other end of the scale it is known as "working class solidarity". Blunt was a member of many networks great and small and he was not unusual in this. Everyone has his PPN. We may not recognise it but we all belong to networks. Some are the fundamental ones of kith and kin; some are motivated almost entirely by mutual self-interest; some are quite frivolous, their obligations easily ignored; others are, literally, matters of life and death. Networks are all around us, ubiquitous and pervasive. Success is largely a matter of nurturing one's own and always being aware of your enemies.

For all of us, if we will only see it, one man leads to another.

Networks: A Vocabulary

Booster: Artificially created or **ersatz network** designed primarily for advancement of members (despite frequent protests to the contrary). First coined by Sinclair Lewis, the American novelist.

Cold Contact: Potential benefactor with whom you have only second-hand personal relationship.

Colonial OBN: Old Boy Network in old white Commonwealth countries based on imitations of British public schools and their traditions, viz Upper Canada College, Toronto, or Geelong Grammar, in Australia.

Ersatz Network: See **Booster**.

Ethnic Network: Network based on nationality or race.

Horizontal Network: Network of contemporaries, often used of families – brothers, sisters, cousins of the same generation.

Hot Contact: Potential benefactor who you know at first-hand, member of your **PPN**.

Major Public School: Leading School or First-Rate on **Waugh Scale** (see appendix I). School with genuine network qualities at a national level.

Massingberd 500, The: Five hundred key network families who have consistently produced "men and women of prominence" over at least three generations. First classified by genealogist Hugh Montgomery-Massingberd.

Minor Public Schools: Good Schools and Schools on **Waugh Scale**. Few network properties.

Negative Network: Rather like inverted snobbery, a situation in which network membership is a liability rather than an advantage and a member is discriminated against. Thus an Oxbridge college may try not to admit a candidate whose family have all been to the same college or a set of barristers' chambers will refuse to admit Old Boys of the same school.

243

Network(s) of Association: Network based on actual friendship or first-hand connection.

Network(s) of Expectation: Network based on membership which implies certain characteristics. For example (sometimes mistakenly), that Balliol men are very clever, or that Wykehamists have very good manners.

Network (verb): To take advantage of or exploit friendship, contact or similar link in order to by-pass usual channels.

Network (noun): Association of people with shared interest(s), background, aim or almost any bond imaginable which is prepared to make use of individual members.

New Girl Network(s) (NGN(s)): **Boosters** for women.

Old Boy Network (The OBN): Network of former public school boys and/or Oxbridge graduates (Foundation Branch); or of recognised success stories (Establishment Branch).

Other Chap's Network(s) (OCN(s)): Networks for those not belonging to the **OBN** (either branch).

Old School Tie: Necktie with stripe or other recurring motif (heraldic device or monogram) to demonstrate wearer's educational background or (sometimes) other network membership.

Personal Private Network (PPN): The individual's network of friends and contacts.

Sergeant Major's Network(s) (SMN(s)): Network of senior NCOs in military or civilian life whose power is often greater than it appears. Often a satellite of an officer class network, viz: barristers' clerks, courtiers, butlers etc.

Stigmatised or Stigmatic Network: Network of the oppressed or underprivileged.

Tafia, The: The Welsh network, especially in London.

Vertical Network(s): A historical network which encompasses different generations – most usually an expectation-generating family network of ancestors such as Hill-Nortons or Bickersteths.

Waugh Scale, The: Division of public schools into four grades, Leading, First-Rate, Good and simply School. First mentioned by Evelyn Waugh in his novel *Decline and Fall* (see Appendix I).

APPENDIX I

Heald's List of Major Public Schools

There are several hundred fee paying, independent schools in Britain all of which think of themselves as "public schools" within the meaning of the act. As far as networks go it seems to me that the great majority are surprisingly ineffectual. Attending one of the "minor" public schools, by which I mean "Good School" or "School" on the Evelyn Waugh scale, does not arouse particularly high expectations among either pupils or potential employers or competitors; nor are there many influential networks emanating from these lower orders.

There are occasional specific exceptions to this so that minor schools may network brilliantly in particular areas. London's Hampton is disproportionately successful in the world of rowing; George Heriot's produces more great rugger players than seems reasonable; Gresham's School, Holt, has, at times, done a similar line in aesthetes. But in general network terms – not academic, or social, or sporting – it seems to me that these are the only schools which *really* count. All others are, like it or not, "minor" public schools.

Leading Schools	First-Rate Schools	
Ampleforth	Bedford	Malvern
Charterhouse	Bradfield	Millfield
Eton	Bryanston	Oundle
Harrow	Cheltenham	Radley
Marlborough	Clifton	Repton
Rugby	Downside	St. Paul's
Shrewsbury	Fettes	Sedbergh
Westminster	Gordonstoun	Sherborne
Winchester	Haileybury	Stonyhurst
	Highgate	Tonbridge
	King's, Canterbury	Uppingham
	Lancing	Wellington

This is the state of play early in the 1980s, but like any league table it has room for promotion and demotion. The network schools of the next decade may be quite different (though I doubt it).

APPENDIX II

Heald's List of Great British Networks

Networks are seldom in direct competition. In small town Britain, membership of the Rotary Club cuts far more ice than membership of White's. If you're talking about a national moneyed aristocracy with international ramifications, the reverse is true. Because of this any list of "top" networks is arbitrary and subjective, but, in their very different ways and alphabetical order, these ten take a lot of beating.

Balliol – still the most effective Oxbridge network.

The barristers' clerks – a sergeant majors' network that even surpasses the sergeant majors, at least as powerful (and prosperous) as most of the lawyers for whom they work.

Eton – no school, in network terms, to touch it.

The Garrick – smartest working men's club in London.

The Guards – a passport to prosperity for officers *and* men. Number one network in easily the most network conscious of the three Services.

Nobody's Friends – the Church's talking shop, where the episcopacy meets the believing laity.

Rotary – the Garrick of Middletown, UK.

The royal family – a model for all family business.

The Tafia – England's most powerful foreign legion, dominated, naturally, by the London Welsh.

White's – smartest non-working men's club in London (with arguably industrious exceptions).

APPENDIX III

Old School Ties Available 1981
from P. L. Sells

Old Boys (stripes only)

Old Ackworth
Old Albanian
Old Aldenhamian
Alderman Newton Old Boys,
  Leicester
Old Alleynian (Dulwich College)
Alleyn Old Boys (Alleyn's
  School)
Old Aluredian (Narrow)
Old Ardinian (Ardingly)
Aston, Old Edwardian
Old Barnard Castle
Old Barrovian (King William's
  College)
Battersea, Old Grammarian
Old Beaumont
Old Bedfordian
Old Bedford Modern
Old Berkhamsted (Wide)
Old Berkhamsted (Narrow)
Old Birkonian
Old Blues (Christ's Hospital)
Old Blundellian
Old Bradfieldian (Narrow)
Old Breconian
Old Brentwood
Old Brightonian
Old Bristolian
Old Bromsgrovian (Wide)
Old Bromsgrovian (Narrow)
Old Brutonian
Camp Hill, Old Edwardian
Old Canfordian
Old Cantabrigian (Cambridge
  High School)

Old Carthusian (Wide)
Old Carthusian (Narrow)
Old Centralian (Birmingham)
Old Cheltonian
Old Chigwellian
Old Cholmeleian (Highgate)
Old Citizens (City of London)
City Old Boys, Leicester
Old Cliftonian
Old Conway (Training Ship)
Old Cowper
Old Cranbrook
Old Cranleigh (Wide)
Old Cranleigh (Narrow)
Old Decanian (Dean Close)
Old Denstonian (Wide)
Old Denstonian (Narrow)
Old Dixonian
Old Dovorian (Narrow)
Old Dovorian (Wide)
Old Downside
Old Dunelmian (Durham)
Old Dunstonian (St. Dunstan's,
  Catford)
Old Eastbournian
Edinburgh Academicals FP
Old Edwardian (New Street,
  Birmingham)
Old Edwardian (Sheffield)
Old Elean (King's School, Ely)
Old Elizabethan (Worcester)
Old Emanuel (Wandsworth)
Old Epsomian
Old Etonian
Old Feistedian

Old Fettesian-Lorettonian
Five Ways (Old Edwardian)
Old Framlingham (Wide)
Old Framlingham (Narrow)
Old Fullerian (Watford)
Gateway Old Boys, Leicester
Glasgow Academicals FP
Old Glenalmond
Old Gregorian (Downside)
Old Gresham (Norfolk)
Old Grocers
Guild of Leopards (Skinners School)
Old Haberdashers
Old Haileybury (Magenta)
Old Haileybury (Black)
Harrow Association
Old Heleian (Exeter)
Old Hurstpierpoint (Hurstjohnian) (Narrow)
Old Ipswich
Old King William (IOM) (Narrow)
Old Lancastrian
Old Lancing (Wide)
Old Lancing (Narrow)
Old Latimerian
Old Leysian
Old Llandovery
Old Lorettonian
Old Lyonian
Old Malvern
Old Marlborough (Wide)
Old Marlborough (Narrow)
Old Merchant Taylors
Old Merchiston
Old Mill Hill (Wide)
Old Mill Hill (Narrow)
Moat Road Old Boys Leicester
Old Novocastrian (Newcastle)
Old Oakham
Old Olavian
Old Oundle
Old Parkonian
Old Pauline

Old Peterite (Narrow)
Old Queenian (Taunton)
Old Quintinian
Old Reading
Old Repton
Old Rossallian
Old Rugby
Old Rydal (Colwyn Bay)
Old St. Bees (St. Beghian)
Old Salopian (Wide)
Old Salopian (Narrow)
Old Sedbergh
Old Shirburnian (Wide)
Old Shirburnian (Narrow)
Old Skinners (Guild of Leopards)
Old Silhillian (Solihull)
Old Stationers
Old Stowe (Black)
Old Stonyhurst
Old Stratfordians
Old Stortfordians
Old Sutton Valence (Narrow)
Old Taunton
Old Tonbridge (Wide)
Old Tonbridge (Narrow)
UCS Old Boys (Hampstead)
Old Uppingham (Wide)
Old Uppingham (Narrow)
Old Watsonian
Old Waverley
Old Wellingborough
Old Wellington (Berkshire)
Old Westminster
Old Westminster Citizens
Old Weymouth
Old Whitgift
Old Wilsonian
Old Wolverley
Old Woodbridge
Old Wrekin (Wellington Salop)
Old Wycliffe
Old Wyggeston (Leicester)
Old Wykehamist (Wide)
Old Wykehamist (Narrow)

APPENDIX IV

The Sherborne School 1982 Appeal

President: The Rt. Hon. Viscount Boyd of Merton, PC, CH, DL

Vice-Presidents: Sir Arthur Norman, KBE, DFC (Chairman of
    Governors)
Sir Alan Campbell, GCMG (Vice-Chairman of Governors)
K. A. Abel, Esq.
R. W. Aldridge, Esq.
Gen. Sir John Archer, KCB, OBE
M. J. L. Attfield, Esq.
The Rt. Rev. John Baker, Bishop of Salisbury
H. E. M. Barnes, Esq., FCA
H. J. N. Chapman, Esq.
Sir Derman Christopherson, OBE, FRS
Sir Robert Clark, DSC
His Hon. Edward Clarke, QC
Maj. Gen. J. E. Cordingley, OBE
Adml. Sir Victor Crutchley, VC, KCB, DSC, DL
Lt-Col. Sir Thomas Devitt, Bt
Maj. Gen. Sir Charles Dunphie, CB, CBE, DSO
M. R. G. Earls-Davis, Esq.
The Rev. J. Eddison
The Rt. Hon. Sir John Eden, Bt, MP
C. R. J. Eglington, Esq.
The Rt. Rev. Gerald Ellison, PC
D. F. R. Evans, Esq., TD
Dr. R. A. Fletcher, D.Phil., DSC
Field Marshal Sir Roland Gibbs, GCB, CBE, DSO, MC
The Rev. Canon F. P. P. Goddard
Field Marshal Lord Harding of Petherton, GCB, CBE, DSO, MC
T. V. Heald, Esq.
R. Hodder-Williams, Esq.
Col. H. F. W. Holmes, TD
J. A. Hopkins, Esq.
D. H. L. Hopkinson, Esq., RD
The Rt. Hon. Lord Iliffe
J. J. Irons, Esq.
Lt. Gen. Sir Ian Jacob, GBE, CB, DL

Lt. Gen. Sir Maurice Johnston, KCB, OBE
Dr. R. A. Keable-Elliott
Adml. Sir Horace Law, GCB, OBE, DSC
Capt. A. A. Lockyer, MVO, RN
Sir Robert Marshall, KCB, MBE
M. McCrum, Esq.
A. A. E. Morgan, Esq.
Lt. Gen. Sir Thomas Morony, KCB, OBE
T. R. Parry, Esq.
Sir Alastair Pilkington, FRS
D. W. Pittard, Esq.
R. W. Powell, Esq.
G. Pring, Esq.
Sir John Rix, MBE
D. C. D. Ryder, Esq.
J. W. Spicer, Esq., MP
H. P. Stewart, Esq.
G. F. Symondson, Esq.
J. A. Tallent, Esq., CBE, TD
The Rt. Hon. Lord Thomas of Swynnerton
W. E. Tucker, Esq., CVO, MBE, TD, FRCS
O. Van Oss, Esq., FSA
M. M. Walford, Esq.
The Very Rev. Canon Alexander Ross Wallace
J. D. Watney, Esq.
Col. Sir Joseph Weld, OBE, TD, JP
M. E. K. Westlake, Esq.
Dr. D. I. T. Wilson, MBE
The Rev. A. R. Wingfield Digby
Simon Wingfield Digby, Esq., TD, DL

APPENDIX V

Balliol College 1982 Appeal

Coincidentally my college, Balliol, also launched an appeal in 1982. Their target of £2,000,000, as against £700,000, neatly reflects the difference between a "leading" rural public school and one of the country's foremost academic networks. So does the composition of the two appeal committees. Notice that although the Balliol committee is much stronger on political figures it contains no admirals or generals. Also that, whereas the Sherborne group is drawn from well disposed local residents, parents and other friends of the school as well as Old Boys, the Balliol committee is entirely composed of Balliol men. The Balliol committee that launched the appeal was:

Patron: The Rt. Hon. Harold Macmillan
Chairman: The Rt. Hon. Lord Kilbrandon
Secretary: Rodney Leach
Members: Eric Anderson
   Lord Avebury
   Lord Balogh
   R. P. Bell
   Sir Thomas Bingham
   Sir Robert Birley
   Lord Fulton
   The Rt. Hon. Sir Ian Gilmour
   Sir Alexander Glen
   Graham Greene
   Ronald Grierson
   The Rt. Hon. Denis Healey
   The Rt. Hon. Edward Heath
   Christopher Hill
   The Rt. Hon. Roy Jenkins
   Brian Knox
   The Rt. Revd. and Rt. Hon. G. D. Leonard
   George Malcolm
   Russell Meiggs
   Sir Walter Oakeshott
   John Platts-Mills
   Anthony Powell
   Sir William Rees-Mogg

Sir Richard Southern
Sir Anthony Wagner
Laurence Whistler
Sir Edgar Williams

APPENDIX VI

Public School Boys/Fathers at Same Schools

School	Percentage	School	Percentage
Eton	47%	Glenalmond	16.58%
Ampleforth	35.8%	Sherborne	16.03%
Downside	33% (circa)	Radley	16%
Uppingham	28.2%	Repton	15.8%
Harrow	28.16%	Malvern	15.5%
Oundle	28%	Fettes	15%
Wellington	25.2%	Eastbourne	9.3%
Rugby	25%	Tonbridge	7.85%
Charterhouse	24%	Whitgift	7.6%
Winchester	23.6%	Lancing	7.47%
Loretto	22%	Kings School,	
Stowe	21%	Canterbury	7.2%
Sedbergh	20.4%	Gordonstoun	5.57%
Shrewsbury	18%	Hurstpierpoint	5.5%
Clifton	18%	Brighton	5%
Haileybury	17.29%	Westminster	4.3%

Average: 18.36%

The Old School Tie by Kenneth and George Western (1934)

Rah, Rah, Rah Rah Rah, Rah,
Rah, Rah Rah Rah,
    Hello cads, we're going to sing
    you a song.
Rah Rah Rah, Rah Rah Rah,
Rah, Rah, Rah Rah Rah,
    About the old school,
Horray, Rah!
    Listen you fellas, now look here
    you chaps,
Let's think of the old school today,
    Of Eton and Harrow and
    Borstal as well.
Three cheers, follow up and
horray.
    Let's wear that pullover we won
    at Narkover,
Let's all walk about in small caps,
    And let every mug be a tribute
    to Rugby,
And bravo, bravissimo, chaps.
    Any old Alsatians here?
There's one or two old
Dalmatians, George.
    Really?
Spotted around!
    A cannibal chief sat and
    sharpened his knives,
Wearing his old school tie.
    Solomon slept with his five
    hundred wives,
Wearing his old school tie.
    Two hundred and fifty a side it
    was,
Was it really?
    Yes, that hot weather.

H'm it was warm.
    Very close, almost touching
    really.
Lloyd George often spoke of his
school so they say,
    But now he's a platinum blonde
    in his way,
He sits up in bed looking like
Frances Day,
    Wearing his old school tie.
Toujours la Polytechnic!
    Of course.
Cochran sat down in a gallery
queue,
    Wearing his old school tie.
Moses was found in the bullrushes
too.
    Wearing his old school tie.
The Royal Garden Party was the
smartest for years,
    Jimmy Thomas arrived and they
    gave him three cheers,
He turned up in evening dress, top
hat and spurs,
    Wearing his old school tie,
Sic transit Gloria Swanson,
    Oh yes?
Don't forget Marlborough,
remember St. Paul's,
    And Dulwich and Hamlet and
    Stowe,
And Wormwood and Dartmoor
and Pentonville too,
    And Dr. Barnardo's,
Say there!
    Oh up the Scrubs!

Let's talk about batting and physics and Latin,
   And Classics we took in our stride,
And famous school fellows like Laurel and Hardy,
   And Crippen and Jekyll and Hyde,
But you're forgetting the Shell, you hounds,
   And the Remove, you know.
There's a man in the moon so astrologers say,
   Wearing his old school tie.
They're going to make Hitler the Queen of the May,
   Wearing his old school tie.
At the debts talks when Montague Norman came in,

They said Oxford or Cambridge? And so with a grin,
He lifted his beaver and under his chin,
   He was wearing his old school tie.
Pro bono public house-o.
   Really?
Gandhi's disciples all kicked up a din,
   'Cos Gandhi said "If we can fight we can win,"
Then his loin cloth fell off but he wasn't run in,
   He was wearing his old school tie.
Rah Rah Rah, Rah Rah, Rah, Rah, Rah, Rah Rah Rah.
   Good hunting cads.

APPENDIX VIII

Christ Church/Old Westminsters

The relationship between Westminster and Christ Church, Oxford, has traditionally been one of the strongest OBN Oxbridge-public school links. This list is by no means comprehensive, but it is Westminster's selection of distinguished old boys who made the connection. The dates refer to the year of matriculation.

1897 Sir Maurice Gwyer KCB (d. 1952)
      Hon. Student of Ch. Ch.
1901 Rt. Rev. G. K. A. Bell (d. 1958)
      Bishop of Chichester
1902 W. T. S. Stallybrass (d. 1948)
      Vice-Chancellor, Oxford University
      Lord Green (d. 1952)
      Master of the Rolls
1908 Sir Adrian Boult CH
1912 J. G. Barrington-Ward (d. 1946)
      Student of Ch. Ch.
1914 Rt. Rev. R. W. Stannard
      Suff. Bishop of Woolwich
1915 Sir Ronald Howe (d. 1977)
      Dep. Commissioner Met. Police
1917 F. J. Warburg
      Publisher
1918 Lord Rea (d. 1981)
1919 Sir Henry Chisholm CBE (d. 1981)
      Sir Roy Harrod (New Coll.) (d. 1981)
      Student of Ch. Ch.
      Sir Philip Hendy (d. 1980)
      Director, Nat. Gallery
1920 Humfry Payne (d. 1936)
      Archaeologist
1921 J. J. Byam Shaw CBE
      Hon. Student of Ch. Ch.
1926 Sir John Winnifrith KCB
      Dir. Gen. National Trust
1927 C. H. V. Sutherland CBE FBA
      Student of Ch. Ch.

1928 H. Lloyd Jones CMG
        Sec. to Ashmolean Museum
      L. J. D. Wakely CMG
        HM Ambassador to Burma
1929 Rt. Rev. J. G. H. Baker
        Bishop of Hong Kong
      A. F. L. Beeston
        Laudian Professor of Arabic
      Sir William Deakin DSO
        First Warden of St. Antony's
      Sir Peter Pain QC
        Judge of the High Court
1932 Hon. Sir John Latey
        Judge of the High Court
      G. W. Stonier
        Author and journalist
      D. P. Walker FBA
        Professor of the History of the Classical Tradition, Warburg
        Institute
1933 Jack Simmons
        Professor of History, Univ. of Leicester
1934 Sir Richard Barlas KCB
        Clerk of the House of Commons
      R. M. Robbins CBE FSA
        London Transport Executive
      Lord Byers
      P. L. Shinnie
        Professor of Archaeology, Univ. of Calgary
1937 Brian Urquhart MBE
        Under Secretary-General, United Nations
1939 D. F. Pears (Balliol Coll.)
        Student of Ch. Ch.
1940 P. L. Gardiner
        Fellow of Magdalen
      Hugh Lloyd-Jones
        Regius Professor of Greek
1941 Donald Swann
      T. J. Brown FSA
        Professor of Palaeography, Univ. of London
1943 Sir Richard Faber KCMG
        HM Ambassador to Algeria (1977)
1944 J. A. Robinson CMG
        HM Ambassador to Algeria (1974)
        Minister, Washington DC (1977)
      Anthony Sampson
        Author and journalist

1945 R. A. Denniston
      Academic Publisher, Oxford University Press.
1946 R. W. Young
      Principal, George Watson's College, Edinburgh
1949 Sir Crispin Tickell
      HM Ambassador to Mexico
      D. F. Whitton
      Fellow of Lincoln
1951 Nigel Lawson MP
      Secretary of State for Energy
      J. King-Farlow
      Professor of Philosophy, Univ. of Alberta
1952 Anthony Howard
      Journalist

Later Westminster–Christ Church men are often too young to have made their mark although the post-Anthony Howard generations do include the BBC's economic correspondent, Dominick Harrod (whose father was a Christ Church don for many years), the novelist Tim Jeal and the pianist Anthony Peebles. Since the abolition of closed scholarships the number of Westminster boys going on to Christ Church is, in the words of Westminster's headmaster, "significantly down on the past". He adds that "the relationship whilst still alive is not as strong or ever will be as strong as in the past".

APPENDIX IX

A List of the Dynasties of England and Wales as Compiled by Hugh Montgomery–Massingberd

Acland
Acton
Addington
Adeane
Adrian
Agnew
Aitken
Albery
Alderson
Alington
Allsopp
Amery
Heathcoat Amory
Anson
Arden
Arkwright
Armstrong
Arundell
Asprey
Asquith
Assheton
Astor

Babington
Bacon
Bagot
Bailey
Balston
Bankes
Barclay
Baring
Barlow
Barran
Barrington
Bates
Bathurst

Hicks Beach
Beauclerk
Beaumont
Beecham
Benn
Curtis-Bennett
Benson
Cavendish-Bentinck
Berkeley
Berry
Bertie
Bethell
Bibby
Biddulph
Birkbeck
Birkin
Birley
Blackwell
Blandy
Borwick
Bosanquet
Boscawen
Bourdillon
Bourne
Pleydell-Bouverie
Bowater
Bowring
Brackenbury
Brand
Brassey
Brett
Bridgeman
Brinton
Brocklebank
Brooke (×2)
Brudenell-Bruce

Cumming-Bruce
Prideaux-Brune
Brunner
Buckley
Bull
Butler
Buxton
Byng

Cadbury
Cadogan
Nall-Cain
Cairns
Gough Calthorpe
Carey
Carington
Rivett-Carnac
Carter
Bonham Carter
Cavendish
Cayley
Cayzer
Cazalet
Cazenove
Cecil
Chamberlain
Chance
Channon
Charrington
Chitty
Cholmondeley
Christie
Spencer-Churchill
Clark (×2)
Clay
Clifford

258

Clive
Windsor-Clive
Cobbold
Cockerell
Somers Cocks
Codrington
Cohen
Cokayne
Coke
Collingwood
Colvile
Colville
Compton
Congreve
Cook
Cooper
Ashley-Cooper
Copeland
Cornish
Courage
Courtauld
Courtenay
Coventry
Cripps
Cromwell
Crossley
Cubitt
Capel Cure
Curzon
Cust

Dalgety
Darwin
Dashwood
Dawnay
Deedes
de Ferranti
de Grey
de Havilland
de Hoghton
de Lisle
Denison
de Salis
de Trafford
Devereux
Dickens

Wingfield Digby
Dimsdale
Donaldson
Cottrell-Dormer
Conan Doyle
d'Oyly-Carte
Drax
Duckworth
Dugdale
du Maurier
Duncombe
Dunn
Dymoke

Eden
Egerton
Eliot
Scott-Ellis
Elmhirst
Elwes
Empson
Engleheart
Evelyn
Eyre

Faber
Fane
Farrer
Feilding
Fenwick
Festing
Fiennes
Fisher
Fitzherbert
Fitzmaurice
FitzRoy
Fitzwilliam
Fleming
Fletcher
Floyd
Foley
Foljambe
Foot
Ford
Fordham
Fortescue

Foyle
Fremantle
Frere
Freud
Frewen
Fry
Furness
Furse

Gage
Garnett
Garton
Gascoigne
Gatacre
Lloyd George
Gibbs
Gibson
Giffard
Gilbey
Gladstone
Glyn
Gooch
Goodall
Gorges
Gorst
Goschen
Gosling
Leveson-Gower
Grade
Graham
Lycett Green
Greenall
Greene
Greenwell
Grenfell
Greville
Grey
Grigg
Grimston
Grisewood
Grosvenor
Guest
Gurdon
Gurney

Haggard

259

Halsey
Hambro
Hammick
Hamond
Hanbury
Hankey
Harcourt
Hardinge
Gathorne-Hardy
Harington
Harmsworth
Harris
Harrod
Hastings
Finch-Hatton
Hawtrey
Henderson
Heneage
Herbert
Hervey
Hesketh
Joynson-Hicks
Hildyard
Hill
Hoare
Hobhouse
Hodgkin
Hogg
Hood
Horlick
Hornby
Howard
Fitzalan-Howard
Huxley

Inge
Inglefield
Inskip
Rufus Isaacs

Jackson
James
Jay
Jellicoe
Jenyns
Joel

Johnstone
Joicey
Jolliffe
Joly de Lotbinière

Keble
Kenyon
Keppel
Keyes
Keynes
Kindersley
Kleinwort
Knatchbull
Knollys
Knox

Lamb
Lambton
Lascelles
Law
Lawrence
Layard
Laycock
Legge
Legh
Leigh
Le Marchant
Gordon-Lennox
Lever
Llewellyn
Lloyd
Loder
Lopes
Lowther
Luard
Lubbock
Fairfax-Lucy
Lunn
Lushington
Luttrell
Lyle
Lyttelton
Lytton

McCarthy
McLaren

Makins
Malet
Mallalieu
Mann
Manners
Marks
Holland-Martin
Martineau
Maugham
Meinertzhagen
Merton
Messel
Methuen
Meynell
Millar
Mitford
Moberly
More-Molyneux
Monckton
Mond
Monson
Montagu (×2)
Sebag-Montefiore
Morris
Morrison
Mosley
Mostyn
Mountbatten

Nettlefold
Nevill
Nicolson
Noel
Norman
Northcote

Oglander
Olivier
Onslow

Paget
Palmer
Parker (×2)
Peake
Pearson
Pease

Peel

Pelham

Pelly

Denison-Pender

Douglas-Pennant

Pepys

Percy

Perowne

Philipps

Phillimore

Phipps

Pilkington

Pitman

Player

Plowden

Carew Pole

Portman

Potter

Pratt

Pretyman

Pryor

Pym

Quilter

Raikes

Ralli

Ramsbotham

Randolph

Read

Rhys

Ricardo

Ridley

Pitt-Rivers

Roberts

Rodd

Romilly

Trevor-Roper

Rossetti

Rothschild

Rous

Rowley

Rowntree

Rumbold

Runciman

Russell (×2)

Ryder

Ryle

Sainsbury

St. Aubyn

St. John

Salt

Samuel

Sandeman

Sassoon

Savile

Scott

Scrope

Seebohm

Seely

Segrave

Seymour

Shackleton

Sherbrooke

Shirley

Shuttleworth

Siddeley

Sidney

Sieff

Silkin

Sitwell

Skipwith

Smith (×3)

Abel Smith

Dorrien-Smith

Soames

Somerset

Spencer

Stamp

Stanhope

Stanley

Stephen

Vane-Tempest-
   Stewart

Stone

Stonor

Stourton

Strachey

Streatfeild

Strutt

Studd

Sumner

Surtees

Sykes

Talbot

Taylor

Terry

Thackeray

Thesiger

Thynne

Tiarks

Tollemache

Townshend

Tree

Trefusis

Trevelyan

Trollope

Turton

Unwin

Vane

Vanneck

Vaughan

Verey

Verney

Vernon

Vestey

Vickers

Villiers

Vivian

Wake

Waldegrave

Walker

Wallop

Walpole

Walter

Walwyn

Ward

Warde

Lee-Warner

Waterhouse

Waterlow

Watney

Watson

261

Waugh
Wedgwood
Weld
Sackville-West
Whitaker
Whitbread
Wigram
Wilberforce

Monier-Williams
Willoughby
Wills
Wingate
Wodehouse
Wontner
Worthington
Wrottesley

Wyatt
Wyndham
Williams-Wynn

Yorke
Young
Younghusband

APPENDIX X

The One Hundred and First Meeting of the Saintsbury Club

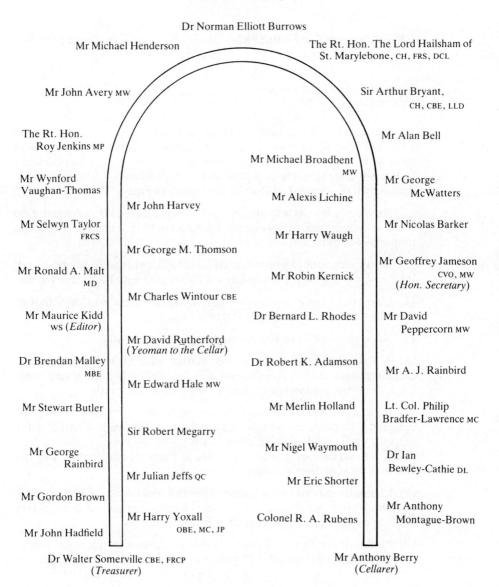

Dr Norman Elliott Burrows

Mr Michael Henderson

The Rt. Hon. The Lord Hailsham of St. Marylebone, CH, FRS, DCL

Mr John Avery MW

Sir Arthur Bryant, CH, CBE, LLD

The Rt. Hon. Roy Jenkins MP

Mr Alan Bell

Mr Wynford Vaughan-Thomas

Mr Michael Broadbent MW

Mr George McWatters

Mr John Harvey

Mr Alexis Lichine

Mr Selwyn Taylor FRCS

Mr Harry Waugh

Mr Nicolas Barker

Mr George M. Thomson

Mr Ronald A. Malt MD

Mr Robin Kernick

Mr Geoffrey Jameson CVO, MW (*Hon. Secretary*)

Mr Charles Wintour CBE

Mr Maurice Kidd WS (*Editor*)

Dr Bernard L. Rhodes

Mr David Peppercorn MW

Mr David Rutherford (*Yeoman to the Cellar*)

Dr Brendan Malley MBE

Dr Robert K. Adamson

Mr A. J. Rainbird

Mr Edward Hale MW

Mr Stewart Butler

Mr Merlin Holland

Lt. Col. Philip Bradfer-Lawrence MC

Sir Robert Megarry

Mr George Rainbird

Mr Nigel Waymouth

Dr Ian Bewley-Cathie DL

Mr Julian Jeffs QC

Mr Eric Shorter

Mr Gordon Brown

Mr Anthony Montague-Brown

Mr Harry Yoxall OBE, MC, JP

Colonel R. A. Rubens

Mr John Hadfield

Dr Walter Somerville CBE, FRCP (*Treasurer*)

Mr Anthony Berry (*Cellarer*)

VINTNERS' HALL

THURSDAY, 21st OCTOBER 1982

263

APPENDIX XI

Regulations for Debutantes in the Year of Abolition (1958)

The following regulations for the formal presentation of ladies at Court were in force in 1958:

(1) Ladies who have already been presented in their present name and style and wishing to make presentations, should forward the names as soon as possible and in any case should reach the Lord Chamberlain's Office not later than the first post on Friday, December 13th, giving the date they last attended a Court or Presentation Party.

(2) Any lady who has attended, or has been presented, at, a Presentation Party in 1956 or 1957 is not eligible to attend in 1958, except to present an unmarried daughter.

(3) No applications can be accepted from ladies wishing to be presented; their names must be forwarded by the ladies who wish to present them.

(4) Unmarried ladies are ineligible to make presentations even though they themselves have been presented.

(5) No applications can be accepted for attendance only.

(6) A lady eligible to make a presentation who wishes to present her daughters and/or daughters-in-law may, in addition, present one other lady. Otherwise ladies are limited to one presentation only.

(7) Invitations will be extended to the husbands of ladies making presentations, or being presented, only if their names are submitted in the original application and if space permits.

The attendance of gentleman at these Presentation Parties will not count as presentation at Court.

(8) Ladies domiciled in the Commonwealth and Colonies wishing to be presented must make application to the High Commissioner or Secretary of State concerned, for presentation by his wife.

(9) Ladies of Foreign Nationality, either by birth or by marriage, can be presented only through the Diplomatic Representative of the country concerned, except when they are in possession of British passports.

264

APPENDIX XII

The Devonshire and Dorset Regiment (1981)

SURVEY STATISTICS

Forms returned: 608

Home Towns	Total	Percentage
Devon	372	61%
Dorset	104	17%
Other	132	22%
Devon and Dorset	476	78%
Plymouth alone	148	24%

Family Connections

Father in regt.	22	4%
Father in Devons	37	6%
Father in Dorsets	25	4%
Total "sons of fathers"	84	14%
Brothers in regt.	85	14%
Other relatives	87	14%
Total of soldiers with family connections	256	42%

Residential Connections

Live(d) in Devon	364	60%
Live(d) in Dorset	114	19%
Total in counties	478	79%
Educated in Devon	338	56%
Educated in Dorset	98	16%
Total in counties	432	72%

APPENDIX XIII

Outline Family Tree for Sgt. Janes of The Devonshire and Dorset Regiment 1981

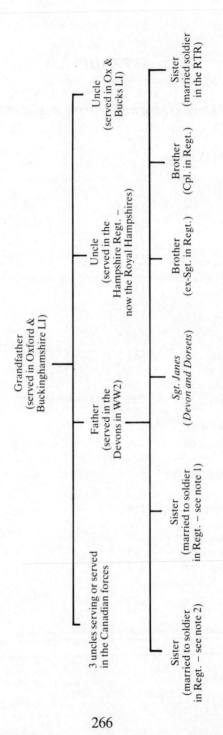

Notes

1. Sister is married to a Pte. Lomax, who says he has a great many cousins connected with the regiment, either serving or now left the Army.

2. Another sister is married to a Cpl. Rixon, who has two brothers currently serving in the regiment.

APPENDIX XIV

Select Family Tree of Admiral of the Fleet Lord Hill-Norton

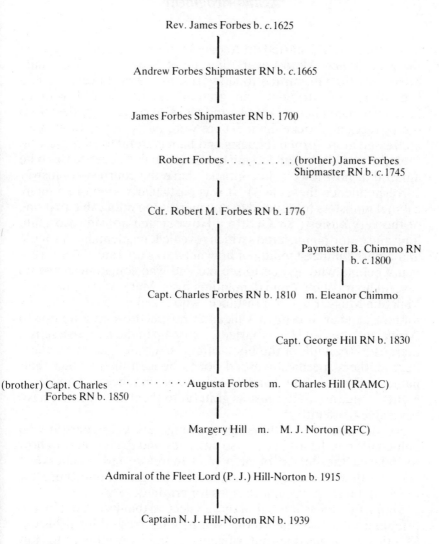

Rev. James Forbes b. *c.*1625

Andrew Forbes Shipmaster RN b. *c.*1665

James Forbes Shipmaster RN b. 1700

Robert Forbes . . . . (brother) James Forbes
Shipmaster RN b. *c.*1745

Cdr. Robert M. Forbes RN b. 1776

Paymaster B. Chimmo RN
b. *c.*1800

Capt. Charles Forbes RN b. 1810   m. Eleanor Chimmo

Capt. George Hill RN b. 1830

(brother) Capt. Charles · · · · · · · · ·Augusta Forbes   m.   Charles Hill (RAMC)
Forbes RN b. 1850

Margery Hill   m.   M. J. Norton (RFC)

Admiral of the Fleet Lord (P. J.) Hill-Norton b. 1915

Captain N. J. Hill-Norton RN b. 1939

In nine generations only one did not have a naval officer, in a period which (so far) extends 315 years.

Acknowledgments

Since 1979 when I started on *Networks*, the subject has verged on the obsessional. Almost every time I met someone professionally or socially the talk turned to networks, and almost everyone had something to contribute. I am grateful to all those with whom I have exchanged network news and views at cocktail parties or on the terraces at Twickenham. There were many others to whom I addressed more formal requests and I am grateful to all those who took the trouble to reply to my letters (though I never cease to be amazed at how few "cold contacts" have the courtesy to answer correspondence these days). It was particularly kind of so many cabinet ministers to respond to my queries and noticeable that one of the very busiest, Sir Geoffrey Howe, came up with two quite long and entertaining letters which revealed, incidentally, an acute and amused understanding of how networks operate. There were many people who agreed to see me and who sometimes gave up several hours of busy and demanding lives. Many of their names – Malcolm Muggeridge, for instance, who asked me down to Sussex for lunch and an afternoon walk and who first drew my attention to Attlee and the Old Haileyburians – crop up in the text. In a sense, therefore, the bulk of the book offers acknowledgment on every page. Others specifically asked not to be identified so that their names will not be found in the book nor among these acknowledgments. I am, naturally, just as grateful to them as to those I have been able to identify.

At one point I was thinking of listing here every person who helped me but the list became so unwieldy and the problem of how to indicate the degree of help (and therefore indebtedness) so complex that I decided to be invidious and single out only those few to whom I have particular reasons for gratitude.

I hope that those left out of these selective thanks will not be too offended, and also that no one will be embarrassed by inclusion. Mention of names does not, of course, imply any attempt to shift responsibility. Errors of fact or interpretation are entirely mine and in no way the fault of those who have been so generous with their time and help.

268

If I begin with my editor, Ion Trewin, of Hodder and Stoughton, it is not simply because I think it is the tactful thing to do but because he has nursed this project through from beginning to end. It was he who commissioned it early in 1980. Throughout my research he arranged regular briefings – at the Garrick – where lunch guests included such network experts from his own PPN as Andrew Boyle and Anthony Sampson. When I retreated to North America to write the text he maintained a regular correspondence spiced with relevant anecdotes and newspaper clippings. When he arrived for a final week of editing and organising, he came not only with shrewd professional advice and expertise, but also duty free cigars, a large jar of Marmite and a huge Union Jack for hanging over the front door. A proper editor.

One of his great strengths was to read material very fast and then offer detailed and incisive advice about it. The same applies to my agent Richard Simon and his colleague Vivien Green who were able to turn my copy round with almost indecent haste, enabling me to embark on another draft almost before I had time to draw breath from completing the last.

Of all those who helped with material I most regret Sir Geoffrey de Freitas, a cold contact introduced by way of Malcolm Muggeridge and Lord Longford, who died between my talking to him at the Reform Club and publication. It was Sir Geoffrey who told me about George Thomas and the Old Etonian tie (a story later confirmed to me by Mr. Speaker himself) and in the course of our talk he produced several other pertinent and funny anecdotes whose provenance astute readers will easily recognise.

Various men of war contributed genially to my naval and military knowledge, notably Admiral of the Fleet Lord Hill-Norton and Colonel David Webb-Carter of the Irish Guards, but I must record special thanks to Colonel John Wilsey, then commanding the Devon and Dorset Regiment, who not only invited me to spend a day with the regiment in their barracks at Colchester but also organised a questionnaire to be filled in by every man under his command – a detailed summary of this can be found in Appendix XII on page 268. The Bar and the Church were also generous, none more so than John Bickersteth, Bishop of Bath and Wells, who lent me a copy of his enormous family tree and provided a comprehensive interpretation of it over lunch at his club.

Although much of my research was pursued through cold contacts I have been fairly ruthless in my exploitation of the hot contacts of my own PPN. Hence, naturally, much of the material on Sherborne, where I am particularly grateful to Alan Howard, the careers master, for letting me take part in the careers' convention; and Balliol, where I would like to record my lasting gratitude, not just for "network" information, but in a more general educational sense to my former tutors, Professor Richard Cobb and Dr. Maurice Keen. How lucky for me and the book that an old Shirburnian friend, Colin Lucas, should now be a Fellow of Balliol, and that I should also have Balliol friends and contemporaries at Eton (Martin Hammond), *The Times* (Edward Mortimer) and in the House of Commons (Chris Patten).

I am indebted, too, to my regular employers, William Deedes, editor of the *Daily Telegraph* and John Anstey, editor of the *Telegraph Sunday Magazine* for sending me to places and people who have often proved useful in my researches, as well as offering continuing financial and other practical support. Journalism is a great contact maker.

One journalistic friend, Andrew Duncan, has been of considerable assistance in my understanding of such diverse subjects as the royal family and Rotary; another, Hugo Vickers, told me about Sergeant Preston and King George VI's game book; while a third, Hugh Montgomery-Massingberd, loaned me his invaluable creation: the Massingberd 500. Philip Howard of *The Times* whom I have known since we both reported a Tariq Ali Oxford Union debate in the early 1960s provided a useful gloss on *Who's Who* and other Establishment organs.

The book has been through several drafts, first being written in fragmentary form as each individual piece of research was completed. I am very grateful to Peter Chant, Mrs. Euler and the staff of Mount Pleasant at Reigate for their continuing hospitality and understanding. They provide an unsurpassed writer's retreat. It was there that I first met Harry Hoff (alias novelist William Cooper) who devoted much time and patience to trying to explain the Civil Service and its links with Oxford and Cambridge. I am particularly grateful for his rigorous insistence on dealing only in what he calls "ascertainable facts". I am even more indebted to Dorothy B. Hughes, Grand Master of the Mystery Writers of America, who lent me her lovely house in New Mexico where the last stages of the book were completed.

Finally my family. Emma, Alexander, Lucy and Tristram may still be too young to understand precisely why their father spends so many hours hacking away at his portable Olivetti, but they have developed a fine instinct for leaving him alone when it matters and disrupting when he is in need of a break. Despite appearances, I do appreciate it. My wife Alison has had to listen to almost every word of every draft read out loud, often when the author was in a mood of suicidal despair. This seems to me to be above the call of connubial duty and without such dedicated support the book would almost certainly never have been completed.

Bibliography

Just as my oral evidence was eclectically garnered so my written evidence came from a wide variety of often unexpected sources. I relied quite heavily on the *Daily Telegraph* and *The Times*, particularly their correspondence columns and court pages with those endless network nuggets of christenings, weddings, regimental dinners and all that. Also useful were *Gay News*, the *Devon and Dorset Regimental Journal*, the *Balliol College Review* and various other publications.

As with conversations, so with the reading of books. Everything became relevant. I expected in reading Evelyn Waugh, Anthony Powell, Simon Raven and C. P. Snow to come across numerous references to networks in action. But once I was attuned to the idea of *thinking network* I found network references and allusions in the most unlikely places, even running across them in the books of contemporary North American women writers such as Margaret Atwood and Laurie Colwin.

What follows is a list of those books on which I have drawn directly for my text or which have influenced my thoughts on networks most consciously.

Agnew, Sir Geoffrey, *Agnew's 1817–1967*, Bradbury and Agnew, London, 1967.

Atwood, Margaret, *Bodily Harm*, Jonathan Cape, London, 1982.

Barr, Ann and York, Peter, *The Official Sloane Ranger Handbook*, Ebury Press, London, 1982.

Bence-Jones, Mark and Montgomery-Massingberd, Hugh, *The British Aristocracy*, Constable, London, 1979.

Bishop, T. J. H. and Wilkinson, R., *Winchester and the Public School Elite*, Faber, London, 1967.

Bottomore, T. B., *Elites and Society*, C. A. Watts, London, 1964, Penguin, London, 1970.

Boyle, Andrew, *The Climate of Treason*, Hutchinson, London, 1979. Revised edition, Coronet Books, London, 1980.

Braddon, Russell, *All the Queen's Men: The Household Cavalry and the Brigade of Guards*, Hamish Hamilton, London, 1977.

Bradley, Ian, *The English Middle Classes are Alive and Kicking*, Collins, London, 1982.

Butterworth, Eric and Weir, David (editors), *The Sociology of Modern Britain*, A Fontana Original, London, 1970.

Fidler, John, *The British Business Elite: Its Attitudes to Class, Status and Power*, Routledge & Kegan Paul, London, 1981.

Gathorne-Hardy, Jonathan, *The Public School Phenomenon, 597–1977*, Hodder and Stoughton, London, 1977.

Gilbert, Michael, *The Final Throw*, Hodder and Stoughton, London, 1983.

Goffman, Erving, *Asylums: Essays on the Social Situation of Mental Patients and Other Inmates*, Anchor Books, Doubleday, New York 1961, Pelican, London, 1968.

Goffman, Erving, *The Presentation of Self in Everyday Life*, Allen Lane, The Penguin Press, London, 1969.

Goffman, Erving, *Stigma: Notes on the Management of Spoiled Identity*, Prentice-Hall, New Jersey, USA, 1963, Pelican Books, London, 1968.

Harrison, David, *The White Tribe of Africa: South Africa in Perspective*, BBC, London, 1981.

Herman, Edward S., *Corporate Control, Corporate Power*, Cambridge University Press, Cambridge, 1981.

Kellner, Peter and Crowther-Hunt, Lord, *The Civil Servants: An Inquiry into Britain's Ruling Class*, Macdonald, London, 1980.

Korn Ferry, *British Corporate Leaders – A Profile*, A Korn Ferry International Study in conjunction with the London Business School, London, 1981.

Laver, James, *Dandies*, Weidenfeld and Nicolson, London, 1968.

Lees-Milne, James, *Ancestral Voices*, Chatto and Windus, London, 1975.

Lees-Milne, James, *Prophesying Peace*, Chatto and Windus, London, 1977.

Levy, Roger, *Rotary International in Great Britain and Ireland*, Macdonald and Evans, Plymouth, 1978.

Lurie, Alison, *The Language of Clothes*, Heinemann, London, 1981.

Marwick, Arthur, *Class: Image and Reality in Britain, France and the USA since 1930*, Collins, London, 1980.

Masters, Brian, *Great Hostesses*, Constable, London, 1982.

Mullally, Frederic, *The Silver Salver: The Story of the Guinness Family*, Granada, London, 1981.

Mullin, Chris, *A Very British Coup*, Hodder and Stoughton, London, 1982.

Pakenham, Thomas, *The Boer War*, Weidenfeld and Nicolson, London, 1979.

Payn, Graham and Morley, Sheridan (editors), *The Noel Coward Diaries*, Weidenfeld and Nicolson, London, 1982.

Rae, John, *The Public School Revolution: Britain's Independent Schools 1964–79*, Faber, London, 1981.

Sampson, Anthony, *Anatomy of Britain*, Hodder and Stoughton, London, 1962.

Sampson, Anthony, *Anatomy of Britain Today*, Hodder and Stoughton, London, 1965.

Sampson, Anthony, *The New Anatomy of Britain*, Hodder and Stoughton, London, 1971.

Sampson, Anthony, *The Changing Anatomy of Britain*, Hodder and Stoughton, London, 1982.

Scott Welch, Mary, *Networking: The Great New Way for Women to Get Ahead*, Harcourt Brace, Jovanovich, New York, 1980.

Smith, Leif and Wagner, Patricia, *The Networking Game*, Network Research, Denver, Colorado, 1980.

Sterling, Claire, *The Terror Network: The Secret War of International Terrorism*, Weidenfield and Nicolson, London, 1981.

Wareham, John, *Secrets of a Corporate Headhunter*, Playboy Paperbacks, New York, 1981.

Wellman, Barry, *Network Analysis from Method and Metaphor to Theory and Substance*, Department of Sociology, University of Toronto, Toronto, 1981.

Westergaard, John and Resler, Henrietta, *Class in a Capitalist Society. A Study of Contemporary Britain*, Heinemann Educational, London, 1975.

Wildeblood, Peter, *Against the Law*, Weidenfeld and Nicolson, London, 1955.

Young, Michael and Willmott, Peter, *Family and Kinship in East London*, Routledge & Kegan Paul, London, 1957.

I have also had, perforce, to rely to some extent on two flawed but indispensable annual volumes:

Who's Who, A. and C. Black, London.
Whitaker's Almanack, J. Whitaker and Sons, London.

Index

Compiled by Douglas Matthews

Index